Anglish/Yinglish

Anglish/Yinglish

Yiddish in American Life and Literature

SECOND EDITION **Gene Bluestein**

University of Nebraska Press   *Lincoln and London*

1st edition © 1989 by Gene Bluestein,
published by the University of Georgia Press, 1989

2nd edition © 1998 by the University of Nebraska Press
All rights reserved
Manufactured in the United States of America

∞ The paper in this book meets the minimum requirements of
American National Standard for Information Sciences—Permanence
of Paper for Printed Library Materials, ANSI Z39.48-1984.

Library of Congress Cataloging-in-Publication Data
Bluestein, Gene, 1928–
Anglish/Yinglish : Yiddish in American Life and literature /
Gene Bluestein.—2nd ed.
p.   cm.
Includes bibliography and discography.
ISBN 0-8032-1225-9 (cloth: alk. paper).—ISBN 0-8032-6147-0
(pbk.: alk. paper)
1. English language—Foreign words and phrases—Yiddish—
Dictionaries.   2. Yiddish language—Influence on English—
Dictionaries. I. Title.
PE1582.Y5B58   1998
423'.391—dc21
98-10943
CIP

For Ellie again
and to the memory of
Marx Wartofsky

Contents

Preface

It was Walt Whitman who first described the United States as a "nation of nations." He also gave a remarkably prophetic vision of American English:

> The English language befriends the grand American expression. . . . it is brawny enough and limber and full enough. On the stock of a race who through all change of circumstance was never without the idea of political liberty, which is the animus of liberty, it has attracted the terms of daintier and gayer and subtler and more elegant tongues. It is the powerful language of resistance . . . it is the dialect of common sense. It is the speech of the proud and melancholy race and of all who aspire. It is the chosen tongue to express growth faith self-esteem freedom justice equality friendliness amplitude prudence decision and courage. It is the medium that shall well nigh express the inexpressible.

He clearly meant that the Anglo-Saxon element of our early history has luckily attracted to itself a variety of the world's speech, thus giving us a national stature that also encompasses a great portion of humanity. The term "chosen tongue" is a conscious play on the Jewish notion of a "chosen people," which does not mean what most people think. The Jews were chosen, according to the Hebrew Bible, to be messengers to the world; and it has often been assumed that part of their role was to take upon themselves the punishment for the trespasses of their brethren. (This explains the joke that describes Goldberg arriving in Heaven. "Lord," he asks, "is it true that the Jews are the chosen people?" To an affirming nod, he continues: "Then, would you mind choosing someone else next time?")

Rather than suggesting an exclusive relationship to God, Whitman proposes that the unique fate of our language is to develop and change by incorporating the traditions of those millions who left their homelands yearning for freedom. Far from being chauvinistic, he affirms the international quality and the multiethnic nature of the American experience. It has been a process fraught with ambivalence, but one that continues to this day.

People in this country still find it difficult to acknowledge that our language thrives on the ideas and dialects of all those who came, not to mention the influence of those Native Americans who were already here. But although the process Whitman was describing had just begun to go into its major phase, he saw the future with great clarity.

Anglish (Anglicized Yiddish), which turns Yiddish words into colloquial English (as in shmo), and Yinglish (Yiddishized English), which gives English words and expressions the qualities of Yiddish syntax and intonation (as in "a Heifitz he isn't"), show perhaps better than any other development how our language has benefited from its immigrants and how they have in turn kept elements of their linguistic tradition alive. The phenomenon includes interactions with sources from Native American and African-American to Anglo-Celtic, European, Cajun, and, most recently, Southeast Asian traditions. We have just begun to study the implications of many of these relationships, and we have a long way to go before the whole picture is presented clearly.

But there is a special irony in the fact that Yiddish and American English have both been described as inferior dialects in relation to Hebrew and British English, respectively. In both cases a folk-based strategy of humor has been the main survival technique, along with a dogged insistence that the cultural values expressed in the language are worthy of being passed on to the next generation. At the present time Anglish/Yinglish is a phenomenon that reveals a great deal about American as well as Yiddish studies. No one can say where the process will lead. But despite Roland Barthes's clever, au courant transformation (we need to unexpress the expressible), Anglish/Yinglish may be one of the sources that bring us close to fulfilling Whitman's prophecy.

Acknowledgments

Wayne Colver first suggested this study. Aimée Brigham will use it better than anyone else. Kermit Vanderbilt and Marx Wartofsky provided some useful suggestions. Jack Zeldis gave me the benefit of his expert knowledge of Hebrew and his sensitivity to YIDishkait. Jemmy Bluestein read the text with intelligent scrutiny and held me to his high standards. I owe a deep debt of gratitude to Sharon Ihnen for her sensitive reading of the manuscript. The errors are mine.

A Note on Pronunciation

All the Yiddish words in the dictionary text are spelled phonetically according to the system described here. Yiddish is written in an alphabet that is Semitic, reads from right to left, uses no capital letters, and, with the exception of words from Hebrew, is essentially phonetic. Thus, Yiddish has two separate spelling systems, one for itself and another for its stock of Hebrew and Aramaic words.

Since there is no universally accepted system of transliteration, writers often spell the same word differently, in accordance with their own dialects or the spelling conventions of their individual languages. Since my own family background was Bessarabian Romanian, I tend often to give that dialect. Among the obvious dialect differences are pronunciations of vowels and certain consonants. When my mother wanted to characterize her speech, she would say, "MUHme, TUHte, kuhts" (mama, father, cat) instead of "MAme, TAte, kats," which is the way many of our neighbors from other parts of Europe spoke. But it's clear that those are not crucial distinctions.

There's almost always a problem in transliterating the word that appears as chutzpah in American dictionaries. In the Anglish/Yinglish dictionary it is KHOOTSpe, so as to prevent the *ch* (as in the German *ach*) from being pronounced like the *ch* in chicken. Many years ago the sound was rendered by an *h* with a dot under it. When that practice passed out of use we ended up with such puzzlers as the name Yitzkhak misspelled Yitzhak and mispronounced "Yitzak."

Writers' ways of transliterating words beginning with *sh* are especially interesting. In Yiddish a single letter denotes the sound "sh"; hence it should never be transliterated *sch*, which is the German convention. As we shall see, Yiddishists are very sensitive to what they consider to be "Germanisms" in their language usage.

Scholars have attempted to establish a standard Yiddish based on a combination of Russian and Lithuanian dialects, which are very different from Jewish-German dialects. But such attempts have been no more successful than comparable efforts to establish a standard English. Yiddish (like American English) is a fusion language, very rich in its diversity. Again, like American English, the history of Yiddish is multifold and the story of its development is clearly indicated in its diverse sources, which include Hebrew, Aramaic, German, French, Italian, and Slavic materials.

Despite these dialectical differences Yiddish is an international language among Jews, and my pronunciation guide will provide as accurate a rendering as is necessary for comprehension. It is always best if you can find native speakers to help, though chances are they will try to convert you to their own dialectical preferences.

a as in father	MAzl
uh as in above	puhts (the schwa sound)
e as in egg	KEtsele (Every *e* is pronounced as a separate syllable. None is ever silent. This word is KE-tse-le.)
ea as in bear	khaLEARye
ee as in see	BYAlee
i as in it	knish (Don't add vowels between consonants. This is not kaNISH or kuhNISH.)
o as in over	shmo
oo as in book	shnook
u as in blue	nu
ai as in aisle	khai
ay as in pay	DRAYdl
oy as in oil	goy
k as in kick	kaBAle
kh	There is no equivalent sound in English, but it's like trying to cough up something from the back of your throat. Or like the German *ach.*
j as in joy	nooj
r	There are several authentic pronunciations, ranging from a very trilled Russian sound to one that sounds French. The extremely sharp Ameri-

	can *r* is the most inappropriate. One says, "Er ret mit a SHARFn raysh" ("He speaks with a sharp *r*"), meaning he is probably an American.
s as in sit	NAKHis (*s* is never substituted for *z*.)
ts as in fits	TSAtskele
tsh as in catch	kvetsh (Don't say kaVETSH.)
z as in zero	iz
zh as in Zhivago	zhluhb

Introduction to the First Edition

Before World War II there were an estimated eleven million Yiddish speakers in the world. Six million (at least) were murdered by the Nazis and their allies in many European countries. Most of the survivors left the cities and towns where their families had lived, in some cases for centuries, before the nations that helped to destroy them were even in existence. In what is now Hungary and in areas on the northern shores of the Black Sea, for example, there were ancient Jewish communities that were declared "alien" by the settlers who came later and established nation-states. Although there are remnants of Jewish communities that still function (in Poland and Romania as well as in Germany), the great European centers of Yiddish culture and learning have practically disappeared. And they are not likely to be revived in the near future.

The prospects for Yiddish in the United States do not appear to be much better. The language is disappearing along with the older generation of New York City's Jewish population. This is best reflected in the demise of the Yiddish-language press in New York City, which has had as many as twenty Yiddish dailies. Now there are two—the *FORvits* (*Jewish Daily Forward*), founded in 1897 by Abraham Cahan, (pronounced "kan"); and the *MORgn FRAIhait*, founded in 1922. The name means "morning freedom," but it is never referred to that way. The *Forward*, once the most influential of the Yiddish dailies, with a circulation of close to half a million, today claims fewer than fifty thousand readers. The *FRAIhait*, an unofficial but virtual Communist party organ, is barely surviving.

It may well be this bleak prospect that has spawned the flurry of books about Yiddish in recent years. These include a number of quickie word lists, Leo Rosten's popular compendiums, and the scholarly works of Max Weinreich and Uriel Weinreich. Perusal of all these and others, however, should make us hesitant about predicting the demise of Yiddish; it is a prophecy that has been made for hundreds of years. Actually, it is always difficult to make long-range predictions about the future of any language. There are times when it appears that George Orwell's prognostications are right on track, that we are being overwhelmed by what he called Newspeak, with its combination of euphemism and mindless conformity. Or, in the long run, we may end up with something approximating the English-Russian MISH-mash that Anthony Burgess employs in *Clockwork Orange;* or the final solution may even be the dream of most engineers I know: an electronic attachment that will transmit thoughts directly from brain to brain, bypassing all existing languages.

But, all these possibilities aside, it is likely that our conventional languages will persist, and very possibly Yiddish will continue to be among them. To begin with, as we shall see, Yiddish is a language of survivors, including the remnant of those who miraculously lived through the hell of Hitler's concentration camps. Since Yiddish was their language, it is supremely the voice of those who amazingly overcame the most brutal plan of genocide ever devised by anyone in any time or place; the greatest miracle is that they are still around to discuss it in their own language.

Second, as Isaac Bashevis Singer noted in his Nobel Prize speech (which is also printed in Yiddish):

One can find in the Yiddish tongue and in the Yiddish style expressions of pious joy, lust for life, longing for the Messiah, patience, and deep appreciation of human individuality. There is a quiet humor in Yiddish and a gratitude for every day of life, every crumb of success, each encounter of love. The Yiddish mentality is not haughty. It does not take victory for granted. It does not demand and command but it muddles through, sneaks by, smuggles itself amid the powers of destruction, knowing somewhere that God's plan for Creation is still at the very beginning. There are some who call Yiddish a dead language, but so was Hebrew called for two thousand years. It has been revived in our time in a most remarkable, almost miraculous way. Aramaic was certainly a dead language for centuries, but then it brought to light the Zohar, a work of mysticism of sublime value. It is a fact that the classics of Yiddish literature are also the classics of the modern Hebrew literature. Yiddish has not yet said its last word. It contains treasures that have not been revealed to the eyes of the world. It was the tongue of martyrs and saints, of dreamers and Kabbalists—rich in humor and in memories that mankind may never forget. In a figurative way, Yiddish is the wise and humble language of us all, the idiom of frightened and hopeful humanity. (Singer *NL*, 8 9)

It does seem as if some contrivance is at work to save Yiddish from the annihilation that has seemed to be its fate. There remain Yiddish speakers in many parts of the world—Canada, Mexico, South America, and South Africa—and there is a large corpus of printed Yiddish materials for anyone who wants to read it or to learn the language. Not to mention the third- and fourth-generation Jews in this country, many of whom are determined to revive cultural patterns earlier generations rejected in the zeal to become Americanized. This sometimes includes the desire to study Yiddish and what is more and more being called YIDishkait, the Jewish values specifically evoked by Yiddish. Even in Israel, which pointedly revived Hebrew as its national language because it so vehemently opposed Yiddish as a language of the ghetto and of Jewish passivity, there has recently developed a scholarly and educational interest in MAme LUHIslui (Yiddish, the mother tongue).

Perhaps the most amazing and unpredictable source of hope for the survival of Yiddish comes from a circumstance no one could have imagined. An unexpected result of the Holocaust was the tenacious and near-miraculous survival of Orthodox sects such as the khSEEdim, who came very close to being totally destroyed in their population centers of Eastern Europe. But they not only survived, they have taken root in New York City and in Israel. Their Israeli connection is ironic, since some groups do not recognize the Jewish state, adhering to the biblical prediction that it will be established only when the Messiah comes. But with or without recognition, they are a strong and expanding population. You can see teachers leading their black-costumed charges like a string of goslings with PAYes (curly sidelocks) through the streets of Brooklyn, where you may be accosted by their MITSvuh-mobile, with its exhibits encouraging orthodoxy of all kinds.

What is most interesting about the khSEEdim is that Yiddish is both their everyday language and the language they use to study the Talmud, which, as fundamentalists, they maintain to be their main reason for existing. The choice of Yiddish is based on the fact that the Holy Scriptures and the synagogue ritual are in Hebrew (LUHshn KOYdesh, the language of holiness, the sacred tongue). Therefore, it is their conclusion that Hebrew should not be used for everyday activities nor in discussing and interpreting the Scriptures themselves. Consequently, Yiddish is still for them and their children a viable, living speech. However much they relegate it to a second-class position in relation to Hebrew (an old story for Yiddish), the khSEEdim have guaranteed that at least for the foreseeable future it will survive as, in many senses, "the wise and humble language of us all, the idiom of frightened and hopeful humanity."

This study is concerned with the function of Yiddish in American life and literature. Curiously (and without reference to Orthodox retentions) the presence of Yiddish is being felt more pervasively in American culture than ever before, not only in literature but also in the mass media. It is difficult to imagine how anyone can read Saul Bellow's *Herzog* or Philip Roth's *Portnoy's Complaint* without a gloss of the Yiddishisms they employ so frequently. The same must be said for a book like *Sophie's Choice*, even though the author is not Jewish. Consequently, I have keyed my references to the works of writers whose use of Yiddish requires explanation of the vocabulary and of the important connotations.

Language is the great carrier of cultural values, and that has led me to expand this study to include more than the words that appear in what we consider to be important literature. Formal literature is only one of the sources for the infusion of Yiddish into the American consciousness. By far the largest impact has come from the ubiquitous fields of entertainment, which include burlesque and nightclubs, legitimate theater and musical comedies, and such media as radio, television, film, and the recording industry. The only comparable impact from a specific minority in America comes from black culture, through the influence of jazz musicians and black comedians. The comparison is worth making because it highlights the extent to which our language is influenced by such strongly folk-based traditions as Yiddish and black English. And it is especially worth noting because both Yiddish and black speech have been subject to the same kind of condescension from highbrow sources.

Critics in many fields, however, have begun to take note of the power exerted by traditions hitherto considered outside the mainstream of high culture—if indeed the United States can talk at all of "high culture." Although it is an exaggeration to say (as a writer in the *Times (London) Literary Supplement* insisted not long ago) that "the voice of literary America is heard by many as an essentially Jewish voice—the voice of Bellow, Malamud, Gold, the two Roths," nevertheless there is a special sense in which the development of Jewish-American literature illuminates uniquely American circumstances that we too often fail to acknowledge. I question the *TLS* writer's assertion because it smacks of special treatment of Jewish issues. This sort of approach has clouded our understanding of some truly central inferences that should be drawn from the Jewish-American experience. On the other hand, the list of Jewish literary figures might very well be expanded to include Nathanael West, J. D. Salinger, Arthur Miller, Leslie Fiedler, S. J. Perelman, Clifford Odets, Bruce Jay Friedman, Norman Mailer, Isaac Bashevis Singer, Allen Ginsberg, Stanley Elkin, Grace Paley, and Cynthia Ozick.

What has not been emphasized sufficiently in discussions of Yiddish is that Jewish Americans (writers as well as others) have been concerned mainly with telling us about the values of life in the United States, rather than (as has often been the case with European Jewish writers) with filling in the outlines of the history of the Jewish people. As I explain in appendix 1, just such a conflict was the central theme of *Portnoy's Complaint,* which is why it received such hostile reviews from traditionalists in the Jewish community. Yiddish has played a prominent role in the attempt by "hyphenated Americans" to understand the meaning of the American experience. Although similar explorations have been carried out by other groups (the analyses of blacks, Latinos, and Native Americans bring comparable insights), there has been for some time a major symbiotic relationship between Yiddish and English that is linguistic as well as ideological—and that may help to explain why there has been a rash of Yiddish studies in recent years.

I will describe two aspects of this relationship, using the terms Anglish, or Anglicized Yiddish, in which a Yiddish word is integrated into English usage, as with *shmo* and *shmoozing;* and Yinglish, or Yiddishized English, in which an English word is integrated into Yiddish usage, as with *allrightnik* or the expression "a Heifetz he isn't." Both of these developments are more extensive than we might expect, although as a fusion language American English has always been quick to accept words from other sources; as Walt Whitman was among the first to argue, "the English language is the accretion and growth of every dialect, race, and range of time, and is both the free and compacted composition of all. From this point of view, it stands for Language in the largest sense, and is really the greatest of studies. It involves so much; is indeed a sort of universal absorber, combiner, and conqueror." Here is another connection between English and Yiddish, for the latter, as we will see in the following brief history, is also a notable fusion language, one that has become richer for all of its international connections. Yiddish helps us to understand what Whitman said about the nature of the American experience when he noted that we are a "nation of nations," that to be an American is to have a multicultural experience, like it or not.

One can almost never embark on a discussion of Yiddish without encountering the erroneous notion that it is simply an inferior dialect of German. Linguists maintain that Yiddish and Modern High German are both dialects of the same language—German. Similarly, one can argue that American and British are both dialects of English. But the pressures of the need for cultural identity and the history of national insecurity have made the relations between Yiddish and German, and between American and British English, much more complicated. In both connections, partisans of Yiddish and of American English have had to fight for their right to a clear cultural identity. A major aspect of the ideological conflict can be seen quite clearly in a comment by a German-Yiddish scholar around the end of the seventeenth century. The Jews, he argued, have given German "an entirely foreign tone and sound; they have mutilated, minced, distorted, the good German words, invented new unknown [words], and mixed into German countless Hebrew words and phrases with the result that he who hears them speak German must conclude that they speak nothing but pure Hebrew, for practically no single word comes out intelligible" (Weinreich *HYL*, 103–14). This is meant to be insulting, of course, but it also shows the longstanding tensions between Yiddish and German. The condescension on one side has been met by a fervent reaction on the other. Despite the dispassionate views of experts, the conflict in many quarters remains heated.

Until recently the history of Yiddish was ordinarily discussed in terms of three periods. But Max Weinreich, the great historian of the language, gives four:

1. Early Yiddish (ca. 1100–ca. 1250). The period of Ashkenaz I in the basins of the Main, Upper Rhine, and Upper Danube.
2. Old Yiddish (ca. 1250–ca. 1500). The period of Ashkenaz II that marks the movement east.
3. Middle Yiddish (ca. 1500–ca. 1700). A period of merging Western and Eastern Yiddish.
4. New Yiddish (ca. 1750 to the present). The period of emancipation, the flowering of literary tradition, the Holocaust.

Max Weinreich argues that Yiddish came into existence when Jews from France and Italy moved into the area in Germany that he calls Loter. They brought with them Hebrew, as well as dialects related to Old French and Old Italian. These were the main components that mixed with the Middle High German (MHG) of the time. That is to say, this was a period when the German language was beginning to develop toward its modern forms, and at this moment Yiddish also went its own way. (This phrase is roughly comparable to the stage of English during the time of Chaucer.) From the outset Yiddish contained elements from Hebrew, Aramaic, Old French, and Old Italian, which made it very different from MHG. As it continued on its separate path from MHG, Yiddish in its next stage of development also began to show the influence of Slavic traditions.

So although there are similarities with German, there are also enough differences to have provided Yiddish with its own integrity, linguistically as well as ideologically. Although MHG is one of its components, the influence of the others is so strong as to make it almost impossible for German speakers to comprehend the Yiddish they hear. Weinreich gives a model Yiddish sentence that shows the four main elements, which also makes the point that even someone well versed in German will not comprehend the basic meaning of the sentence: "NUHKHn BENTSHn huht dear ZAYde geKOYFT a SAYfer." The sentence says: "Following the benediction after the meal, grandfather bought a religious book." SAYfer is Hebrew; BENTSHn is from the Loez, and ultimately from the Latin *benedicere*; NUHKHn, huht, dear, and geKOYFT are from German; ZAYde is from Slavic. The differences in this sentence and elsewhere are not only lexical but syntactical and cultural, and they indicate some essential differences between Yiddish and German that go back to their very beginnings. Even though there is more vocabulary from the German source, words from Hebrew and Slavic make it extremely difficult for a German reader to follow the meaning of the sentence.

From at least the thirteenth century the integration of elements from Slavic languages increased the distance between Yiddish and German, the result of eastward migrations through central Europe, Poland, Bielorussia, the Ukraine, and Russia. Words like TSHAInik (tea kettle), BLUHte (mud), and BLUHNjen (to get lost), among many others, reveal these sources.

Viewed in this framework Yiddish turns out to have more YIKHis (prestige by way of distinguished antecedents) than most people have suspected. Nevertheless, this MISH-mash of sources has worked to keep the term zharGUHN associated with Yiddish. It suggests a hodgepodge rather than a real language. Not only condescending critics but many Jews as well were encouraged to define Yiddish as an inferior dialect. No language is in fact pure, but obviously fusion languages like Greek, Latin, German, French, and English are universally acknowledged to have their own integrity. No one feels the need to describe any of them as a zharGUHN—the word my parents' generation routinely used to describe their language. But the attempt to diminish the cultural integrity of Yiddish continues, even in educated circles, despite assurances by linguists like Uriel Weinreich that "Yiddish in its entire European diaspora developed with a dynamic of its own."

One key element in the evolution of Yiddish is that it never had a country to call its own; and it is just the luck of Yiddish (a shliMAZL from the beginning) that when the Jews created their own nation in

1948 they revived Hebrew (which had never totally disappeared as a spoken language) and seemed effectively to have extinguished the mother tongue. (So it goes, as Kurt Vonnegut says; the Yiddish is aZOY gayt es.) No SABra (native-born Israeli) wanted to be mistaken for a Yiddish shliMAZL, and despite the fact that there was an over-whelming majority of Yiddish speakers in Israel at first, "the language of the ghetto" is today unknown to most young Jews there— as it is to most American Jews, who cannot speak or read Hebrew either. And although the Israelis have shown a recent interest in Yiddish, they are still very uptight about its connection with the "ghetto mentality."

According to Max Weinreich, the earliest example of Yiddish writing is some glosses made by the sage Rashi in a commentary that dates from around 1100. Before the commentary was discovered, the Cambridge Manuscript of 1382 was considered the oldest example. It was found in a Cairo genEEze (a repository for unused scrolls and sundry manuscripts) and contains the repertoire of a Jewish minstrel (SHPEELman) who apparently traveled to Egypt, which in the four-teenth century was a refuge for persecuted European Jews. The texts comprise several poems and a fable about a sick lion. Two of them bear the date 1382. It is always difficult to correlate the relationships between speech and writing, but it seems likely that Yiddish was spoken for a time before being written down; and of course there is no telling how many examples of early writing were lost to us.

From the beginning, Yiddish was associated with women and their activities. Hebrew prayers, not suitable to be spoken by females in the sacred tongue, were translated into Yiddish, as were folk tales, fables, and poems. Yiddish also became the vernacular language among Jews in general, much of the vocabulary being developed to deal with the details of mundane matters in Jewish communities, while more prestigious activities were still the subject of Hebrew and Aramaic, a language closely related to Hebrew, probably brought from Babylonia. Aramaic served as the vernacular throughout the Middle East. The Talmud was written in Aramaic, which was also the language of Jesus; had he appeared in Germany in the Middle Ages he would have spoken Yiddish. Ultimately Aramaic was replaced by Yiddish, in which vocabulary from the former shows up frequently. A major prayer in the Passover celebration is still recited in Aramaic.

(It begins "Behold the bread of affliction . . .") The association of Yiddish with women's activities and other mundane affairs considered to be less than serious contributed to the lowbrow status of Yiddish, despite the sentimental attachment to the idea of MAme LUHshn.

On the other hand, it is just this functional relationship with many levels of folk culture over a long period of time that gives Yiddish its impressive, vital, poetic qualities. A shliMAZL, it turns out, is not entirely without virtues, as readers in the twentieth century have begun to discover. Ultimately, though at what precise moment no one knows, Hebrew became the language of the synagogue, and Yiddish took over everywhere else in the lives of European Jews, including everyday speech and scholarly discussions of sacred texts. Although there are other Jewish vernaculars (like Ladino, still spoken among Jews of Spanish and Portuguese ancestry), MAme LUHshn won a strategic hold in the culture of European Jewry. Today in Europe, and even in Israel, Yiddish still provides an avenue of communication despite whatever other language blocks exist.

The differences between Hebrew and Yiddish are important and instructive. Although Yiddish uses Hebrew orthography and is also written from right to left, a person may know how to read one but not the other. Most Israelis hearing a Yiddish folk song need a translation, though they probably know the Hebrew words to the tune. An American or European Jew who reads, writes, and speaks Yiddish would be at a loss among Hebrew speakers and might not be able to make out a simple street sign in Tel Aviv or the headline of any Israeli newspaper. This is confusing to people who think Hebrew and Yiddish are the same. On a segment of the Dick Cavett show, Richard Benjamin, the actor who played the leading role in the film version of *Portnoy's Complaint*, couldn't translate the meaning of the song title "HAva naGEEla," that famous Israeli song regularly played at weddings and baseball games in the United States. Benjamin had explained the meaning of several Yiddish expressions in response to Cavett's complaint that without some working Yiddishisms he felt terribly WASPy. (It's true that knowing a certain amount of Yiddish is a mark of urbanity.) But "HAva naGEEla" is Hebrew, and as far as the actor was concerned it might have been Greek. Several weeks later, folksinger and actor Theo Bikel (who knows both Hebrew and Yiddish) gave the translation: "Let us rejoice." But by that time

Cavett didn't quite know what was going on, assuming perhaps that Benjamin didn't know any Yiddish at all—which may have been the case. Some time later Cavett, who has a sincere interest in learning languages, had a long, on-the-air conversation with Isaac Bashevis Singer about the word *shmuhk*. He kept pressing Singer for a precise definition, and only after an embarrassing round of hedges and euphemisms did it become clear to Cavett that the word could not be defined literally on a nationally televised program. (See the entry to discover how it does in fact get wide exposure on TV.)

According to Uriel Weinreich, Hebrew words appear in Yiddish with a frequency sometimes exceeding 15 percent, depending on the level of usage, and retain their own spelling; thus Yiddish uses two separate systems. Hebrew is written in consonants without vowel indications. The vowels were originally understood by native speakers and it was not necessary to provide them in writing. In the seventh and eighth centuries of our own era, scholars supplied the major system of vocalizing points (still in use) because people were forgetting the pronunciation of certain words, especially in areas where Hebrew was not in common use. It is still a matter of principle not to vocalize the TOYre scrolls used in the synagogue, partly on the ground that the meanings of the texts must remain flexible, and partly in response to the injunction in Deuteronomy that one must not add anything to the Holy Scriptures. Modern Hebrew writing is not vocalized except for children's books and beginning texts.

Written Yiddish, on the other hand, includes the vowels (like German or English), but when a Hebrew word occurs in a Yiddish sentence it retains its own spelling, although given a Yiddish pronunciation. The Hebrew word toRA, for example, is pronounced TOYre. Many books on Yiddish persist in giving the Hebrew pronunciation rather than indicating how the word sounds in Yiddish. A further complication is that modern Hebrew is based on Sephardic (Spanish) pronunciation, which differs from the European Ashkenazic tradition. Israelis say eMET (truth), while Europeans say Emes; the Yiddish is Emis. Hebrew is khutsPA (admirable impudence), Yiddish is KHOOTSpe. Given the pronunciation and stress, the word is often not at all the same to Hebrew and Yiddish speakers. This is not surprising since Hebrew is a Semitic language, and Yiddish is Indo-European. Still, as Shaw liked to say about the English and

Americans, Jews are regularly separated by the common elements of their heritage.

In Hebrew you may have the equivalent of LVR, a word that you know means LiVeR. If you were dealing with an archaic word in an unfamiliar text, however, there might be other vowel possibilities that would indicate a different meaning. Regularly one encounters sentences in Yiddish that are the equivalent of "I am a LVR," in which the Hebrew words stand out from the text. In this case the word is probably LoVeR, but there are contexts where it could be LiVeR. You can see clearly the two systems of spelling: The Yiddish is always phonetic (you never run into anything like *knife* or *although*), while the Hebrew must be learned according to its own system, and that has often meant simply memorizing the Hebrew words rather than learning the language itself.

It is sometimes argued that Hebrew is a lofty, formal language, well suited for abstract discussion, as against the folksiness of Yiddish. But that is only another side of the attempt to define MAme LUHshn as innately inferior to the sacred tongue. It is difficult to support such assertions, and it is notable that biblical Hebrew manages to deal with the whole range of human expression, from the rules of Deuteronomy to the ecstasy of the Song of Songs. Moreover, many of the Hebrew words regularly used in Yiddish are quite down-to-earth, like those for hour, truth, and impudence. Modern Hebrew, of course, is effective for everything from advertising to poetry. Still, there remains for some modern writers the sense of Hebrew having been wrenched from its sacred context, as this verse from Israeli poet Yehuda Amichai suggests:

> To speak, now, in this tired language
> Torn from its sleep in the Bible—
> Blinded, it lurches from mouth to mouth—
> The language which described God and the miracles,
> Says:
> Motor car, bomb, God.

At the same time there is ample evidence that Yiddish is also capable of encompassing the whole range of literary and philosophical discussion.

Leo Rosten and other nostalgic writers notwithstanding, there is nothing special about the ability of Yiddish to express ideas or emotions idiomatically or metaphorically. Every language has the capability; if you pick the right level of diction in American, Irish, or any folk speech you get similar effects. Yiddish can be used as genteelly (but not quite as gentilely) as any other language, and can be quite as dull. Sholom Aleichem was one of several classic writers who consciously used folk speech as the basis for his exceptional insights into the condition of European Jewry around the turn of the century. One of his standard humorous techniques was to have a vernacular character mistranslate the Hebrew components in his speech. In one story the narrator quotes a famous line in Hebrew about the virtue of a good name and says, "I'll translate it for you: We were better off without the train." On one hand, the wrecked translation pokes fun at the character's ignorance; but on the other, it shows the author's wonderful ability to make up his own proverbs and aphorisms with puns and malapropisms along the way. This is very much like the approach of Mark Twain, to whom Sholom Aleichem is rightly compared. When they met in New York, Sholom Aleichem noted that he was flattered to be known as the Yiddish Mark Twain; Mark Twain graciously noted that he was equally pleased to be known as the American Sholom Aleichem.

Other Yiddish writers (like I. L. Peretz) often employ a drier and more formal diction very much removed from the folk, vernacular style of Sholom Aleichem. Saul Bellow, who knows Yiddish very well, has commented, "I do not wholly admire the stories of I. L. Peretz. This is heresy, I know, but I find them slow going; they depend too much on a kind of Talmudic sophistication which the modern reader, and I along with him, knows very little of." Recent responses to Yiddish tend to emphasize its folksy qualities, which is perhaps a predictably nostalgic reaction. But if that explains the basis for interest in Yiddish by American writers, much influenced by the Mark Twain tradition in our own literature, it also underestimates the impressive range of the language.

Perhaps the most remarkable aspect of Yiddish in modern literature can be seen in the accomplishments of Isaac Bashevis Singer, winner of the Nobel Prize for literature in 1978. Born in Poland, Singer spent most of his life in the United States, but he continued to do all his writing in Yiddish, even though not all of his works are published in their original language. When asked how he intended to spend the Nobel Prize money, he indicated that part of it would go to bring his books back into print in Yiddish. At first Singer's work was published in the Yiddish newspaper the *Jewish Daily Forward*, but more recently the short stories appeared in English in the *New Yorker*, with Singer as translator or cotranslator. Thus he managed to provide accurate and effective versions in English. The circumstances tell us a great deal about Yiddish in the United States; only a Jewish writer living in America could win the Nobel Prize in literature for work written entirely in Yiddish.

The problem of translating the Yiddish classics remains a serious one. There have been many attempts to translate the masterworks of Yiddish but they are not always successful. Among the best translations are Saul Bellow's, which include renderings of Sholom Aleichem's long story "Eternal Life," and Singer's classic "Gimpel the Fool." Bellow shows that it is indeed possible to translate Yiddish effectively. One always needs to keep in mind Robert Frost's quip, "Poetry is what is lost in translation." But it is also true that when a fine writer translates, a good deal of the original is transmitted.

It would be wonderful if Bellow could be persuaded to spend all his time translating the remainder of Sholom Aleichem's work. But it's not likely—there are more than forty volumes in the collected works. We will simply have to do the best we can with what there is; and of course there is no telling what will come up. Perhaps the long-sought-for computer translator may prove functional someday soon. But in the meantime the history of Yiddish warns us to be wary of dogmatic statements about its life and death. It will probably muddle through. And if it continues to tell us things we might otherwise never hear about, it's no accident that the message often comes in the form of a joke. Like the one about the grandma and her grandchild on a bus in Tel Aviv. Grandma loudly and consistently speaks to the child in Yiddish. One of the other passengers on the bus finally says to her, "Lady, this is the land of Israel. Why don't you speak Hebrew to that child?" "Well, there's a good reason," the old lady says. "I don't want him to forget that he's Jewish."

Introduction to the Second Edition

When I put together the first edition of this book in the 1980s, it was widely felt that American literature spoke in the voices of Jewish writers. The list was long and impressive, ranging from Saul Bellow to more obviously radical writers like Norman Mailer. There were also several women among the list, including Cynthia Ozick and Ruth Rubin. Just as it was amazing that our nation's literature should be represented in the voices of Jewish writers, so it was equally remarkable that some women were included as well.

As we look back at those years, it becomes apparent that the ascendancy of Jewish writers was only the beginning of a national tradition that has come to include Native Americans, African Americans, Latinos, Asians, and a host of women writers who span all of the aforementioned backgrounds; indeed the women have established their own special niche in this movement, which has finally realized the great promise of American life. All these outsiders attained a position on the same level occupied by our earlier WASP-ish writers, who still hold their own dignified position.

In view of this development we might suspect that Yiddish would simply have taken its place in the mosaic that now defines American literature. But that is not the case. The influence of Yiddish has continued and is now found in almost all of the other ethnic sources of American literature, as well as in the mainstream language itself. Some words, like KHOOTSpe (chutzpah) and SHMOOZing, have become standard and are not written in italics or any other special print. Other words, especially dietary terms like BAYgls and BYAlees, are equally well known among most Americans. Certain scatological words, like drek and shmuhk, have entered into wide usage that simply overlooks their taboo status. So drek means simply dirt and shmuhk (or shmo) just means a jerk, or nerd. We no longer refer to "glad rags" but prefer SHMAtes, which literally means rags but has come to mean clothes in general.

In the course of time we can see certain changes in some Yiddishisms, while other words retain their traditional meanings. SHMOOZing (from the Yiddish SHMOOes) used to mean inconsequential, trivial chatter but has now come to mean influential talk, or power conversation. TCHOTCHke, from Yiddish TSAtskele (a little doll or plaything), now refers to any trivial ornament or insignificant object.

These and many other words reflect the logical absorption of Yiddish words into American usage, the needs and humors of one language quite overtaken by another. Although there are many fewer Yiddish speakers worldwide, the influence of many Jewish stand-up comics and other show business performers has contributed strongly to the invasion of American English by MAme LUHshn— the mother tongue.

These movements are likely to continue, now not as exceptions to but as examples of the normal progress of hitherto uninfluential traditions, outsiders to American life and literature. All of them have something to contribute to our fusion language, which is richer and more expressive than ever before. Although not alone now, Yiddish holds its own among the many sources that underlie our native tongue. We can welcome them all to the family and say to them, MAzl tuhv!

Anglish/Yinglish

Anglish/Yinglish Dictionary

adeSHEM *n.* A Hebrew euphemism for the Tetragrammaton (YHVH). Since it is prohibited to write or speak the name of God (some Orthodox Jews write G–D, even though that is in no sense a name), there are a number of euphemisms, such as adoNOY (my Lord) and adeSHEM. It is standard for a cantor to say adeSHEM when singing a sample of the liturgy outside the synagogue. AdeSHEM is a composite of adoNOY and haSHEM (the Name).

afiKOYmen *n.* From the Greek word for dessert. It refers to the special piece of MATse that is hidden during the Passover meal and then served as "dessert." The child who finds the afiKOYmen is usually given a small reward. In our family it's a kiss and a hug from everyone present.

A Heifetz iz er nisht A Heifetz he isn't—or, a Heifetz he's not.

Few critics have found it possible to resist the force and wit of this direct translation from Yiddish. It's not exactly a damning with faint praise, in fact a good review may follow, but the performer is held up to the highest standard and evaluated from its height. For writers it might be "a Shakespeare he isn't"; for conductors "a Leonard Bernstein he isn't." I once heard a sportscaster characterize a rookie ball player similarly: "A Joe DiMaggio he isn't." A "Peanuts" comic strip shows Charlie Brown trying to sign up players for his football team. Recalling Charlie's career as a baseball manager, Lucy says, "Vince Lombardi he isn't." The inversion sounds like German, but the Yiddish locution has wit and expression rather than standard syntax.

S. Schoenbaum in a *TLS* review: "*Young Shakespeare*, Fraser may call his book, but the work of young Shakespeare *The Two Noble Kinsmen* isn't" (12 January 1997).

A *New York Times* headline: "Deficit: Public Enemy No. 1, It's Not" (16 February 1997). A subheadline to a story on crime: "Civil, It Isn't" (*New York Times*, 18 May 1997).

aKOOSHerke (accoucherka) *n.* Friddish for midwife. Bellow loves to use French in his work and this is his coinage. The suffix -*ke* defines the person. We say in Anglish "the next-doorike," meaning the one next door. For a male the suffix is -*ker*. A well-known term is BUHMeke (bummeke), a woman who fools around.

"'Who is to blame?' said Grandma Lausch when I came home. 'You know who? You are, Augie, because that's all the brains you have to go with that piss-in-bed *accoucherka*'s son'" (Bellow *AAM*).

a LAYBn oif dain KEPele In the remake of Alfred Hitchcock's anti-Nazi film *The Lady Vanishes*, Elliot Gould consistently speaks Yiddish, pretending it's German. At one point he takes Cybill Shepherd's head in his hands and says the phrase, which translates roughly as "a blessing on your little head." It's similar to a Jewish mother's wish when something unfortunate has happened to one of her children: "Mir far dir" (It should happen to me).

Alef bays The first two letters of the Yiddish (and Hebrew) alphabet. The English word alphabet is made up of the first two letters of the Greek alphabet (alpha, beta), which derives from the same Semitic linguistic sources as the Yiddish and Hebrew alphabets.

Ale ZIBn GLIKn Literally, all seven blessings, perhaps as mentioned in the Jewish marriage ceremony. It means blissful to the highest degree. "Alone he came to America and sent for me. But you—you want *alle siebn glicken*" (Bellow *H*).

allRAITnik *n.* A conformist, one who is all too willing to accept the status quo, to say "all right" even when resistance is called for. The expression was coined by Abraham Cahan, author of *The Rise of David Levinsky*.

"In the leftist publications they dubbed Sam Dreitman an American 'all-rightnik' and a 'Golden Calf'" (Singer *S*).

Edmund Wilson, writing about the biblical story of Joseph: "He gratifies his father Jacob and arranges for him a serene old age. There are moments when we feel about Joseph that he is a little what is meant by the Yiddish word *allrightnik*, when we are tempted to sympathize with the brothers, in their resentment at his reading of dreams that is always to his advantage" (*RBBO*).

From a review by Bryan Cheyette of *The Oxford Book of Hebrew Short Stories:* "The story describes the misguided emigration of an aged mother from Lithuania, who has joined her allrightnik son in America, where the old woman's gradual disgust at her son's assimilation is memorably conveyed" (*TLS,* 12 April 1997).

ALter KAker *n.* Literally, an old shitter. *The Dictionary of American Slang* gives "an old cock" as the literal meaning, but that is to confuse *KAkn* (to shit) with cock (the fowl). Figuratively, the term refers to an old man, especially one with youthful pretensions, and particularly with a tendency to chase after young women. Hence it suggests something like lecher or dirty old man, and the *DAS* may have provided an accurate though unintentional pun. A more general reading refers to anyone past his prime, similar to what is conveyed by the German *Ausgespielt* (played out). The term is often abbreviated: "He's just an a.k."

"You young bloods have got it over us alter cockers" (Malamud *TT*).

"Then why do you go around with an *alte kocker's* beard and wearing your playground clothes—and with whores!" (P. Roth *ST*).

aMORets *n.* A peasant (literally, people of the earth), hence an uneducated person. An Israeli friend commented to me that the average Israeli is not religiously oriented. "Their parents reacted against the orthodoxy of the old country," he noted. "But now they fear a child brought up without religion will be not only a skeptic but an aMORets."

"That was Lazansky, in the bakery, a giant teamster from the Ukraine. A huge ignorant man, an *amhoretz* who didn't know enough Hebrew to bless his bread" (Bellow *H*).

antiseMIT *n.* Anti-Semite. In "The Jew Bird" Malamud spells it "anti-Semeets," which suggests a Lithuanian accent.

Fiedler's character is attacking defenders of Stalin: "And what had Jacob been, after all, defending for so many years that monster, that *antisemit* in the Kremlin?" (Fiedler *LJA*).

apiKOYris *n.* Atheist. The term is based on the misapprehension of Epicurus (342?–270 B.C.E.) as the author of a godless system of belief, especially because of his strong philosophical materialist tendencies. He was, in fact, not irreligious. ApiKOYris is often used to identify the village atheist, who is accepted as a useful gadfly, though standing outside the conventional values of the society.

This is the basis of classical scholar Arnaldo Momigliano's comment: "[M. I.] Finley and myself, being Jews, have behind us the good old tradition of the Jewish *Epikoros*" (*NYRB*, 16 October 1975).

"To Adam Ha-shem [the Lord] spoke one way and when He finishes with Moses he talks another way. In a dream, in a wish. That *epikoros* Sigmund Freud, he also figured this out" (Ozick, "Usurpation," *BTN*).

ARbiter-ring *n.* Workman's Circle. The name of a Jewish fraternal and cultural organization with mildly socialist inclinations. The more radical group was the Jewish People's Fraternal Order, which was effectively destroyed by the McCarthy purges. Not uncharacteristically, the JPFO took a dogmatic and purist approach to Yiddish in the United States, while the ARbiter-ring was much more flexible and willing to accept linguistic change.

"Only a Jewish woman of a good, culture-respecting background—her father had been a tailor and a member of the Arbeiter-Ring, a Yiddishist—could sacrifice her life to a great artist as she had done" (Bellow *H*).

ashkeNAzi *n.* The term used for Jews originally from Germany. It refers in general to Western European Jewish communities and reflects an ancient split between the Palestinian and Babylonian traditions. Jews from the latter tradition (who settled in Spain and Portugal) are usually called seFARdim, as opposed to the ashkeNAzi Palestinian group. In recent years seFARdim has come to refer to the Jews who have emigrated to Israel from places other than Europe, especially Africa and the Middle Eastern countries. There is also a "racial" opposition in the sense that seFARdim are often dark-skinned.

The origin of these names [Sephardim and Ashkenazim], or rather of the application of these two biblical designations to the inhabitants of Spain and Germany, has long puzzled scholars, and no wholly satisfactory explanation has yet been offered. It appears that with the gradual shift of the Jewish geographic outlook to the western lands some biblical students were impressed by the similarity of sound between Hesperia [the Roman name for Spain] and Seferad, between Saxony or

"As-Skandz" and Ashkenaz. The identification of Seferad with Spain appears fairly well established in geonic writings [as early as the sixth century]. That of Ashkenaz with Germany did not appear in literature until after the first millennium. . . . The Sephardim, on the other hand, long included in the vast Muslim civilization and Jewishly centered in Babylonia, fell heirs to the Babylonian outlook and lore. Ashkenazic Jewry's divergences from its southern neighbors thus continued on a novel plane the ancient dichotomy between Palestine and Babylonia (Baron, *SHJ* 4).

More recently Sephardi refers to ultra-orthodox Jews from the Middle East and North Africa. They often refer to Ashkenazim as having a "soul-less Zionism."

AYDl mentsh *n.* A noble or genteel person. In contemporary usage it more likely refers to someone who puts on airs.

"You travel in style, with ostrich feathers. You're an *edel-mensch*. Get your hands dirty? Not you" (Bellow *H*).

az mi laybt, derLAYbt men Alis Literally, if you live, you will live through everything. There are interesting connotations: It's a way of saying that as long as you are alive, you can survive anything. And it also suggests that if you live long enough, you will experience all that life can give, both good and bad.

Leslie Fiedler used the expression (not quite accurately) to begin his piece "On Being Busted at Fifty": "'*Az m'lebt, m'lebt alles,*' my grandfather began telling me when *he* was fifty and presumably thought me old enough to understand, 'if you live long enough, you live through everything'" (*FR*).

aZOY vee a luhkh in kuhp Like a hole in the head. The source of what has become a standard American expression, as in "This I need like a hole in the head."

"From such a *meshiach* [savior] the public needed service like a *luch in kup*" (Heller *GG*).

aZOY zuhgt men A phrase from a joke with many variations: An anti-Semitic remark is addressed to an old man. He replies, "aZOY ret men tsu an ALTn REbn?" (Is that a way to talk to an old rabbi?)

Joseph Heller uses the expression when someone says to Henry Kissinger, "Henry you're full of shit." Gold comments: "*Azoy zugt men* to such *machers* [big shots] as a General and a Secretary?" (*GG*).

BADkhn *n.* The official jokester at a Jewish wedding. A BADkhn is a little like the court jester in the sense that he can get away with outrageous behavior not allowed anyone else. During the wedding he introduces the bride and groom, but usually in derisive and insulting contexts that poke fun at them, their families, and the whole institution of marriage. The use of a BADkhn has almost totally disappeared, but some of the routines survive in the repertoires of contemporary KLEZmer bands.

baGROOBn *part.* Buried. It also means beaten up, which provides some good punning possibilities. In a satirical song about the REbe, when he dies the disciples are "baGROOBn" (buried or just beaten up).

"That crooked cop? *Bagruben.* In *d'rerd* [in Hell] also" (Heller *GG*).

bai mir BIStu sheyn ("Bei Mir Bist Du Schoen") A famous song from the Yiddish theater, composed by Sholem Secunda. Literally, the song title means "you're beautiful to me." Secunda sold it cheaply and it became a pop hit when recorded by the Andrews Sisters.

A review of a Japanese group by critic Leonard Feather: "This incongruous interlude was good for a chuckle when Fujika brought on his tall, willowy singer, Chaka. As if 'I Wanna Be Loved by You, Boop-Oop-E-Doo' was not enough, she followed with 'Bei Mir Bist Du Schoen.' If anyone can break the listener's Hebraic heart with this song, Chaka can" (*Los Angeles Times*, 22 August 1989).

baleBUSte *n.* In European tradition, a title of high praise for a Jewish housewife. The masculine, baleBUS, means master or lord of the house; the baleBUSte is the sovereign in her own domain. Contemporary Jewish-American writers often associate the term with Jewish puritanism; for them the baleBUSte is a compulsive housewife whose obsession with cleanliness is one of a series of tortures inflicted upon her children.

"A *ballabusta*—she practically sleeps with a dustcloth in her hand" (P. Roth *GC*).

"He saw in her a sort of a *bahlabustuh*-cum-duchess who would survive her husband by twenty years" (Elkin, *CKKC*).

In his critique of Henry Kissinger, "Gold shivered anew at the sophomoric lunacy and preposterous intellectual claims of that noisy *balaboss*" (Heller *GG*).

"As my father said, '*Bolbotish.*' This generous, lovely, *bolbotish* success continues to kowtow to a putz" (P. Roth, *ST*).

In a *New Yorker* profile John Lahr describes Frank Sinatra's mother as a "typical Italian *balabusta*" (3 November 1997).

bal shem tuhv Literally, the Lord (or Master) of the Good Name. It is usually a reference to Israel Eliezer Bal Shem (ca. 1700–1760), also known as the BESHT (an acronym from bal shem tuhv), the founder of the Chasidic movement in modern times. Bal shem tuhv refers to a saintly man who performs miracles by invoking the secret names of God. It is a traditional term applied to many mystical figures (in ancient times Baal was the name of a pagan god), but since the eighteenth century it is usually associated with Eliezer, who founded the modern sect of Eastern European jews known as khSEEdim. Bal Shem Tuhv became a folk hero whose life and deeds spawned numerous legends, largely dealing with his powers as a miracle-working faith healer. Later these deeds became the target of numerous anti-Chasidic songs that ridiculed the alleged power of the Chasidic REbe (leader or teacher). My mother used to sing one: "Miracles, miracles, miracles—I saw it with my own eyes—the REbe walked right into the water—and came out wet." Bal Shem Tuhv consciously kept himself close to the common people and pointedly used Yiddish (rather than Hebrew) even in prayer. He encouraged his followers to express their religious enthusiasm in song and dance, even in the synagogue, thus providing a countermovement to the intellectualism of some rabbinical traditions. The khSEEdim liked to quote the Talmudic comment that explained that one of the gates of heaven could be entered only by song. Although Bal Shem Tuhv left none of his own writings, his reputation was propagated by many disciples after his death. The tradition has been continued by Martin Buber, the great modern interpreter of Bal Shem Tuhv's philosophy, especially in *Legends of the Baal-Shem* (1931) and *The Origin and Meanings of Hasidism* (1960). See also Isaac Bashevis Singer, *Reaches of Heaven: A Story of the Baal Shem Tov* (1980).

banDIT *n.* Literally, bandit. But also used endearingly, as in the expression "little devil."

Sophie Portnoy says of her darling Alex: "This *bonditt?* He doesn't even have to open a book—'A' in everything. Albert Einstein the second" (P. Roth *PC*).

BANkis *n. pl.* A thick glass cup about the size of a small light bulb used for medicinal purposes. Barbers in New York (continuing a medieval tradition) used to advertise "cupping" in addition to shaves and haircuts. I learned how to shtel BANkis (place cups) in order to alleviate the pain in my father's aching back, where BANkis are ordinarily placed, though occasionally the chest is treated as well. Working with a small torch made of a stick wrapped with cotton, dipped in alcohol, and lit from a candle, you hold the BANke in one hand, insert the torch quickly into its open end, and withdraw it, creating a partial vacuum. Then you immediately place the cup on the skin, where it sticks firmly. The object is to get as many on the area as possible—in my father's case that was about fifteen or twenty. After the BANkis have been applied, you cover them with a large towel (to prevent drafts) and let them set for about twenty minutes. Then you remove them gently, placing a finger under the lip of the cup to release the vacuum, producing a lovely popping sound for each one. The treatment concludes with a brisk alcohol rub. In the Middle Ages, when cupping was practiced widely in Europe, barbers, known as surgeons, made a small cut under each cup or inserted a leech to draw out the "bad blood." My father used to examine the ring made by each cup, pointing out that the darker spots marked the place where his "cold in the back" was—and where I had gotten a particularly good vacuum. I never got good enough to move the BANkis around once they were placed—that way you covered more ground without having to add cups. A virtuoso could do that with water glasses! A Mexican-American friend of mine in California knows the practice from his family. In Spanish the cups are called *ventosas.*

"Sit im HELFn vi a TOITn BANkis" (H. Roth *CIS*). Roth is quoting a famous saying: "It will help as much as putting BANkis on a corpse." ("Sit" is slurred speech for "es vet" [it will].)

bar MITSvuh *n.* Literally, a son of the commandment. It refers to the ceremony in which a Jewish boy acknowledges his heritage as a Jew, binds himself to the religious and communal values of his faith, and in turn is welcomed by the community. In the United States the ceremony takes place during the thirteenth year on a Sabbath morning close to the date of the boy's birthday. From that time the bar MITSvuh BUHkher (boy) is considered to be an adult and is eligible to take part in a MINyen (the quorum of ten men necessary for official occasions). In earlier times the preparation for the event was rigorous. An ethical treatise recommends the following schedule for educating the child prior to bar MITSvuh: from five years of age, study the Scriptures; at ten, study MISHne (the first section of the Talmud); at thirteen, fulfill the commandments; from fifteen, full study of the Talmud. In America, training for bar MITSvuh often consists of a series of crash courses aimed at making it possible for the boy to read some selected passages from the Scriptures. The highlight of the occasion is a speech in which the young man accepts his new role and thanks his parents, teachers, friends, and relatives. A standard opening line used to be "Today I am a man." In the past the youth could expect endless numbers of fountain pens as gifts—they were reasonable and appropriate. A famous parody line was "Today I am a fountain pen." A friend of mine used to make it a point to bring a pen to any bar MITSvuh she attended to keep the tradition alive. (Israel Horowitz is the author of a play entitled *Today, I Am a Fountain Pen.*) The modern bar MITSvuh is usually followed by a catered affair that often overshadows the traditional function of the ceremony and has become a notorious opportunity for conspicuous consumption. (See I. B. Singer's "A Bar Mitsvah in Brownsville.") A gag record describes the ultimate occasion: a "bar MITSvuh safari," preceded by the son's speech addressed to the United Nations and accompanied by Leonard Bernstein and the New York Philharmonic Orchestra. Reform and Conservative Jews sponsor a celebration for daughters, bas MITSvuh, partly to correct the lack of a comparable public occasion to acknowledge the girl's coming of age at twelve. Orthodox Jews will have no part of the ceremony. Gentiles are often confused about proper behavior, gifts, and attire. My friend, poet Philip Levine, when asked about proper clothing and behavior, used to recommend, "Wear a blue suit and don't say fuck." It's good advice for most occasions.

"Conversationally, Simon said, 'You know what I should, had better do, is take down her number.' He uncapped slowly the last of his *bar mitzvah* pens" (Markfield *TW*).

An advertisement in the *New Yorker* offers "A very special experience: Bar Mitzvah on Massada in Israel."

From an article on reporter John McCandish Phillips Jr. by Ken Auletta: "Gelb and Rosenthal held the story, hoping to confirm that Burros had been bar mitzvahed; when they did, Phillips wrote an insert, and the story was published" (*New Yorker*, 6 January 1997). Since the meaning is to become a son of the commandment, we should say "to become bar MITSvuh," rather than "to be bar MITSvuhd."

On Steven Spielberg's *Schindler's List*: "In a bizarre mixed metaphor, the *New Yorker*'s media critic suggested that the film 'has had the effect of a giant bar mitzvah, a rite of passage'" (Adam Bresnick, *TLS*, 18 July 1997).

David Mamet, quoted in a *New Yorker* profile: "'Being a writer out there is like going into Hitler's Eagle's Nest with a great idea for a bar-mitzvah festival'" (John Lahr, 17 November 1997).

BAYgl *n.* A breakfast roll shaped like a doughnut but not sweet and much harder. In fact, a stale BAYgl might make a dangerous missile. There are basically two kinds: the water BAYgl (the dough is boiled in water and then baked) and the egg BAYgl, which is slightly larger and of a softer consistency. The classic breakfast is a BAYgl with cream cheese and lox (smoked salmon); like chop suey, this is an American invention rather than a traditional dish. The BAYgl was formerly associated almost exclusively with eastern urban Jewish culture, but is now produced in many different parts of the country. A San Francisco baker calls them baygulls.

There is a joke about two Martians who land next to a bakery in New York. One of them spots a BAYgl in the window and asks, "What do you suppose that strange thing is?" The other answers, "I don't know, but I bet it would be terrific with cream cheese and lox."

BAYglhead was a common epithet in my old Brooklyn neighborhood—it meant dummy. One of my high school friends was known as BAYgls because he always had one in his mouth on the way to school.

Under the headline "The Schmear Campaign" and captions proclaiming "More than Just a Bagel" and "No hole? Oy Vay!" a *Newsweek* story describes the latest food fad: a "bagel with cream cheese baked right into it"—thus the Un-Holey bagel. "Frozen bagels led the way in the bagelization of America" (10 February 1997).

Calvin Trillin on "Killer Bagels": "I was surprised to read that bagels have become the most dangerous food in the country. I've lived in New York—which is to bagels what Paris is to croissants—for a number of years, and I've never been injured by a bagel. When I go back to Kansas where I grew up, old friends never say, 'Isn't it scary living in New York, what with the bagels and all?' My answer to that question would be that New Yorkers who were asked to name foods they think of as particularly benign would mention bagels as often as chicken soup" (*New Yorker*, 12 February 1966).

From an article entitled "American Fast Food in Israel: The Bagel": "Here's the epitome of Jewish food, right up there with knishes and latkes, right? Yet until not very long ago the closest thing to one in the Jewish state was either a rock-hard biscuit ring called a 'beygel' (the original Jewish name). Or a large, soft and sweet Arabic loaf." (*New York Times*, 9 March 1997).

No one has ever found a European equivalent.

bays MEdrish *n.* The house of study and prayer, from the Hebrew bet miDRASH. In many European communities such a place of study was kept so that scholars and students could read the Talmud and other commentaries on the Scriptures. Where possible the bays MEdrish was a separate structure from the synagogue itself.

"But what had the Young Jacob been remembering in fact, and the coming of what demon had he been hastening—slipping off more often than not from the beth midrash to read Werther and Heine's poems" (Fiedler *LJA*).

bays OYlem *n.* Cemetery. It derives from the Hebrew bet oLAM, literally the house of eternity, hence the final dwelling place of everyone.

"It was obligatory to wash when you returned from the cemetery (*Beth Olam*—the Dwelling of the Multitude)" (Bellow *H*).

BECHer *n.* A goblet. A Yiddish song has the lines "Dear Malke, may you be well, fill up the goblets, fill them with wine." (A Jewish *drinking song?* Right.)

In her critique of John Updike's Jewish novel *Bech: A Book,* Cynthia Ozick notes: "But while none of Updike's people has ever attained salvation, salvation is the grail they moon over. Bech's grail is cut in half, like his name, which is half a kiddush cup: *becher*" (Ozick *AA*). BECHer is not necessarily the KIdish cup, an ornamented silver goblet used for the blessing over the wine.

beHAYme *n.* Animal, or animal-like, behavior. From the Hebrew word that gives us behemoth. Often used sarcastically to compare a stupid person to an animal. In a recent political correctness issue, a black woman claimed she had been called beHAYme by an Orthodox student.

Bellow describes an old man who wouldn't eat lettuce: "He raised that intelligent face of his, demented by prejudices and harrowing ironies, and said, 'Give this to the *behemah*'" (*MDH*).

Evaluating Henry Kissinger, Gold saw "the strangest contrasts preserved between the ridiculous aura of success and knowledge that surrounded the self-satisfied *behayma* and the legacy of diplomatic wreckage and *tsuris* [troubles] he had left in his wake" (Heller *GG*).

BENKert *n.* An illegitimate child. Unlike the synonym MAMzer, BENKert connotes a love-child, not one merely born out of wedlock.

The father exclaims, "I tell you she'll bring me a 'benkert' yet, shame me to the dust. How do you know there isn't one in that lewd belly already" (H. Roth *CIS*).

BENTSHn *v.* To give the benediction after a meal or other gathering. From the Latin *benedicere,* it is a good example of one of the main influences on Early Yiddish that help to distinguish it from German.

BILig vee borsht Cheap as borsht. Borsht (pronounced borshtch in Russian) is beet soup, the common fare of peasants in many parts of Eastern Europe. Hardly anything is cheaper.

BISl *n.* A little bit.

Former Chairman of the Joint Chiefs of Staff, General Colin Powell, was reported to have spoken to former Israeli prime minister, Yitzkhak Rabin, in Yiddish, much to the latter's amazement. Powell apparently learned Yiddish in the Bronx, where he grew up. Confronted with the story, Powell replied: "It's definitely not true that I speak Yiddish. Well, maybe a *bissel*" (*New York Times*, 5 April, 1991).

black Jews In *Jews without Money* Mike Gold describes an occasion on which his father brought a black man home to dinner:

Harshly and firmly, he insisted he was a better Jew than anyone present. He was an Abyssinian Jew, descended from the mating of King Solomon and the Queen of Sheba. We others had wandered among the Gentiles, he said, and had been corrupted. But his people had kept the faith pure. For instance, we prayed only at morning and evening. His congregation prayed four times a day. We used seven twists in binding the phylacteries. His people used nine. . . . Reb Samuel was dumbfounded. My father hung his head in shame. At last the Negro left, haughtily kissing the *mezzuzah* again. By his manners one could see he despised us all as backsliders, as mere pretenders to the proud title of Jew.

Since the establishment of the Jewish state in Israel, many dark-skinned and Oriental Jews have settled there, resulting in serious and widespread racial problems. They highlight the fact that Jewish tradition has develpoed in many different directions and is hardly the homogeneous faith many Western Jews and Gentiles assume it to be. Still, the transportation of Ethiopian Jews to Israel in the mid-1980s reveals that country's commitment to saving the remnant of co-religionists, even though it raises problems. (At one point the Orthodox establishment thought of demanding that the Ethiopians undergo recircumcision! Fortunately there is a statute that says a little drop of blood will do. A general immersion in the MIKve was demanded and refused.)

A similar case is the black Rastafarian group in Jamaica, which worships Haile Selassie as a god. Since Selassie claimed to have descended from Solomon, by way of the Queen of Sheba, the Rastafari have defined themselves as one of the Lost Tribes, who will eventually return from their "Babylonian captivity" to their homeland in Africa. The Rastas practice many Jewish customs (including a basically KUHsher diet) and are close readers of the Hebrew

Scriptures. Bob Marley, one of the great Rasta reggae artists, referred often to Jah, an ancient name of God. This is not a localism but a reference to Psalm 68:4: "Sing unto God, sing praises to his name, JAH, and rejoice before him."

BLINts *n.* Anglish for BLINtse, a rolled pancake, filled usually with cheese but sometimes with fruit. The BLINts has become a specialty of American cooking and is often not associated with Jewish cuisine. Next to the BAYgl it has become the most assimilated of Jewish foods in the United States.

From a review of *Eve's Apple* by Jonathan Rosen: "He can describe a baby 'swathed like a blintz in a white blanket,' or a blank suburban house so unlived in it is 'like the clothing of a spy who has torn out all the labels so that he is "untraceable,"' or the way in which the somewhat aimless Joseph keeps the idea of law school 'lodged at the back of my mouth like a cyanide tablet'" (Susie Linfield, *Los Angeles Times Book Review*, 22 November 1996).

BOObee *n.* A term of endearment, originally for a child. It has been extended to such general meanings as kid, kiddo, honey, and baby. (Be careful not to pronounce it booby, as in booby hatch.) Since BOObee is used for both male and female, it is probably not derived from the German *Bube*, boy or lad. The Yiddish etymology suggests that it is based on BOObe (grandmother) and its diminutive, BOObele. A mother addressing her child is actually saying "my little mother." More recently (mainly through the agency of Jewish comics) BOObee has taken on a wider usage. It is an effective way to deflate what might otherwise be a pompous or pretentious statement, and in that respect it is comparable to "baby" in black speech.

In describing a video featuring the Rat Pack, Tom Kuntz writes, "Sinatra [to Sammy Davis Jr.]: 'We have plenty of time, booby— I think we just bought the building'" (*New York Times*, 8 June 1997).

Referring to his nose, Portnoy says, "Sorry, but there's no escaping destiny, *bubi*, a man's cartilage is his fate" (P. Roth *PC*).

"So what did you learn in school today, BOObee?" the mother asks. "I learned that my name is Irving."

boolVAN *n.* A brute, powerful but stupid. The word is based on the notion that a physically powerful person is likely to be a dummy. The word boolYAK has the same implication.

"But Lieberman veered like a *bulvan* and with his elbows clubbed his way between them to the bar, knocking an ashtray to the floor and blindly plopping a stubby paw smack into the center of a bowl of dried nuts with the atavistic luck of something Neanderthal and hungry" (Heller *GG*).

BOORtshe *v.* To rumble or gurgle. BOORtshe implies an inept attempt at expression.

"Kissinger, that *klutz*, Gold noted in salient triumph while chewing wolfishly, had *boorrchet* [should be geBOORtshet] and cried real tears like a *nebbish* in Salzberg when questioned about perjury and had beamed like a clever *shaygetz* [Gentile] in Washington later when the suspicions appeared well founded" (Heller *GG*). Heller later writes "*er hut boorrrchet* [geBOORtshet]." His consistent misspelling of the word is apparently onomatopoeic.

BOYtshik *n.* A young boy. In America BOYtshik is often used as the equivalent of buddy or kiddo: "Listen, BOYtshik, you're not such hot stuff."

"I've seen firetraps in my time, boychick, but this ain't for real" (Perelman *RG*).

"'Ho, boychik, you just missed some rhubarb,' he said one afternoon, slurring the word in a southern way" (Pete Hamill, *SIA*).

BRANZvil *n.* Yinglish for a section of Brooklyn actually called Brownsville. Until World War II Brownsville was a main center of Jewish settlement and activity. If a person hadn't climbed out of the Lower East Side ghetto (in Manhattan), then the next most prestigious place to be from was BRANZvil. In recent years the mainstream Jews have disappeared and it has been settled by blacks and Puerto Ricans along with khSEEdim.

In *Call It Sleep* Roth gives a fine transliteration—"Bronzeville." Arriving in New York City the mother asks, "Gehen vir voinen du? in New York?" (Will we live here in New York?) The father responds, "Nein, Bronzeville. Ich hud dir schoin geschriben." (No. In Bronzeville. I wrote you about it already.) Roth's characters are Austrian and speak a heavily dialectical GermanYiddish.

bris *n.* Circumcision, from the Hebrew bris MEEle, which means contract or covenant of circumcision. The bris takes place on the eighth day after birth and commemorates the covenant between the Jews and their God, as described in the Hebrew Scriptures:

And God said unto Abraham, Thou shalt keep my covenant therefore, thou and thy seed after you; every man-child among you shall be circumcised. And ye shall circumcise the flesh of your foreskin; and it shall be a token of the covenant betwixt me and you. And he that is eight days old shall be circumcised among you, every man-child in your generations, he that is born in the house or bought with money of any stranger which is not of thy seed. . . . And the uncircumcised man-child whose flesh of his foreskin is not circumcised, that soul shall be cut off from his people; he hath broken my covenant. . . . And Abraham took Ishmael his son, and all that were born in his house, and all that were bought with his money, every male among the men of Abraham's house; and circumcised the flesh of their foreskin in the selfsame day, as God had said unto him. . . . And Abraham was ninety years old and nine when he was circumcised in the flesh of his foreskin. In the selfsame day was Abraham circumcised, and Ishmael his son (Genesis 17).

As is often the case, Judaism has provided its own historical meaning for a tradition that has many varying implications for different cultures. Arnold van Gennep, in *The Rites of Passage*, has pointed out that circumcision "is exactly equivalent to pulling out a tooth (in Australia, etc.), to cutting off the little finger above the last joint (in South Africa), to cutting off the ear lobe or the septum, or tattooing, scarifying, or cutting off the hair in a particular fashion." The mutilated person, van Gennep argues, is separated from the mass of humanity by such rites and at the same time is permanently incorporated into a precise group. "The Jewish circumcision," he continues, "is in no way extraordinary; it is clearly a 'sign of union' with a particular deity and a mark of membership in a single community of the faithful." If the Jews had associated themselves with their God, he points out, "by perforating the septum [instead], how much fewer would have been the errors in ethnographic literature?"

An African folktale explains the origin of male and female circumcision (the latter is called excision): In the beginning, human beings were male and female at the same time. In the male, the foreskin represents the female principle; in the female, the clitoris represents the male principle. The practice of circumcision or excision ensures the masculinity of the male and the femininity of the female and makes possible the propagation of the race (from Susan Feldman, ed., *African Myths and Tales*). Sigmund Freud argues in *Moses and Monotheism* that circumcision represents "a symbolical substitute of castration, a punishment which the primal father dealt his sons long ago out of the fullness of his power; and whosoever accepted this symbol showed by so doing that he was ready to submit to the father's will, although it was at the cost of a painful sacrifice." There are no overt references to the sexual implications of circumcision in formal Jewish tradition—it is clearly different from the many circumcision rituals in tribal cultures that usually occur at the time of puberty. But the famous shnit (cut) figures prominently in Jewish humor. One joke concerns a moyl (the man who performs the operation) who hangs a clock outside his shop. "But you're a moyl, not a watchmaker," someone complains. To which the moyl responds, "So what then should I hang outside?" Then there was the famous geneticist, August Weismann, who kept cutting off rats' tails to disprove the idea that acquired characteristics could be inherited. If he had taken Jewish tradition into account, one of his colleagues remarked, he could have spared himself the trouble.

There has been a great deal of discussion as to whether circumcision heightens or impedes the pleasure of sexual intercourse. Similarly, medical advice about the necessity for circumcision varies with the times. Until recently it was generally recommended as a precaution against infection. At this writing there seems to be a movement against circumcision on the ground that all unnecessary surgery ought to be avoided.

At the bris someone traditionally offers to buy back the foreskin for Israel. One of my uncles used to suggest that the foreskin be fried and passed around to the guests. It was a gag, but the suggestion would have easily been understood by most tribal societies, where conservation of magical resources is highly valued.

From a review of Cynthia Ozick's novel *Puttermesser Papers:*

"And she has the son she never had on earth: 'They circumcised him and planted the tiny golden foreskin under an olive tree, and every olive on every branch began to take on the color of gold'" (Jack Miles, *New York Times Book Review*, 15 June 1997).

From a health digest: "Mohels, the practitioners of the ancient Jewish rite of circumcision, appear to inflict less pain on their subjects than do most doctors, possibly because of the tools they use, a researcher says" (*Fresno [California] Bee*, 21 August 1997).

BROOder *n.* (*pl.* BREEder) Brother. In addition to identifying the family relationship, BROOder also has the connotation (as in English) of buddy or fella.

"One thing you can be sure, *bruder*, I have no axe to grind" (Bellow *H*).

BRUHkhe *n.* From the Hebrew, meaning benediction, blessing. There are large numbers of benedictions for most of the major (and some minor) aspects of life and ritual. A standard formula, such as buhRUKH aTUH aduhNOY (Blessed art thou, Lord our God), is followed by whatever is prescribed or proscribed.

Writer Howard Jacobson recalls, "As I remember, most sentences boiled down to 'Blessed art thou O Lord' because of something or other that thou hast given us, or 'Blessed art thou O Lord' because of something thou hast taken away" (*TLS*, 3 May 1985).

Portnoy, worrying about his mother's biopsy: "And then there is that word we wait and wait and wait to hear, the word whose utterance will restore to our family what now seems to have been the most wonderful and satisfying of lives, that word that sounds to my ear like Hebrew, like *b'nai* or *boruch*—benign! *Benign!* Boruch atoh Adonai, *let it be benign*" (P. Roth *PC*).

BUbu *n.* Anglish for a mistake or obvious error; also a minor scratch or cut. The basic meaning probably comes from Yiddish theater slang. When an actor muffed a line, he was said to have spoken as if he had a potato (BULbe) in his mouth. BULbe then gradually became BUbu. I can remember as a child bringing BUbus to my mother so she could take the pain away with a kiss.

Admitting a mistake: "This, I now acknowledge, was a provocative booboo" (Bellow *HFM*).

"I want Mr. Zuckmayer to check on a couple of scenes—you know, to make sure you don't pull a booboo" (Perelman *RG*).

BUHbe-MAlse *n.* An old wives' tale; a fanciful story. Literally, grandma's tale, such as might be told by an old woman, far-fetched and full of superstition. The word for grandmother may be pronounced BUHbe, BOObe, or BAbe, according to the dialect. It's possible that the term comes from a book of fanciful romances written specifically for women, called the *Bova Buch*, hence not believable. A corny Phil Silvers joke: "I just went to see my grandma and got a haircut. She's my BAbe, you see."

Mike Gold explains, "I don't believe in Dybbuks. . . . It is all a grandmother story. . . . How full I was of all the Baba stories that were told in my village about America" (*JWM*).

From a review of Gish Jen's novel, *Mona in the Promised Land:* "And while this miniculture may be synthesized from Chinese *bobbe-mysehs* and Yiddish tonalities, it is nourished simply by their pleasure in each other's company" (Anna Shapiro, *New Yorker*, 8 July 1996).

BUHPkis *n.* Literally, beans. But the word is also used to indicate something absolutely worthless, very much like our expression "not worth a hill of beans." You might say, "What did I get for my effort—BUHPkis!" BUHPkis also works as an expletive, not as strong as "bullshit" but carrying the same connotations.

Mike Gold here uses the literal meaning (which may also be BEBlech): "A humpbacked old witch in a red kerchief hobbles by, pushing a baby carriage covered with cloth. There is no baby in there, but a big pot full of hot black-eyed beans. 'Bubkes!' she wails in a sort of Chinese falsetto, 'buy my hot, fresh bubkes'" (*JWM*).

" 'Short list doesn't mean a thing,' Barker said. 'I've been there many, many times. I'll wager I've been on more short lists than any other tenured professor in the United States. Short list is bubkas'" (Anne Bernays, *PR*).

buhTINskee *n.* Yinglish for one who specializes in minding someone else's business; a busybody. The Slavic-sounding suffix personifies the one who butts in, as if it were Mr. or Mrs. Buttinsky.

"She was a buttinsky. She tried to 'reform' everybody, and fought people because they were 'bad'" (Gold *JWM*).

BYAlee *n.* Anglish for BYAlistuhke PLEtsl (the roll from Bialystok), a breakfast roll. It takes its name from the city that has been shunted back and forth between Poland and Russia. The bakery item is round, with a depression (but not a hole) in the middle. The dough is of a distinctive consistency similar to that of pizza. Although there are onion flakes on a BYAlee, it should not be confused with an onion roll (TSIbele PLEtsl). BYALees may be unique to New York City—I'm not sure they ever existed in Bialystok. Although BAYgl bakers have defected as far west as Los Angeles and San Francisco, BYAlee bakers haven't budged. Outside New York City one often encounters a roll that looks like a BYAlee but, perhaps because a different kind of flour is used, it always turns out to be an ersatz concoction. Like the "egg cream" (a popular New York drink made of carbonated water, chocolate syrup, and a dash of milk), the BYAlee is rarely advertised. But it can be purchased in almost any bakery or deli in New York City. It is the BAYgl's only rival as a breakfast roll—in terms of cream cheese and lox, of course. (With the disappearance of soda fountains, the egg cream is all but extinct.)

A *New Yorker* cartoon depicts a bookstore-cum-café, where a woman says to the clerk: "A bialy, a latte, and 'A Farewell to Arms'" (Michael Maslin, 23 and 30 June 1977).

From a profile of Robert Morgenthau: "When we went inside for a lunch of toasted bialys and smoked salmon, Morgenthau dutifully showed me the family heirlooms" (James Taub, *New Yorker*, 28 July 1997).

Chasidim—see KHOOsid

CHOTCHke—see TSAtskele

chutzpah—see KHOOTSpe

daiYAYnu *n.* Hebrew for "that would suffice." Also the title of a lively Hebrew song popular during the celebration of Passover. It says "If the only thing God had done was to take us out of slavery—that would suffice. If the only thing God had done was to give us the TOYre—that would suffice."

DAVn *v.* To pray. In Anglish the participle is DAvening.

In "The Jewbird" the bedraggled fowl announces that he is Jewish and then proceeds to prove it: "The bird began dovening. He prayed without Book or talith [prayer shawl] but with passion" (Malamud *IF*).

"He watched Rosa *dovening. That's* what was bringing out the Jew in him: a Catholic down on the floor. Always did" (P. Roth *ST*).

From John Lahr's review of *Ragtime*, the musical: "The novelist
E. L. Doctorow can't bow. He may write like an angel, but he bows
like an undertaker. He sort of davens from the shoulders up" (*New
Yorker*, 20 January 1997).

DIbik (Usually dybbuk) *n*. A wandering soul that seeks to find rest
by inhabiting the body of another, from whom it must ultimately
be exorcised. The idea is usually associated with the medieval tradition of the kaBUHLe, but it is probably a much older conception related to similar beliefs that abound in the folklore of many
peoples. In Orthodox Jewish tradition God is the source of all spiritual power, and when an individual dies the soul simply reverts
to Him. The basis for belief in a DIbik is thus heretical because it
suggests that some souls are in limbo and not controlled by God.
The underlying notion is related to the idea of transmigration of
souls (metempsychosis), which was in fact one of the concerns
of the Kabbalists. (James Joyce in *Ulysses* associates the idea of metempsychosis with his Jewish protagonist, Leopold Bloom.) Jewish
folklore retained the tradition of the DIbik, and it became the subject of an impressive drama by the Russian-Jewish writer S. Ansky
(Solomon Z. Rappaport, 1863–1920). *The Dybbuk*, originally written in Yiddish, is still occasionally staged, but the classic presentation was in Hebrew by Habima, an Israeli theater group that was
an offshoot of the Moscow Art Theater. In Ansky's play the DIbik
is exorcised by the sound of the SHOYfer (the ram's horn traditionally blown to usher in the new year). The place of the DIbik
in Jewish demonology is described by one of the characters in
Ansky's play: "The souls of the dead *do* return to earth, but not as
disembodied spirits. Some pass through many forms before they
achieve purification. The souls of the wicked return in the forms
of beasts, or birds, or fish—even of plants, and are powerless to
purify themselves by their own efforts. They have to wait for the
coming of some righteous sage to purge them of their sins and set
them free. Others enter the bodies of the newly born, and cleanse
themselves by well-doing. . . . Besides these, there are vagrant
souls which, finding neither rest nor harbor, pass into the bodies
of the living, in the form of a Dybbuk, until they have attained
purity."

Igor Stravinsky commented on his condition after a series of operations: "I was pale as a dybbuk, and so thin that I resembled my former self like a photograph taken by a thermal camera" (*NYRB,* 23 October 1969).

DRAYdl *n.* A top used in a game played during the celebration of KHANike. The Hebrew letters N, G, H, Sh (standing for the words of the Hebrew phrase "a great miracle occurred there") are inscribed on the sides of the top. In terms of the game, the letters stand for the Yiddish words nisht (nothing), gants (all), halb (half), and shtel (put in). You follow suit according to the way the top falls, the tokens being nuts or candies (we also used M&Ms).

"When I play the game of dreidel with myself, and the dreidel falls on the same letter five or six times because I will it to do so, I can assume that it happened by chance. However, when I spin the dreidel ten times and it comes out the same, I know that chance has nothing to do with it" (Singer *S*).

"'And he intends to follow the story just as it stands?' 'Down to the smallest financial and emotional *drehdel,* he swore'" (Perelman *RG*). Here DRAYdl means detail, in the sense of "following every turn"—not a precise usage.

In a *New Yorker* profile of disk jockey Howard Stern, his cohort John "Stuttering" Melendez is quoted: "Melendez approached the bearded group ZZ Top and asked, 'Since you look Jewish, Why dddd—don't you call yourselves ZZ Dreidel?'" (David Remnick, 10 March 1997).

"In his grave Franklin Roosevelt is spinning like an atomic dreydl" (P. Roth *ST*).

drek *n.* Shit. The literal meaning is almost always passed over in American usage, where drek more often means shoddy or cheap rather than feces or dirt. There is a story (probably apocryphal) that one of the large detergent manufacturers had a new product almost ready to be put on the shelf, when an employee pointed out the irony of the slogan: "The All New Drek." The adjective in Yiddish is DREKish, in Anglish usually DREKee. A headline in the *Fresno Bee* reads: "Art Dreco—One Man's Junk is Another Man's . . ." (29 March 1980). The body of the article gives the etymology as a cross between "dreadful and Deco," coyly refusing to state the literal meaning—the way "some translate the Yiddish expression."

Standard billing for a cheap act: "Drek from Las Vegas."

"'Look I'll handle the whole thing for you,' Sandor assured him. 'You'll come out of all this *dreck* smelling like a roast'" (Bellow *H*). Heading of a review by Christopher Porterfield of J. F. Powers's *Wheat That Springeth Green:* "The separation of Church and Dreck was a matter of life and death for the World" (*Time,* 29 August 1988).

A TV review in the *San Francisco Chronicle:* "It's a disgrace that [Michael] Learned is on dreck like 'Dolls'" (25 September 1989).

"Well, that's something I guess, a tribute to our ability to homogenize and package dreck. In my more pessimistic moments it strikes me that dreck's one of our principal products. In view of this monolithic corporation-sponsored dreckness settling on the land, it's grotesque to work up a lather about a 20-watt alternative radio station" (Stanley Poss, op-ed, *Fresno Bee,* 6 July 1996).

William Safire: "'School uniforms, the evils of tobacco and the mindless dreck on television,' wrote Michael Elliott in the *Washington Post,* are the '*quotidian* issues' engaging so many of us today. (*Dreck,* first cited in print by James Joyce in 'Ulysses,' is a Yiddish word that today is euphemized as 'rubbish, nonsense, junk')" (*New York Times,* 2 February 1997). I doubt the Joyce reference. Ever the great bowdlerizer, Safire neglects to inform us that the literal meaning of the word is shit. In writing about shmuhk, he translated it erroneously as penis. (See entry below.)

EMiss *n.* Truth. The Hebrew is eMET.

"Presumption! Atheist! Devourer! For us there is the Most High, joy, life. For us trust! But you! A moment ago I spoke your own heart for you, *emes?*" (Ozick *BTN*).

"Gold's father grunted at Sid in a touching undertone. '*Emmis?*' He was discontented when Sid nodded" (Heller *GG*).

Epis *pron.* Something. In Yiddish Epis is often a crutch word: "er iz geVUHRn Epis a RAIKHer man (he has become something of a rich man). Or, "vuhs iz Epis geSHEN?" (what has [something] happened?).

farBISn *adj.* Grim and obstinate, embittered.

"Muriel had always been embittered and self-centered—the *farbisseneh* one, his mother would say, an observation made more in woe than reprimand" (Heller *GG*).

farKLEMT *adj.* Distraught. A character in drag on "Saturday Night Live" complains about "her" life and concludes by saying, "I'm so farKLEMT!" It actually means distraught but carries the image of being stuffed up or repressed.

farSHTEENKener *adj.* Stinking. A good strong term of derision. A gag "Chinese kosher" cookbook lists Fah Shtunk Ken Ah Fish Rolls.

"And when Sophie again affirmed all that she had been saying, he looked at her with compassion and murmured, very bitterly for him, '*Oy vey*, what a *farshtinkener* world is this'" (Styron *SC*).

"The professors are always schlepping in Swift to defend some farshtunkeneh nobody" (P. Roth *ST*).

FARtig *adj.* Finished, the end, period.

"If I said black he said white. If I said white he said . . . niggers, they're ruining the neighborhood, one and all, and that's it. *Fartig*. That was when he was in real estate. Far back, that peremptory cry of *Fartig* would instantly create an obedient silence that everybody in the family would be in horror of breaking, including Gold's mother" (Heller *GG*).

FAYgele *n.* (*pl.* FAYgelekh) Little bird, the diminutive of FOYgl. FAYge is also a woman's name (often translated into English as Florence). FAYgele can also connote effeminacy.

As is often the case, Joseph Heller doesn't get it right. "'Not so fast,' objected the old man. 'I got a couple of dead *faygelehs* [FAY-gelekh] I want to watch on television tonight'" (*GG*).

fe An exclamation of distaste. Its effective range extends from malodorous substances to political or critical comments.

"'Feh,' says a voice in the rear" (Malamud *TT*).

fin *n.* A five-dollar bill. Anglish from FINif, the Yiddish word for five. It has long been used in gambling and underworld jargon.

FINsternish *n.* Literally, "a darkness." As Bellow uses it in *Herzog*, it refers to a moment of dark foreboding.

"'Blame your own weak nature,' said Zipporah. 'Az du host a schwachen natur, wer is der schuldig? [Whose fault is it if you have a weak nature?] You can't stand alone. . . . A *finsternish!*'"

FORshpais *n.* Literally, an appetizer.

"Squeezing. Manages a pre-come that way, a *forshpeis*, squeezing the whole cunt hard as she can, and now she has decided: she doesn't want to stop" (P. Roth *ST*).

forts *n.* A fart. It can also mean nil or zero, as in the comment, "It isn't worth a forts."

FRAYlekh *adj.* Merry, cheerful, gay. Also the name for a special Jewish dance tune often played at weddings. During the 1930s jazz trumpeter Ziggy Elman recorded a version of the traditional "SHTILer bulGAR," which he called "Fralich in Swing." Benny Goodman heard it, asked Johnny Mercer to supply some English lyrics, and recorded it with vocalist Martha Tilton in 1939. The tune became popular under the title "And the Angels Sing." In the middle of the record the band performs it in the traditional style, with Elman playing the lead. (See the discussion of KLEZmer music in appendix 2.)

freg nit Don't ask. To the question "How are you doing?" the response is "Don't ask." Poet Philip Levine has a volume of interviews entitled *Don't Ask.*

fres *v.* To eat excessively or vulgarly; ordinarily used to describe an animal's eating. Es means to eat, fres means to gorge oneself or behave outrageously in the process of eating. It has a lightly sardonic tone and results in terms like FRESer (a heavy eater) and Anglish FRESing (pigging out).

"I'm telling you because I know him, he'll be taking it easy on the daybed. Oh boy, he'll be *fressing* an egg and onion sandwich" (Markfield *TW*).

FUHLKStimlech *adj.* In folk style; folksy. It's a useful term, borrowed from German, to describe something based on folk tradition but the result of known authorship. It covers a lot of what in our tradition is called pop—based closely on authentic folk styles but significantly removed from them. I call it poplore (Bluestein *P*).

FUHNfe *v.* An onomatopoeic word that describes the sound made when someone slurs words or speaks nasally and unclearly. It has largely become a show business term—an actor will be cautioned not to FUHNfe when saying lines. But it also refers to a nervous hesitation when a person is uncomfortable about making a statement, as if not quite wanting to say the words in a way that can be understood.

Writing about his ambivalent attitude toward capital punishment, Norman Mailer states, "When my host asked about the death penalty, I *phumphered.* 'I'm not for it,' I allowed, 'but I'm not against it, altogether, either. I think we need a little capital punishment'" (*Parade,* 8 February 1981).

"'What's wrong with him is he's like Walter Connolly, he goes in for *fumfing.*' 'I don't mind it when Walter Connolly *fumfehs,*' said Simon's mother. 'His *fumfing* I can take. Only when H. B. Warner *fumfehs* he doesn't just *fumfeh.* He *fumfehs* the way Lewis Stone *fumfehs;* he *boorchahs!*' [BOORtshe is to rumble or mutter]" (Markfield *TW*).

"Kissinger was an ingrate to his benefactors ('Kissinger bad-mouths practically everybody he knows, presidents included') and could *funphfeh* like a *gonif* when pressed for the truth" (Heller *GG*).

fuhts *v.* Anglish for puttering around, doing something insignificant or nonfunctional. It may be a combination of "fooling (or fucking) around" with "PUHTSing around." In that case fuhts is a euphemism. In the following example Portnoy means fool around or mess with, a less common usage.

"Oh yeah, when I am holding all the moral cards, watch out, you crooks you! I am nobody to futz around with" (P. Roth *PC*).

"At first she didn't realize. She didn't have to futz around in Paris with all that post-war sleaze. This girl had brains enough to be a chief executive officer of a blue chip corporation" (Bellow *MDH*).

An entry in John Cheever's diary: "I belt down a great deal of bourbon before lunch, futz around. Buy flowers for Mary" (*New Yorker,* 28 January 1991).

galitsiANer *n.* A person from Polish Galicia (Russian Galitsiya), an area in southeastern Poland and the northwestern Ukraine. A galitsiANer has an easily identified accent and is often considered to be a difficult and temperamental individual, perhaps not very well educated. Such regional prejudices also include LITvaks, people from Lithuania.

"Hey, hey, you're a *Galitzianer!*' Mrs. Cheper chuckled. 'Right?' Merz locked fingers and waved like a happy prizefighter. 'Touch a *Galizianer* and you're holding a cucumber,' Mrs. Cheper told the crowd. 'It's an old saying.' 'Scratch a *Litvak* and you're peeling radishes,' Merz countered happily" (Markfield *TW*).

ganAYdn *n.* Garden of Eden. It is two words in Hebrew.

"Puttermesser, while working in the Municipal Building, had a luxuriant dream, a dream of *gan eydn*—a term and notion handed on from her great-uncle Zindel, a former shammes in a shul that had been torn down" (Ozick *L*).

GANif *n.* Thief. A favorite expression is "AMERike GANif," used in grudging admiration for American knowhow or accomplishments.

"And you had to have a partner, a *goniff?*" (Bellow *H*)

"'You little gonif,' my impatient mother used to call me. This didn't signify that I was literally a crook; it meant that I had a masked character" (Saul Bellow *A*).

The headline of a review of a Hunter S. Thompson book: "The Gonif of Gonzo" (*Los Angeles Times Book Review*, 29 June 1997).

gay in drerd Go to hell. Literally, go into the ground.

"'You know, we Chinese have an old proverb—' 'So do we Yankees,' I cut him short. 'It runs, "A fool and his money are soon parted." Well, *geh in d'rerd*, old man'" (Perelman *TMP*).

GAZln *n.* Robber, murderer. It often has a slightly sardonic tone and may be applied to a child or an adult for whom there is a feeling of grudging admiration. A verse in a Jewish folk song:

When a GAZln murders someone, he does it with a knife.
But you, you're worse than a murderer—
You kill and kill me, yet I never die.

It's a classic definition of love. (See "Oyfn yam" in the Bluestein Family album, *Where Does Love Come From?* as listed in the Discography.)

Chiding her husband, Herzog's mother says, "Answer me, *gazlan*. Could you give a blow on the head?" (Bellow *H*).

"A doctor of *medicine* you want? Some fancy *gozlin* from Park Slope that'll rob you blind" (Styron *SC*).

geDEERn *n.* Intestines or innards.

In a *New Yorker* profile of Yip Harburg, the songwriter says everything he wrote came "as they say in Yiddish from my gedeeren," meaning from his guts (30 September 1996).

geFILte fish *n.* A special dish often served during the Passover meal. Literally, filled fish, because it is sometimes stuffed into a covering, like KISHke. The key to making geFILte fish is using a mixture of three kinds of fish: carp, whitefish, and pike. The dish is usually served as fishballs with onions and carrots, and always with a serving of strong horseradish (khrayn) as a condiment. It's always tasty, but for some reason it is served only during Passover. GeFILte fish can usually be purchased in jars in any large supermarket. Except for a little MSG it's not bad as manufactured stuff goes.

From a review of *Barney's Version* by Mordecai Richter: "every rift is loaded with ore, not always precious: a case, one may feel, of over-egged cake, or over-gefilte fish" (D. J. Enright, *TLS*, 5 September 1997).

geNOOG shoyn Enough already. This has become an American expression.

Herzog's mother pleads with her husband, "Yonah—I beg you. *Genug schon.*"

Fresno Bee columnist Dennis Pollock: "Happy anniversary, my hind foot. Every time you turn on the television these days, someone is talking about something that happened 20 years ago or 50 or 15. . . . Enough, already" (3 September 1989).

A *Los Angeles Times* review complaining about the number of times Eddie Murphy's name appears in the credits for his film *Harlem Nights* (as producer, writer, director) is headlined, "Enough Already!" (18 November 1989).

From an article titled "Sexual Politics": "The solution to every ill has been illumination and exposure, even and especially when it comes to the arena of sexuality, man at his most mammalian. Enough already. It's time to dim the lights" (Henry Louis Gates Jr., *New Yorker*, 25 August and 1 September).

geVALT An exclamation meaning "help!"

"Gevalt, a pogrom" (Malamud *IF*).

giMAtreea *n.* Reading words for their numerical meanings, or numbers for their verbal meaning. The possibility arises because the Hebrew letters are also numbers: alef = 1, bays = 2, giml = 3, and so on. Thus every word has a numerical neaning (khai, which means life, equals 18). Every number can also be related to equivalent words. With a little imagination and ingenuity a world of correspondences can be conjured up through words or numbers. My father, who had been trained in giMAtreea in Bessarabia, once sent a check for $14.75 on the occasion of my son's birthday. I suspected there was some special calculation involved and, indeed, he explained that he had added the age, date, number of letters in my son's name and mine; divided by the number of stops between Brighton Beach and Times Square on the subway; and subtracted the numerical equivalent of my son's namesake in the family. Well, if the procedure wasn't exactly like that, it's close enough to give some idea of the complication and playfulness that can be involved.

"The vestibule is this world, and the hall is the world-to-come. Listen. In gematriya, the words 'this world' come out one hundred sixty-three, and the words 'world-to-come' come out one hundred and fifty-four. The difference between 'this world' and 'the-world-to-come' comes out nine. Nine is half of eighteen. Eighteen is chai, life. In this world there is only half of chai. We are only half alive in this world! Only half alive" (Potok *TC*).

glat *adv.* Flat or smooth. It generally means extremely. In New York the term glat kosher often appears in Chinese restaurants, meaning rigorously kosher.

"As an indication of the importance Clinton laid on the Jewish vote, the southern Baptist promised (surely he didn't know what he was doing) that if he was elected President there would be a glatt—that is, rigorously—kosher kitchen in the White House" (*New Yorker*, 11 May 1992).

go figure Anglish, meaning try to figure it out. The Yiddish is gay vays, go know.

Joseph Epstein in a review of Sander L. Gilman's *Smart Jews:* "Less than one-half per cent of the world's population, Jews have won more than fifteen per cent of the Nobel Prizes given since the beginning of the prizes in 1901. Go, as the Jews themselves say, figure" (*TLS*, 7 March 1997).

Goniff—see GANif.

goot YUHNtif Happy holiday. From the Yiddish goot (good), and the Hebrew yom (day) and tuhv (good). It's the standard greeting on holiday occasions. The equivalent for the Sabbath is "goot SHAbis," to which the response is "goot YUHNtif."

"A very pale moon rose slowly. So did a stranger as they approached the bench. 'Gut yuntif,' he said hoarsely" (Malamud *IF*).

goy *n.* The Hebrew word for nation, it came to mean nations other than the Jews. The plural is GOYim, in Anglish often goyz. GOYishe and GOYisher are adjectives. GOYe is the feminine, though SHIKse is more likely to be used. In *Sophie's Choice*, Styron's Gentile narrator, usually accurate in his use of Yiddish, states, "At first Blavkstock . . . was rather distressed that the agency sent him a young woman who was a goy [GOYe]." The famous passage from Isaiah in Hebrew is "lo YISa goy el goy KHERev" (nation shall not raise sword against nation).

Goy and GOYim always have derogatory connotations, unfortunate because there is no neutral term in Yiddish comparable to "Gentile." There have been many attempts to substitute nit-yeed (literally, not Jew) but the term has not caught on. At the same time one frequently sees goy applied to second- and third-generation Jews who have lost contact with Jewish culture. In Philip Roth's *Goodbye, Columbus*, Mr. Patimkin says, "You know more than my own kids. They're *goyim* my kids, that's how much they understand."

Ultraorthodox Jews in Israel who do not acknowledge the legitimacy of the state because they are still waiting for the Messiah to come refer to even devout Zionists and other Israelis as GOYim. ("Why do you think I brought my people from Russia to America and not Eretz Yisroel [Israel]? Because it is better to live in a land of true goyim than to live in a land of Jewish goyim" [Potok *TC*].)

According to Lenny Bruce: "Evaporated milk is goyish even if the Jews invented it. Chocolate is Jewish and fudge is goyish. Spam is goyish and ryebread is Jewish." Bruce has also noted that if you live in New York City you're Jewish even if you're not, and if you live in Montana you're not Jewish even if you are.

The opposite of GOYish is YIDish. YIDishkait refers to the qualities associated with being Jewish, GOYishkait to all those that reflect Gentile values, and the opposition between the terms accentuates the isolation of the Jews from the host countries in which they have been minorities. The resulting ethnocentrism can be seen as a defense or an affirmation—or both. Despite persistent and influential interaction, the distinction between Jew and Gentile continues in varying degrees to the present time. There are periodic warnings that intermarriage will destroy the Jewish identity, and most rabbis will not perform mixed marriage ceremonies. The words to a well-known Yiddish folk song my mother taught me when I was about ten years old emphasize the difference:

> A Jew enters a bar to have a little glass of wine.
> Sober he is and sober must be,
> Because he is a Jew.
> A goy enters a bar to have a little glass of wine.
> Drunk he is and drink he must,
> Because he is a goy.

In Bellow's book *The Victim* a character refers to the song: "You Jews have funny ideas about drinking. Especially the one that all Gentiles are born drunkards. You have a song about it—Drunk he is, drink he must because he is a Goy . . . Schicker [drunkard]."

A joke of Eastern European origin concerns the Jew who is forced to convert to Christianity. But the morning after his conversion he rises early and recites the Hebrew prayer that accompanies the ritual of winding the phylacteries (TFILn) around the arm and forehead. His wife reminds him that he is no longer a Jew. "Ach," the old man says, slapping his head, "GOYisher kuhp!" (Literally, head of a Gentile, but it means "the brains of a goy.") The term of approbation is "YIDisher kuhp."

Jewish-American humor, on the other hand, often emphasizes the extent to which ethnic traditions merge in the United States. A man enters a Chinese restaurant and is greeted by a black waiter. That's odd, he thinks, as he asks for the specialty of the house. "Pizza," the waiter replies. "Unbelievable," says the customer. "How can that be? Here we are in a Chinese restaurant, the waiter is black, and the specialty of the house is pizza!" The waiter replies, "Well, you have to keep in mind—this is a Jewish neighborhood."

Bellow's Yiddish is always correct: "Beside his bed, the goyische lady sat in her long skirts and button shoes" (*H*).

The Last Dragon, described as a kung fu comedy, features scenes in a noodle factory named "Sum Dum Goy."

In the Jewish finger-play game, the thumb is goy, the little finger is Jew.

Gold's father says, "*A goy bleibt a goy* [a Gentile will always be a Gentile; i.e., he will not give up his anti-Semitism]" (Heller *GG*).

"He was amazed by her lack of control—by *anyone*'s lack of control but particularly by the lack of control of the goy who drank. Drink was the devil that lurked in the goy—'Big-shot goyim,' his father said, 'the presidents of companies, and they're like Indians with firewater'" (P. Roth *AP*).

From a review of Michael Steinlauf's *Bondage to the Dead:* "He was villified as a liar and a purveyor of 'distinctive racism,' as was the Editor of the paper, the well-known writer Adam Michnik, who was called a supporter of 'anti-Polonism' and 'anti-goyism' (this from a distinguished Polish historian)" (Abraham Brumberg, *TLS*, 27 June 1997).

Joseph Epstein, reviewing Sander L. Gilman's *Smart Jews:* " 'How odd / Of God,' wrote William Norman Ewer, with malice aforethought, 'To choose / The Jews.' God did so, according to the best response I know, 'Because the *goyim* / Annoy Him'" (*TLS*, 7 March 1997).

From the same article: "In 1959, Robert Graves gave a talk to the Israel Commonwealth Association in Tel Aviv with the title 'What It Feels Like To Be a Goy,' in which he recounted his own attempt, in the intellectual fashion of the day, to scout his genealogy for Jewish ancestors—with, one needs to add, no success. 'Write me down as a *goy*,' Graves reported, 'and as a Protestant *goy:* than which nothing in the world could be more *goyesque*'" (*TLS*, 7 March 1997).

GOYlem (golem) *n.* The GOYlem is a clay figure that has been brought to life through incantations mentioning the secret names of God. This ancient folk tale became the source of a number of legends and literary adaptations. Ultimately, like Frankenstein's monster, the GOYlem disobeys its master. As a general term it refers to a stupid or lethargic person. My Yiddish show business family used to say of the typical audience (OYlem): "der OYlem is a GOYlem." The opposite is "der OYlem iz NISHka GOYlem." (The audience is no dummy.)

"He's been invented, that's what, like Frankenstein, you see, only he's been invented by a rabbi. He's made out of clay or some kind of shit like that, only he looks like a human. Anyway, you can't control him. I mean, sometimes he acts normal, just like a normal human. But deep down he's a runaway fuckin' *monster.* That's a golem. That's what I heard about Nathan. He acts like a fuckin' golem" (Styron *SC*).

In *Leviathan* Cynthia Ozick has collected a series of stories about a female GOYlem. "The creature churned into the living room and hurried back with two volumes, one in either hand; she held the pen ready in her mouth. She dumped the books on the bed and wrote: 'I am the first female golem.'"

"My writer's mind thinks in images and makes connections in metaphor. So I will introduce here a fanciful notion, the possibility that our President is a resolved phantom of cold war, a kind of Golem sprung from national premises and fears that have not been seriously examined in almost half a century" (E. L. Doctorow, *Nation,* 22 March 1986).

From a review of Cynthia Ozick's novel *Puttermesser Papers:* "The original golem, created in the 16th century (as Ms. Ozick explains) by the great Rabbi Judah Loew, cleansed Prague. Puttermesser's golem has a bigger project ahead. She will cleanse New York" (Jack Miles, *New York Times Book Review,* 15 June 1997).

From a review of Peter Demetz's *Prague in Black and Gold:* "Demetz is careful to separate the Rudolfine rabbi Judah Loew from the mystical legend of the golem, which was largely elaborated in later centuries. Today, of course, tourists in Prague can buy golem T-shirts" (*New York Times Book Review,* 3 August 1997).

GRAger *n.* A small hand toy with a ratchet mechanism that makes a grating noise. During the telling of the POOrim story, children turn the GRAger whenever the villain's name (HUHmen) is mentioned.

"They heard him the way Haman hears the *grager* on *Purim*" (Sholom Aleichem *SS*).

GREEvn *n.* Cracklings. A delicacy made from fried chicken skin and other assorted leavings. Anytime a chicken was cooked we would crowd near the stove for a taste of GREEvn.

". . . a total slave to her *kugel* and *grieben* and *ruggelech*" (P. Roth *PC*).

GRUHber yoong *n.* An impolite, unintelligent person. Literally, a thick, young man.

"Schwartz did not answer. What can you say to a grubber yung?" (Malamud *IF*).

"The remedy suggested by the dumb *putz* was limited nuclear warfare. *Zayer klieg* [very smart, ironically] that *grubba naar*" (Heller *GG*). "*Grubba naar*" (coarse or impolite fool) is not idiomatic.

GUHgl-MUHgl *n.* A folk remedy for sore throats and colds. It may be onomatopoeic for the sound of gargling. The recipes vary but usually include tea, lemon, aspirin, and sometimes a raw egg. It's guaranteed to provide relief, as anything hot with these ingredients might very well do. And as with folk medicine in general, if you believe it will help, it probably will.

Former New York Mayor Ed Koch gave his recipe to a radio interviewer: gargling with grapefruit, lemon, and honey.

guht *n.* God. Yiddish characteristically uses a suffix that connotes endearment and familiarity, such as GUHTinyu (my dear [little] God). That's also a good example of KHOOTspe.

greps *n.* A belch.

GUNsl *n.* Thug, gunslinger. According to the *Dictionary of American Slang,* it comes from Yiddish GANZl (goose) and has connotations of homosexuality as well.

"The Chicago Bar is being guarded outside by two of their descendants, kids in George Raft suits, many sizes too big, too many ever to grow into. One keeps coughing, in uncontrolled, dying spasms, The other licks his lips, and stares at Slothrop. Gunsels" (Pynchon *GR*).

On the rebirth of a hoodlum: "Gone was the schlammer [a specialist in breaking limbs] and gunsel of yore" (Fried *RFJG*).

haDAse *n.* The Hebrew form of the Persian name Esther. Most Americans know Hadassah as the name of the Women's Zionist Organization of America and are often surprised to hear it as a popular name in Israel.

haGUHde *n.* The narration describing the exodus from Egypt and numerous other elements of the Passover celebration. During the SAYder (the order of the meal) the haGUHde is read and interpreted. A highlight is the Four Questions, asked by the youngest child present; they begin, "Why is this night different from all other nights?" (My literature professor at Brooklyn College, Harry Slochower, used to begin our study of every new book by asking "the Passover question": Why is this book different from all other books?) The haGUHde text is often elaborately illustrated, and in the United States there are often special versions: politically radical, ecologically oriented, and so on. During World War II the Four Questions were associated with President Roosevelt's proposals for the Four Freedoms. An especially beautiful illustrated version was designed by artist Ben Shahn.

hak flaysh *n.* Chopped meat, hamburger. I have heard the term used mainly in prizefight contexts: "He made hak flaysh out of him in three rounds."

HAKd and SHLUGd *v.* Anglish for the verbs HAKn and SHLOOGn (to chop and hit).

Heller's Yiddish is tenuous at best (he often has the wrong grammatical forms) and is more Anglish/Yinglish than it is the real thing: "So off I went with my men to Keilah and fought with the Philistines, and hocked and *shlugged* them and aggravated them too, until their heads were aching and their bones were breaking and they could not stand it anymore" (Heller *GK*).

HAKn a TSHAInik Literally, to chop a teakettle.

"There is a better phrase for it in Yiddish: *hakn a tcheinik*, which means to chop a teakettle, or in American idiom, to talk up a breeze—or nonsense" (Rosenfeld *AE*).

haliVOODnik (Hollywoodnik) *n.* Everyone who grew up in my neighborhood has a favorite expression that means "you typical lazy American bum!" This was a friend's father's specialty. If my friend ever slept past seven in the morning, his father would call from downstairs, "haliVOODnik, the day is almost gone!" We used it as well thereafter to refer to anyone putting on airs.

HANDling *v.* Anglish for HANDln, to engage in business or commercial activity.

Joseph Heller uses it to mean wheeling and dealing: "He lied about peace and lied about war; he lied in Paris when he announced 'peace was at hand' just before the presidential elections and he lied again afterward by blaming North Vietnam for bad faith when all his *hondling* went *mechuleh* [self-destructed]" (*GG*).

HAYmish *adj.* From the word for home, it means the way you behave there—at ease, in a friendly, unpretentious manner. Plain folks are HAYmishe MENtshn.

"It was not a *shayna Yid* [SHAYner yeed—a good person] who would go down on his knees on a carpet to pray to *Yaweh* with that *shmendrick* Nixon, or a *haimisha* [HAYmisher] *mentsh* who would act with such cruelty against the population of Chile" (Heller *GG*).

Joan Rivers reviewing herself in the *San Francisco Chronicle:* "It's a more *haimish* 'Geraldo' with wit, depending on the day's theme—'a bitchy Dinah Shore'" (14 February 1990).

Hebonics *n.* A takeoff on the term ebonics (a combination of ebony and phonics) as used in basic education, Hebonics has been widely distributed on the Internet as "Jewish English." It's actually a kind of Anglish: "Hardens consonants at the ends of words. Thus hand becomes 'handt.' The sarcastic repetition of words by adding 'sh' to the front is used for emphasis—mountains becomes shmountains." To which we might add "Hebonics, shmebonics." The phenomenon of its appearance on the World Wide Web is an instance of what I call poplore, a modern form of folk tradition.

hocking *v.* Anglish for HAKn, to chop; it looks back to HAKn a TSHAInik (meaningless banter).

"Stop already *hocking* us to be good! *hocking* us to be nice" (P. Roth *PC*).

huhb es in drerd To hell with it. More correctly "ich huhb es in drerd" (literally, I have it in the ground). Bellow uses it as an example of Gersbach's incompetent Yiddish. Herzog notes that Gersbach "loved to use Yiddish expressions, to misuse them, rather. Herzog's Yiddish background was genteel. He heard with instinctive snobbery Valentine's butcher's, teamster's, commoner's accent, and he put himself down for it." Gersbach says, "You're a *ferimmter mensch.*" "Moses [Herzog], to save his soul, could not let this pass. He said quietly, *'Berimmter'* [a distinguished person]." *Ferimmter* is a malapropism and Herzog takes pleasure in being able to note Gersbach's ignorance of proper Yiddish.

Huhb rakhMONes Have mercy. The postscript to Malamud's *Tenants* is a litany of mercy, written out many times to echo huhb rachMONes. "Hab rachmanes, Lesser, I have my own ambition to realize" (Malamud *TT*).

From a review of jazz singer Bobby McFerrin: "He should have a little Christian *rachmanes* and duet only with his peers" (*Nation*, 20–27 July 1985).

HUHmntashn *n.* Literally, HUHmen's pockets. A cookie baked in a triangular shape and supposed to resemble the three-cornered hat of the POOrim story's villain, HUHmen. (Apparently an updating of an old story.) HUHmntashn are made with poppy seed or prune filling.

ikh huhb deer in buhd Literally, I have you in the bath (or bathhouse). But when spoken, it's the equivalent of "go to hell—I have no use for you."

"Some sons I got. *Ich hub dem bader in bud* [ikh huhb zay BAYde in buhd]" (Heller *GG*).

ikh shtarb Literally, I'm dying, but in usage an exclamation of joy, disbelief, or sheer excitement. It was my mother's favorite exclamation when something pleased her.

In MITn derINen Often ironic, it means "in the midst of everything," "on top of everything else."

"*Und vus nuch?* [oon vuhs nuhkh—'and what else?'] *In mit'n d'rinnen* the slippery prick was *shoyn* [already] a Trustee for the Metropolitan Museum of Art because of 'his known commitment to the value of cultural exchange'" (Heller *GG*).

I should live so long Yinglish, from the Yiddish ikh zol aZOI lang LEbn—"may I *not* live so long if I'm lying."

kaBUHle (usually Kabbalah) *n.* The Hebrew word for tradition. The Yinglish term refers in general to Jewish mystical ideas from earliest times, but it also implies the specific mystical conceptions developed in Provence and Spain during the Middle Ages. Major texts include the Sepher Yetzira and the Zohar. The fiction of Thomas Pynchon and the criticism of Harold Bloom reflect the strong influence of the kaBUHle.

"Kabbalah, it must be remembered, is not the name of a certain dogma or system, but rather the general term applied to a whole religious movement. This movement . . . has been going on from Talmudic times to the present day; its development has been uninterrupted, though by no means uniform, and often dramatic" (Scholem *JM*).

"'Kabbalah' has been, since about the year 1200, the popularly accepted word for Jewish esoteric teachings concerning God and everything God created. The word 'Kabbalah' means 'tradition,' in the particular sense of 'reception' and at first referred to the whole

of Oral Law. . . . It seems fair to characterize the history of sub-
sequent Kabbalah as being a struggle between Gnostic and Neo-
platonic tendencies, fought out on the quite alien ground of Judaism, which in its central development was to reject both modes of
speculation" (Bloom *KC*).

KAdish *n.* One of several prayers praising God recited at every synagogue service. The mourner's KAdish is traditionally recited in
commemoration of the deceased, and thereafter once a year. Since
a devout Jew hopes the prayer will be said for him by his son, the
latter is also known as a KAdish. *Kaddish* is the title of a long poem
by Allen Ginsberg (connected with the death of his mother) and
also the title of Leonard Bernstein's Third Symphony. In the conclusion of Malamud's *God's Grace*, a gorilla says KAdish for the
novel's protagonist. Malamud's book leans heavily on evolutionary imagery, and there is a strong implication that the gorilla is indeed the spiritual offspring of the hero.

"Some heir he's got! Some *Kaddish!* Ham and pork you'll be eating before his body is in the grave" (Bellow *H*).

Phillip Lopate on the status of poetry in the United States: "If it
is too early to say Kaddish, it is also too early to celebrate a rebirth"
(*New York Times Book Review*, 8 September 1996).

KAKn *v.* To shit. The Anglish noun is KAka, usually meaning something bad or inferior. My mother used to quote a proverb, "kak
zikh ois, VEStu HUHbn a KLOORn kuhp." (Take a good shit; it
will clear your head.)

Henry Roth gives a different version: " 'In Veljish,' she continued, 'they say that "kockin" will clear the brow of pain' " (*CIS*).

On Henry Kissinger, Gold notes: "The lonesome cowboy was *ba-
kokt* again and it was his allies in South Vietnam who would not accept the *tsedreyt mishmosh* [mixed-up mess] of a truce he had *unger-
patchket* [ungePATSHket—mismanaged]" (Heller *GG*).

KAKuhMAYmee (cockamamie) *adj.* Anything patently ridiculous or
outrageous. KAKuhMAYmee is New York Anglish for decalcoma-
nia (from the French word *decalcomanie*, meaning to trace a de-
sign), referring to the tattoo-like decals children used to buy and
decorate themselves with. KAKuhMAYmee is not Yiddish even
though it sounds like it.

"And this is statistics (I am told by my father), not some cocka-maimy story he is making up for the fun of it" (P. Roth *PC*).

"Well, shortly after, I went up to Utica to do an industrial for the Grotesque Towel people, one of these cockamamey musicals they stage at their dealers' convention" (Perelman *RG*).

KALte KOOZHnye *n.* A cold furnace. Herzog's father thus describes a barren marriage. Bellow's explanation is, "he had brought his iron to a cold forge" (*H*).

kaPUHte *n.* The long gaberdine coat worn by some observant Jews. Like many Early Yiddish words, it derives from a French word, *capote* (coat).

"They sit in their stores in the long capotes and shake over their Talmud like bedouins" (Singer *S*).

KAshe *n.* Cereal, porridge, often buckwheat groats. In my youth, when we bought a knish it was either potato or KAshe. It is also of-ten served as a side order with a meat dish.

"On the same block they went into a cafeteria and ordered two fried eggs for Isaac. The tables were crowded except where a heavyset man sat eating soup with kasha" (Malamud *IF*).

In Pynchon's *Mason & Dixon*, George Washington asks his (Jew-ish) black slave if any "kashe varnikes" (noodles with buckwheat groats) are left.

kaZATski *n.* The famous Russian Cossack dance in which a dancer squats and kicks each leg out separately.

"Thus my Rabbi, Reb Israel, used to say—when he was happi-est, at a wedding or other celebration, after he had had a few glasses of wine and was ready to lift up the skirts of his long coat and dance a *kazatsky*" (Sholom Aleichem *SS*).

KETSele *n.* Pussycat; the diminutive of kats. It is a term of endear-ment and probably the source of all the current pussycat titles hav-ing sexy connotations. A National Public radio correspondent is named Ketsl Levine.

khai *n.* Life. The two Hebrew letters that spell the word life total eighteen (see geMAtreea). Those letters are often worn on a neck-lace (by both men and women) as a good luck charm. It is appro-priate to present one to a person who has just turned eighteen.

khaim YANkel *n.* A nobody, a simpleton. Khaim is the masculine

name derived from khai; the feminine is KHAIye, often KHAIke. YANkel is the Yiddish form of the Hebrew name yaKUHV (Jacob). Putting them together is the equivalent of "Joe Blow"—a nothing.
"Oh, that *shlemiel*. To *him* it was an agony, that *Chaim Yankel*" (Heller *GG*).

KHAle *n*. A white bread made with eggs and flour, the dough often braided, and served on Friday evenings to usher in the sabbath, or on holidays and other special occasions. In Anglish it often becomes KHAlee, or even worse, HAlee. A folktale has it that KHAle was the means whereby the children of Israel crossed the Red Sea: Each dipped a piece of KHAle in the water and drained it away.

"There was singing and dancing. An old granny danced opposite me, hugging a braided white chalah" (Singer, "Gimpel the Fool," in Bellow *GJSS*).

"I could have definitely sat down to eat with her but decided not to as again I had one of Mom's chala sandwiches" (Markfield *TW*).

"'The challah machine,' said Sabbath, 'is the last thing that works. Look at a window full of challah. No two exactly alike, and yet all within the genre. And they still look like they're plastic. And that's what a challah wants to do. Wanted to look like plastic even before plastic. There's where they got the idea of plastic. From challahs'" (P. Roth *ST*).

From a profile of Secretary of Defense William Cohen: "In June I had accompanied Cohen to Bangor, Maine, and to a small bakery where his father, Reuben Cohen, had made bread and bagels— and the Sabbath Challah—for nearly seventy years" (James Carroll, *New Yorker*, 18 August 1997).

khaLEARye *n*. Literally, cholera, but essentially an oath—"a plague on it," "damn it." Despite the specific reference to cholera, khaLEARye applies to plagues in general; hence a familiar oath, a SHVARtse khaLEARye, means the black plague. It's a mild curse: A khaLEARye zol es NEMen—"may it be wiped out by a plague."

"'He may have been right,' Aunt Bertha spat out vehemently. 'But cholera choke him anyway!'" (H. Roth *CIS*).

KHANike (usually Chanukah or Hanukah) *n*. The eight-day Jewish festival that commemorates the rededication of the Temple (165 B.C.E.) by the Maccabees. The story involves a miracle in which one small cruse of oil lasted for eight days; thus eight candles are lit on the meNOra (a candelabra with nine positions, including one for the SHAmis, the "helper" used to light the others). Since both KHANike and Christmas were originally winter solstice celebrations, they often coincide and compete. It is sometimes argued that KHANike is better than Christmas because we get a present each day instead of only once. There is no tradition for that idea. Children used to get KHANike gelt (mostly small change) but that custom is slowly passing. Assimilationist tendencies include a "KHANike bush" or wreath. The DRAYdl game is still often played.

KHAver *n.* Friend, comrade (*f.* KHAverte) In left-wing Jewish circles KHAver came to have the same connotations as the Russian "comrade," meaning a fellow Socialist or Communist. The plural khaVEARim refers to the Reds. The leftist political connotations are lessened by the Israeli use of the word to mean friend or comrade, without the Communist echoes. KHEvre means the gang or bunch.

"So I warn you, *chaver,* get off the lousy details" (Bellow *H*).

"Twenty-two-and-a-half years, hear, you hear? Hey, people, hey, neighbors, hey, *chaverim!*" (Markfield *TW*).

KHAYder *n.* Elementary school. It comes from the Hebrew word meaning room, that is, the room where children study. In European tradition there are several levels of instruction, from the elements of Hebrew to beginning Talmudic studies. In America KHAYder refers to classes run mainly by synagogues and directed mainly toward preparation for bar MITSvuh. There are also private parochial schools that provide a more rigorous curriculum. KHAYder BUHkher means schoolboy or novice.

khayn *n.* Charm. In the Yiddish song by Sholem Secunda, "Bei Mir Bist Du Schoen," the second line is "Bei mir huhstu khayn" (I think you're charming). The song was made famous by the Andrews Sisters in a bilingual version.

A schoolboy parody:

> Bei mir bist du shayn.
> You give my nuts a pain.
> Get flushed down the drain. (Markfield *TW*)

KHAzer *n.* Pig. As in English, KHAzer carries connotations of gluttony, filth, and slovenliness. But because of the taboo on pork in Jewish dietary laws, it also has the general meaning of anything that is not KUHsher. (Despite this, as Philip Roth notes, pork products seem to be all right when consumed in Chinese restaurants.) Not only the whole range of forbidden foods, but any cheap or worthless item can be characterized as khazerAI. In the remake of the film *Scarface,* in which the gangsters are all Cubans, KHAzer, in a variety of mispronunciations, is used to describe a greedy individual.

"You go to Harold's Hot Dog and *Chazerai* palace after school and you eat French fries with Melvin Weiner" (P. Roth *PC*).

"Yet, Gold now found himself in mysterious sympathy with the mercenary longings of the *chozzer*" (Heller *GG*).

KHAzn *n.* (*pl.* khaZUHNim) Cantor, the functionary who sings the liturgy in a Jewish religious service. The function is ambiguous because the participants often prefer to do their own chanting, as was the practice in ancient times and is currently done in Israel. But cantors have been highly prized in Europe and America, especially to present the musical portions of High Holiday services. On those occasions the KHAzn presents a veritable concert of liturgical selections, often with a choir to assist him. Musical instruments, however, are strictly forbidden in Orthodox synagogues, in commemoration of the fall of the Temple, although in ancient times there were often large orchestras in the Temple. (The American Puritans adopted the same proscriptions against using instruments in their churches because the practice, especially the use of organs, smacked of papism.) The KHAzn should have a fine voice—tenor or baritone but not bass; folk tradition has it that a pregnant woman will abort if she hears a bass. The great cantors developed their own special variations on the liturgy, largely on the basis of folk tradition. These are in addition to the cantillations, traditional tunes for sections of the Hebrew Scriptures, indicated by special marks in the text. The cantorial melodies are passed down from generation to generation and have rarely been written down.

Because he was my first cousin, I had many opportunities to hear Moishe Oysher, one of the great cantors. (Aficionados will argue about whether he or Yossele Rosenblatt was the greatest.)

Moishe came from several generations of cantors and learned much of his material from his father, Zelig (my mother's brother), who was a KHAzn in Bessarabia. Listening to his recordings now, I can easily spot the folk melodies introduced into the liturgy as the basis for his virtuoso vocal expression, which often included complex coloratura technique. All this was enhanced by a voice of operatic quality; he could easily handle the ranges of both tenor and baritone and was in fact offered many opportunities to join the Metropolitan and Chicago opera companies. He also made several classic Yiddish films on the theme of a KHAzn who is tempted to leave his calling and become a popular singer and actor.

Despite this film activity and his frequent appearances on the stage, Moishe kept his basic commitment as a KHAzn and was much in demand in even the most Orthodox synagogues. Occasionally the rabbis in Brooklyn watched him so closely that he had to walk from his home in lower Manhattan to the synagogue in order not to break the prohibition against riding in a car on the High Holidays. After the services he would slip away and spend the night at our house in Brighton Beach. Later in his career he performed High Holiday services at hotels in the Borsht Belt, a tradition still maintained by resort owners in the Catskills. Operatic figures like Jan Peerce have made similar appearances and recorded cantorial materials.

Moishe's sister became famous on the Yiddish stage as "Fraydele the KHAznte"—the female cantor. There was no such traditional post, but Fraydele learned her father's repertoire as well as her brother's embellishments and, since she is also gifted with a superb voice, she can sing cantorial styles better than most males. Her Yiddish stage vehicles usually included a situation in which she masqueraded as a young man and consequently had an opportunity to perform the cantorial materials. (She maintains that her roles were the inspiration for Isaac Bashevis Singer's *Yentl*.) There is no doubt that many contemporary liberal Jewish groups would provide her with an opportunity to function as a KHAznte, even if Orthodox groups would still be outraged.

Today Conservative and Reform groups often hire a cantor who doubles as educational director, but wherever possible the cantor is still expected to provide a major musical experience for the High

Holidays. In general, Orthodox Jews will not retain a full-time cantor, out of concern that he might alter the traditional materials, as would inevitably be the case. But, as I have indicated, they often hire a "star" for the High Holidays. Reform Jews for many years resisted having a KHAzn for precisely the opposite reasons, desiring to bring the congregation's music up to date. Compositions like Ernst Bloch's *Sacred Service,* for baritone, chorus, and orchestra, are often performed in place of the ordinary service, to the chagrin of Conservatives, who rightly compare it to the tradition of Protestant church music. Conservative Jews will employ a KHAzn if possible but will not allow an organ or other instrumental accompaniment. I once played traditional Jewish songs on the five-string banjo in a Reform temple for a yuhm KIPer children's service, a practice the rabbi justified by explaining that the banjo is derived from David's harp. Not many of the old-timers in the congregation found it a credible argument.

"Not so long after, Moishe Oisher [Oysher] hopped off the Brighton Theater's stage, pulled Mrs. Teichitz from her seat and waltzed her around the aisle singing, *Ich Hub Dir Tzu Viel Lieb* [I love you much too much]" (Markfield *TW*).

KHOOpe *n.* Wedding canopy. It is supported by four poles, each held by a member of the wedding party. Often a portable affair, it is reminiscent of an earlier, nomadic period when permanent structures were not available. The KHOOpe symbolizes a hallowed area in which the wedding ceremony is performed. To lead someone to the KHOOpe is to get married.

"'My sister-in-law was *there,* Stella. My ex-wife stood under the *chuppa* with this broad, and when the time came she broke the glass. My wife is a shiksa. The two of them are lesbians. This is what Judaism has come to? I can't believe it!'" (P. Roth *ST*).

From a *New York Times Magazine* article on weddings by Susan Shapiro: "'Anything you want' turned out to be plans for a black-tie sit-down dinner at a Bloomfield Hills country club with chuppa, rabbi, sweet table, four courses, six musicians and me, signing the ktubba in a long white gown" (23 February 1997). KeTUba is the Hebrew word for the wedding agreement.

From a review by Juliet Fleming of some English mystery plays in the *Times Literary Supplement:* "With the exception of a tactless marriage scene, which proposes kitsch as the identifying mark of Judaism by uniting Mary and Joseph under a chuppa to strains of *hava nagila, The Creation* is thoroughly enjoyable and, after two and a half hours, over only too soon" (28 March 1997).

KHOOsid *n. (pl.* khSEEdim [usually Chasidim]) A member of the enthusiastic religious sect known as khSEEdim (a word difficult to pronounce authentically because there is no vowel between *kh* and *s,* despite spellings that often provide an *a*). The original Hebrew meaning, pious man, came to refer to the specific piety of the followers of the Bal Shem Tuhv and other Chasidic leaders. The KHOOsid saw himself as the servent of his REbe, to whom magical powers were often attributed. But the main significance of Chasidism was its reaction against the intellectualism of some rabbinical traditions. The KHOOsid devoted himself to mystical traditions (such as kaBUHle) and habitually expressed religious fervor through music and dance—even in the synagogue. The khSEEdim like to cite a dictum that one of the gates of Paradise could be entered only through song. Although not quite the Holy Rollers of Judaism, the khSEEdim come close in their advocacy of "enthusiasm," a term most organized religious groups abhor. An important element in Chasidic tradition is its devotion to Yiddish, even in prayer, which otherwise is usually in Hebrew. The khSEEdim use Yiddish to discuss the Holy Scriptures and also in daily life, thus preserving Hebrew from contamination with secular activities. The large settlements of Chasidic groups in New York City (especially in Brooklyn) and the resurgence of Chasidism in Israel have consequently provided a tremendous new impetus for Yiddish, which has almost totally lost its older generation of native speakers.

As a result of the KHOOsid's exaggerated subservience to his REbe, there developed a genre of satirical songs poking fun at the relationship. According to a famous anti-Chasidic song, "When the rabbi walks, his disciples run; when he drinks, they guzzle; when he sleeps, they snore; and when the rabbi dies, the followers are buried!" (There's a nice pun in the last line because the word for buried, baGROOBn, also means "beaten up.")

KHOOsn, KAle *n.* Groom and bride. A popular song composed by

Sigmund Mogulesco (so widespread it often shows up in jazz solos) says, "KHOOsn, KAle MAzl tuhv." (For more information on Mogulesco and other Jewish-American musicians, see Mark Slobin, *Tenement Songs*.)

KHOOTSpe *n.* (usually chutzpah) Umitigated gall, arrogance, nerve, from the Hebrew word for audacity. A friend of mine visiting in Israel let out a wolf whistle at the sight of a good-looking young woman, who gave him back, loud and clear: "khootsPA!" (the modern Israeli pronunciation). The point is that in Yiddish (as in modern Hebrew) KHOOTSpe is not entirely negative. It may mean the kind of gutsy and outrageous behavior that one cannot help but admire. The classic definition is the story of the young man who murdered his parents and then threw himself on the mercy of the court because he was an orphan. It is probably the most widely used Yiddish word in English.

"A Jewbird, what a chutzpah. One false move and he's out on his drumsticks" (Malamud *IF*).

The comic strip "Hagar the Horrible" shows Hagar alone and trapped on the edge of a cliff. But he gives the opposing army "five seconds to surrender—or else." The leader of the enemy hosts replies: "Boy! *That's* chutzpah."

"Chutzpah is the very essence of modern man, and of the modern Jew as well. He has learned so assiduously from the Gentile that he now surpasses him. The truth is that the element of chutzpah was present even among the pious Jews. They have always been a stiff-necked and rebellious people. Well, there is a kind of chutzpah that is necessary, but I won't go into that now" (Singer *TP*).

"For the inspiring example of her personal chutzpah and her unflappable calm in pursuit of our common interest, I thank my agent, Wendy Well" (Alice Walker *TF*).

A letter from novelist Ishmael Reed in the *Nation: "The Village Voice* book review, run by white and gender supremacists, also printed a negative review of Angela Davis's *Women, Culture, and Politics* because Davis, with characteristic chutzpah, exposed the feminist movement's racist attitudes toward black men" (16 October 1989).

A *Greensboro News and Record* editorial states: "Having succeeded in shifting the burden of low-level nuclear waste disposal off their own shoulder and onto North Carolina's, our neighbors in South Carolina now presume to tell us just where in North Carolina the new disposal facility should be. If there's a Low Country word meaning chutzpah, this is the definition" (5 April 1990).

A headline in the *Los Angeles Times:* "[Sam] Harris Is a Jesus with Chutzpah in Glitzy 'Superstar' Revival" (7 May 1990).

Physicist Richard Feynman is described by Daniel D. Dennett in the *TLS* as "an International Grand Master in the chutzpah department" (10 May 1991).

Frederick Crews on the famous theosophist: "For sheer chutzpah there was no one like Madame Blavatsky" (*NYRB*, 19 September 1996).

From an article on former New York mayor Edward I. Koch: "This was considered a remarkable act of chutzpah, since, as far as the committee was concerned, Giuliani had every right to ignore its recommendation" (James Straub, *New Yorker*, 14 October 1996).

Remembering his and Carl Sagan's defense of evolution in a small southern town, Richard Lewontin writes: "Carl and I then sneaked out the back door of the auditorium and beat it out of town, quite certain that at any moment hooded riders with ropes and flaming crosses would snatch up two atheistic New York Jews who had the chutzpah to engage in public blasphemy" (*NYRB*, 9 January 1997).

"The word chutzpah acquired a new meaning when Newport unrolled its 'Alive with Pleasure' campaign. One ad showed beautiful young achievers playing a fast-action game of beach volleyball, cigarettes still clenched between their teeth" (*New York Times*, 20 April 1997).

From a profile of Garth Drabinsky: "Nonetheless, his taste, tenacity, and chutzpah link him to a distant grandiose producing brotherhood—all of whose members invented flamboyant public events, including themselves" (John Lahr, *New Yorker*, 2 June 1997).

A Sephardic leader in Israel: "'Rabbi Ovadiah gave us the courage to go out and do for ourselves. He gave us the chutzpah of holiness'" (*New York Times Magazine*, 1 June 1977).

From *His Eminence of Los Angeles: James Francis Cardinal McIntyre:* "Franklin Delano Roosevelt was certainly aware of such power, which was why less than a decade after the defeat of Al Smith by

Herbert Hoover in 1928 for the presidency—in part because of Smith's Roman Catholicism—Roosevelt had the chutzpah (to mix metaphors) to invite Cadinal Mundelein of Chicago for an overnight stay at the White House" (Kevin Starr, *Los Angeles Times Book Review*, 22 June 1977).

KHUHkhem *n.* A sage or wise person. But as in English, the meaning slides easily into irony, suggesting a wise guy whose schemings often backfire. We can say, "gay zai a KHUHkhem" (literally, go be a sage, meaning "How could anyone have figured that out?"). Or "he really thought he was a KHUHkhem," meaning he was not. KHUHkhme is a wise saying and also a joke. A Yiddish folk song predicting the great celebration when the Messiah arrives asks who will make wise pronouncements at the fête. The answer is SHLOYme haMElech vet KHUHkhmes ZUHgn (Solomon the King will speak wisely).

Fiedler gives the ironic meaning: "Listen to the Professor, the *chochem*. He knows. Congress don't know, the Pope himself don't know, but Jacob Moskowitz knows. Only how to blow his nose he don't know, how to put a dollar in the bank, the *chochem*" (*LJA*).

KIBits *v.* To interfere in someone else's affairs, especially to give unwanted advice during a card game. The KIBitser is, by extension, anyone who gives unwanted advice. Often mispronounced in Anglish as kibITser. See Stanley Elkin's collection of short stories, *Criers and Kibitzers/Kibitzers and Criers*.

Slothrop and friends are playing a drinking game called the Prince of Wales: "The word has osmosed out into the Casino, and there is presently a throng of kibitzers gathered around the table, waiting for casualties" (Pynchon *GR*).

KIDish *n.* From the Hebrew word for sanctification, it is the prayer recited over a cup of wine on the Sabbath and holidays. A special KIDish cup is often used. Not to be confused with Kadish, the traditional doxology.

kike *n.* Derogatory term for Jew.

From a piece about playwright Alfred Uhry's memories of the attitude of his parents toward Eastern European Jews: "The prejudice was so strong, he says, that some German Jews would even call Eastern European Jews 'kikes.' 'When I was growing up the word 'kike' was not bandied around in my household, but they sure said it' " (Alex Witchel, *New York Times*, 23 February 1997).

KIle *n.* Hernia. We used to refer to a really strenuous task as a double KIle. Max Weinreich defines the level of usage as vulgar.

KIMpet *n.* Childbirth, confinement, or labor.

"'I don't know when I'll be delivered,' Father Herzog whispered. He used the old Yiddish term for a woman's confinement— *kimpet*" (Bellow *H*). Herzog's father is talking about being delivered from his trials in the world.

kineHUHre From a mixed Yiddish-Hebrew expression that means "may no evil eye harm it (kain ayn HUHre). KineHUHre is a verbal device similar to knocking on wood to ward off evil forces.

Henry Roth gives a literal English translation: "He's well grown, no evil eye" (*CIS*).

KISHkes *n.* Intestines or guts. Like guts, KISHkes has many metaphorical connotations. Philip Roth catches the literal meaning and more in describing his father's constipation: "But all catharses were in vain for that man: his *kishkas* were gripped by the iron hand of outrage and frustration." After his own sexual adventure with the Monkey and an Italian whore, Portnoy confesses: "Then I got up, went into the bathroom, and, you'll be happy to know, regurgitated my dinner. My *kishkas*, Mother—threw them right up into the toilet bowl" (*PC*).

At the other extreme, KISHke (usually translated as stuffed derma) is a culinary delight still featured in New York restaurants. It's a piece of beef intestine stuffed with a filling of flour, shMAlts (chicken fat), and spices. (A similar effect can be achieved with a chicken neck, but then it's known as HELDzl.) We never say of a brave person, "That's KISIIkes for you."

"Fight! Fight! Gib'm, haws-fly! In de kishkis—nudder one" (H. Roth *CIS*).

klap *n.* A blow, hit, or stroke. The father of one of my Brooklyn buddies used to threaten regularly, "I'll give you such a klap, you'll crap in your pants."

"'He's the one who hit me in the eye with the ball.' 'No kidding? The clopper himself' " (Potok *TC*).

KLEZmer *n.* (*pl.* klezMOrim) Village musician. The musicians who played for weddings and other celebrations were often virtuosi recognized in the Gentile as well as the Jewish communities of Europe. One of the KLEZmer special instruments was the hammered dulcimer, known as the TSIMbal. With other stringed instruments (and perhaps a flute) such a group would be basically a string band. Another kind of KLEZmer group had the instrumentation of a small military or marching band. In Europe these often became large aggregations, and their recordings there as well as in this country were influential in the revival of KLEZmer music. Based on these recordings and interviews with KLEZmer musicians, a remarkable revival has occurred, not unlike the resurrection of traditional folk and jazz music. Since the KLEZmer musicians were also influential in American jazz and pop music (providing sound tracks for "Betty Boop" and other cartoons), the repertoire of contemporary KLEZmer bands includes not only European but also later American materials. Two important contemporary groups whose recordings are readily available are the Klezmorim and Kapelye (kaPELye means band). (See appendix 2.)

Leonard Bernstein has noted on many occasions that his father refused to pay for his piano lessons "because he didn't want me to become a klezmer."

A note in the *New Yorker:* "It'll never be as big as Bon Jovi, but klezmer music—traditional Eastern European Yiddish music—is enjoying a mini vogue. . . . Also, if you really want to compete in the modern klezmer arena, it might help to be conversant in jazz, minimalism, and an array of international styles, because today's klezmer player is not a rube from the shtetl but an eclectic, versatile musician who is as likely to play at a downtown performance as at a Jewish wedding" (23 July 1990).

From a review of Michael Steinlauf's *Bondage to the Dead:* "Concerts of Yiddish, Hebrew and *klezmer* (instrumental) music, festivals of Jewish culture, conferences on Yiddish theatre have been held with increasing frequency" (Abraham Brumberg, *TLS,* 27 June 1997).

KLIPe *n.* A shrew, an evil person.

"I know Mady is a bitch. And maybe you think I never wanted to kick Phoebe in the ass. That *klippa!* But that's the female nature" (Bellow *H*).

kloog bist du Literally, smart you are, but often used ironically to mean "you're not so bright."
Bellow uses it literally: "Now isn't it time you used your head? You do have one—*klug bist du*" (*H*).

kluhts *n.* A clumsy person, a clod. It has become a standard English expression, often as the Anglish adjective KLUHTSee.
"'You fool,' Nathan interrupted, 'you silly klutz'" (Styron *SC*).
John Cassidy and B. C. Rimbeau are coauthors of *Juggling for the Complete Klutz*, marketed by Klutz Enterprises, Stanford, California.
Sheila Taylor in a syndicated column from the *Fort Worth Star-Telegram*: "The University of British Columbia has discovered that left-handers were 89 percent more likely to have required medical attention for accidents in the preceding two years. And it's not because we're klutzy, as many of you prefer to claim. It's because we're living in an environment designed for the convenience and safety of the 90 percent who are right-handed." (Reprinted in the *Fresno Bee*, 27 August 1989).
"Dump Sam [Donaldson]. He's corny, he's homey, he's out of his element. He's a klutz" (Liz Smith, *San Francisco Chronicle*, 25 September 1989).

KNAYdlech *n.* MAtse balls, usually served in chicken soup.
"On the table, the fresh crisp *matzos* were also waiting, and in the oven a delicious Passover borsht was simmering, and hot *kneidlach* with chicken fat, and maybe even a potato pudding" (Sholom Aleichem *SS*).

KNIPl *n.* A knot. Since people sometimes tied money into the knot of a large kerchief, it also means a hoard of money. It's also a reference to a way of choosing lots. You make a knot in one end of the kerchief and then show only the tips of the four corners. Whoever gets the KNIPl is chosen.

knish *n.* A kind of dumpling, ordinarily filled with potatoes or buckwheat groats (KAshe), though knishes may contain fruit or other fillings. They're a heavy chunk of food, which justifies a friend's description of his tennis partner as a "lunging knish." Because of the way it is folded, knish is a euphemism for vagina.
"'Yuh know w'ea babies comm from?' 'N-no.' 'From de knish.' 'Knish?' 'Between de legs. Who puts id in is de poppa. De poppa's god de petzel'" (H. Roth *CIS*).

"The ice cream cart, attended by a man in a white uniform, is present every day, as are also several broken laundry baskets of salt stengels . . . with shabby old men and women in charge, and a knish wagon, potato and kasha" (Rosenfeld *AE*).

KOOGl *n.* Pudding; fully identified, by type, as LUHKshn (noodle) KOOGl or potato KOOGl. The former often has raisins or other sweeteners, the latter onions and spices. Both are delicacies for special occasions.

"I am reminded at this joyous little juncture of when we lived in Jersey City, back when I was still very much my mother's papoose, still very much a sniffer of her body perfumes and a total slave to her *kugel* and *grieben* [cracklings] and *ruggelech* [cookies]" (P. Roth *PC*).

KOORve *n.* A whore.

"What is to him the heights of human experience? Walking into a restaurant with a long-legged *kurveh* on his arm" (P. Roth *PC*).

kosher—see KUHsher.

KREPlech *n.* (*pl.*) Dumplings, filled with meat and served in soup. KREPlech are very much like the wontons in the soup of that name—we always called them Chinese KREPlech.

Pynchon retells the famous joke about KREPlech in *Gravity's Rainbow:* "Remember the story about the kid who hates kreplach? Hates and fears the dish, breaks out in these horrible green hives that shift in relief maps all across his body, in the mere presence of kreplach. Kid's mother takes him to the psychiatrist. 'Fear of the unknown,' diagnoses this gray eminence, 'let him watch you *making* the kreplach, that'll ease him into it.' She goes through the procedure step by step to the joy and wonder of the child, concluding, 'Now, I spoon some of the hamburger into this little square, and now I fold into a tri—' 'Gaahhhh!' screams the kid, in absolute terror—'*kreplach!*'"

KRIjes *n.* The lower back.

My father's favorite complaint—a pain in the KRIjes.

KRUHTSmich *v.* Scratch me; also an English pun on "Christmas." Both Christmas and Easter were often the pretexts in Europe for attacks on Jewish communities, and it was hard to say either word without some sense of uneasiness. "KRUHTSmich" as a substitute for "Christmas" is a conscious denigration of the celebration of Jesus' birth.

"Christmas. Jesus. Crotzmich. Crotzmich means scratch me. Jesus scratch me" (H. Roth *CIS*).

KUHKHalayn *n.* A summer rental with cooking facilities. It means, literally, "cook for yourself," and that's the point. If you went to a resort area you could rent a KUHKHalayn instead of staying at an expensive hotel.

KUHKHlefl *n.* A cooking or mixing spoon; therefore someone who mixes in everybody's business.

"In the marketplace. A fishwife, a *kochleffel*, everything's his business, you he'll autograph, me he'll get jobs, he listens to everybody" (Ozick *TPR*).

KUHsher (usually kosher) *n.* Acceptable according to the rules of Jewish dietary law, as executed under rabbinical supervision. But in Anglish usage it means O.K., legitimate, acceptable in general terms, almost never in reference to foods. (Is the real etymology of O.K. "officially kosher"?) The ritual notions of what is KUHsher and what is not are spelled out in detail in sections of the Hebrew Bible. In general the principles depend on cleanliness and appropriateness of animals to their habitats. For example, deformed or sick animals can never be KUHsher; birds that don't fly and denizens of the ocean that don't swim (like shellfish) are also forbidden.

It seems clear that many outlawed practices relate to customs of the neighbors from whom the Jews sought to separate themselves. For example, the seemingly strange proscription "Thou shalt not boil a kid in its mother's milk" is a reference to a Canaanite practice. The ban against eating shellfish may also be a reference to rituals associated with worshipers of Venus. To KAsher something is to make it acceptable; in the case of meat, it means draining all the blood by means of repeated soaking in brine.

"'My mother,' he announced bitterly, 'was really out to kasher me, boy, like a piece of beef on the sink, she wanted me drained and white'" (Pynchon *CL*).

"The simple act of eating has become for us a complicated ceremonial, from the preparatory phases of ritual slaughter, through *milchigs* and *fleishigs* [dairy and meat], kosher and *treif,* to benedictions and postprandial prayers. It is for such reasons, among others, that the Jewish religion enjoys the reputation of being one of the most worldly and immanent, one of the most closely connected with daily life. What Sacred Communion is to Catholics, the everyday mealtime is to Orthodox Jews" (Rosenfeld *AE*).

A full-page ad for AT&T in the *Forward* shows a pig wearing a hat and shades, and the text reads: "Something here isn't kosher. Trayf is Trayf, no matter how it's disguised. Like the claims some other long distance companies have been making. They call you up like they're doing you a mitzvah [favor], telling you how much you can save with them. Or put charts in their ads showing their prices compared to AT&T prices. Meanwhile, they're comparing their discount rates to AT&T regular rates. Which is like comparing kugel [noodle pudding] to knishes, bagels to bialys. It's just not the same thing. So make sure you always read the fine print. And if another long distance company calls, before they give you the whole megillah [long story], just tell them to put their claims in writing. Remember, when something sounds too good to be true, it's usually no metsieh [bargain]."

From an article about Jews in TV programs: "And while prime time is Anything But Kosher, it is featuring an increasing number of Jewish characters in new and interesting ways" (Michele Willens, *Los Angeles Times*, 9 September 1989).

From a food column by L. N. Halliburton: "Elite Cuisine of Hancock Park and West Los Angeles serves—are you ready— *Kosher gourmet* food. It would take a couple hundred pages of Talmudic discussion to evaluate that phrase, so I'll refrain. . . . It all reminds me of an old ad campaign for Levy's Rye Bread: You don't have to know your brisket from your *schnitzel,* your *milchig* [dairy] from your *fleishig* [meat] to recognize spankingly fresh food" (*Los Angeles Times*, 15 September 1990). Schnitzel is German for veal cutlet.

A *New York Times* headline reads, "Mock Caviar Is Cheap and Kosher." The story explains, "Kosher dietary laws ban the eating of fish without scales; sturgeon [the main source of caviar] are covered with a series of bony plates instead of scales. The new product, which took three years to develop, is made from a kosher fish that the developers would not identify" (16 May 1990). The new product was invented by Israeli scientists.

kvel *v.* To be delighted, to revel, to beam with joy. "And these two *kvell* also to see a tall, good-looking, young Jewish lawyer" (P. Roth *PC*).

From a *New York Times* article, "Opening a Window on Hasidism": "These lives are filled too with kvelling, or bursts of pride, over the love that binds Hasidim together, and over the faith, courage and tenacity that have led to their regeneration" (David Margolick, 20 July 1997).

kvetsh *v.* To squeeze or pinch. *n.* A complainer—someone who seems to be always in pain from squeezing or pinching. Anglish KVETSHing means complaining.

Often mispronounced kaVETSH, as in the film *Norma Rae*, when Sally Fields says to the Jewish organizer, "Is this the truth I'm delivering up, or is it just plain *kavetshing?*"

"But if she's got a disgusting father and a *kvetsch* of a mother, what else should a man do?" (Bellow *H*)

Heller describes Henry Kissinger: "The only response to this betrayal of an ethnic group was a profound silence, although his Excellency, a fellow of sensitive nature who showed he could *kvetch* and *krechtz* [groan] like a *kronkeh bubbeh* [sick grandma] when his tender feelings were hurt" (*GG*).

From a review of a Robert Coover novel: "That is not to quibble about artistry—Coover couldn't write a dull note to the milkman—but it is to *kvetch* about his preachiness and his refusal to till new soil" (John Schulian, *Los Angeles Times*, 25 October 1987).

A review of the play *Table Settings:* "There's the kvetching mother-in-law, an immigrant who can't forget the hardships of her former life in Minsk, and won't let anyone else, either" (David Hale, *Fresno Bee*, 25 September 1989).

Two New York characters complain about the food in California: "Ditzah was the food kvetch" (Pynchon *V*).

"They went out in back to Van Meter's place and stood on the porch smoking, with the usual full scale kvetchathon proceeding spiritedly inside" (Pynchon *V*).

From a *New York Times* news service report about the musical *Miss Saigon:* "The newest kvetch with the musical, which opened last week, is that fans of Filipina actress Lea Salonga can't find out in advance which performances she will play" (13 April 1991).

From a review of the movie *The Rock:* "This type of role demands a lot of quivering and kvetching, and a daunting number of double takes" (Terrence Rafferty, *New Yorker,* 17 June 1996).

An editorial in *Newsweek* on the change from typewriters to computers: "Reporters hate change. They kvetch if you clean their coffee mugs" (11 November 1996).

From a *New Yorker* article on genetic engineering: "It seems that people who are fretful, crabby, and neurotic—'kvetches,' in the *Times*'s translation into regional dialect—tend to have a shorter version of a certain gene (SLC6A4 on chromosome 17q12, if you want to look it up) than do people of sunny disposition" (Louis Menand, 16 December 1996).

"We've always taken pride from living in the capital of kvetch, the city that never stops complaining" (John Tierny in a discussion of a book on speed in various cities, *New York Times Magazine,* 20 July 1997).

LaDEEno (Ladino) *n.* Judaeo-Spanish (also known as Dzhudezmo). It is the vernacular spoken by Sephardic Jews (whose ancestors came from Spain or Portugal) and is the equivalent of Yiddish. Ladino was also the language of about three hundred thousand Jews who

lived in Morocco, right across the straits of Gibraltar, but mostly in the eastern half of the Mediterranean basin. Their large center, Salonika—which had once been Yavanic [Babylonian], then became Sephardic, and as early as the sixteenth or seventeenth century acquired the name "Little Jerusalem"—was at its apogee at the outbreak of World War I: close to eighty thousand Jews, almost exclusively Dzhudezmo speakers, who accounted for more than half of the total population. Some fifteen years later, when the Greek government replaced the Turkish, Salonika had no more than about fifty thousand Jews and only a few thousand escaped from German hands in World War II (Max Weinreich *HYL*).

"One of the wraiths who briefly make an appearance in 'Usurpation' is the ghost Ibn Gabirol, an eleventh-century Spanish Jewish philosopher and poet. . . . It came to me that if only I had been able to write 'Usurpation' in a Jewish language—Hebrew or Yiddish, or say the Ladino spoken by Ibn Gabirol's descendants—it would have been understood instantly" (Ozick *AA*).

LANTSman *n.* (*pl.* LANSlait) Countryman, someone from the same town or region of the old country. LAlte means people.

"Was Ravitch actually your uncle, or only a landtsman?" (Bellow *H*).

LATke *n.* A potato pancake. One can make LATkes any time, but they're usually served by the panful during KHANike. In the TV program "Taxi," Andy Kaufman portrayed a not-too-bright character who just sort of lay there—named Latka.

From a review of *Marven of the Great North Woods*, by Kathryn Lasky: "His parents teach him to say *bonjour* for hello and line his outerwear with scraps of beaver fur, and his mother places latkes and knishes in his coat pockets and cap to keep him warm" (Meg Wolitzer, *New York Times Book Review*, 17 November 1997).

liKHAIyim To life. This is the standard toast in both Yiddish and Hebrew. When someone says "liKHAIyim" it is appropriate to respond, "SHUHlem" (peace).

"*L'chaim!* We Jews keep on wishing ourselves eternal life, or at least immortality of the soul. In fact, eternal life would be a calamity. Imagine some little storekeeper dying and his soul flying around for millions of years still remembering that once it sold chicory, yeast, and beans, and that a customer owes it eighteen groschen" (Singer *S*).

LIKHTign gan aydn Literally, a bright Eden. It means "may he or she rest in peace."

"'I remember what a fine man he was,' said Uncle Yaffe. 'May he have *a lichtigen Gan-Eden*'" (Bellow *H*).

LIlis (usually Lilith) *n.* Adam's first wife, according to folk tradition. Originally a goddess, LIlis demanded to be treated equally and specifically refused to lie under Adam in what is known as the missionary position. As a consequence, she was banished and became an evil demon. She is held responsible for suffocating children in infancy (an ancient recognition of what we call crib death or SIDs) and for the nocturnal emissions of men. There is extant a prayer to ward off this occurrence, and it is often said by Orthodox men when they spend the night away from their wives. All references to LIlis have been excised from the Hebrew Bible except one, Isaiah 34:14 in the Hebrew version. The King James edition translates LIlis as "screech owl." As a rebel against the male, LIlis has become a symbol of feminist independence and Lilith is the title of a number of feminist magazines. The history of LIlis is fully recounted by Raphael Patai in *The Hebrew Goddess.*

"There existed also the example of the succubus Lilith, who was known to couple in the medieval ghetto even with pre-pubescent boys" (Ozick *TPR*).

LITvak *n.* Lithuanian. The LITvak accent is distinctive and easy to recognize. Among other characteristics, they tend to pronounce *sh* as *s*, so "shayn" (pretty) comes out "sayn." LITvak is similar to the idea of being from Missouri in the United States—that is, a skeptic.

In I. L. Peretz's famous story "If Not, Then Higher," it is a LITvak who follows the rabbi to see if, as rumored, he goes to heaven on the High Holidays. The rabbi actually chops wood and aids an old woman. When asked if the rabbi ascended to heaven, the LITvak answers, "If not, then higher."

LOOFTmentsh *n.* Literally, air man, one who lives on air. It refers to the Jews who lived mainly in the small towns of Eastern Europe and made their livings precariously and by their wits. Such a person lived, in a sense, by floating on the air, without a solid foundation. Marc Chagall often painted these characters literally floating in the air. Herman Wouk's novel *Marjorie Morningstar* has a character named Noel Airman—his real name is Saul Ehrman.

"It is a description frequently in the mouths of some English and American Jews as well, and it might have been partly to counteract such unhappy distortions that George Steiner drew his opposite portrait of the Jew as *Luftmensch,* ennobled by otherness, universalized through wandering, gifted in his homelessness by exceptional sight and judgment, made free by unbelonging" (Ozick *AA*).

MAkee *n.* A derogatory term for Jew. In *The Rise and Fall of the Jewish Gangster* Albert Fried lists a hood named Morris "The Mock" Kaplan.

MAkher *n.* Maker or doer, but best translated as a "mover and shaker." It often has connotations of shady power connections. A GROYSer MAkher is a big shot.

"Not like that *macher,* Alexander. Always some scandal about him" (Bellow *H*).

From a letter to the *New York Review of Books* about T. S. Eliot's grubbing for money: "In short, and in a language he would not like, Eliot emerged as a ganzer macher [wheeler-dealer]" (Signed, Robert [Lawson] Craft, 22 December 1989).

James Atlas on "The Fall of Fun": "Saul Bellow's two older brothers were Chicago real-estate dealmakers—*machers,* in the vernacular" (*New Yorker,* 18 November 1996).

makhiTAYniste *n.* Mother-in-law. Father-in-law is meKHOOTn.

"But surely the dope was at least in part responsible for the close sequence by pushing in front of every camera that bright and thirsting *punim* [face] that only a gentile *machetaynesta* could love" (Heller *GG).*

MAlech-a-MUHVes *n.* Hebrew for the Angel of Death.

Simkin the lawyer: "I have to go to court. Those schmucks are in Bermuda with their brides while I fight the *Moloch-ha-movos* alone" (Bellow *H*).

MAme LUHshn *n.* Mother tongue. It means Yiddish, as opposed to Hebrew, which is LUHIshn KOYdesh (literally, the holy language, but Max Weinreich points out that it should be translated "the language of Holiness"). As in many cultures, "mother tongue" is a sexist notion, which relegates the feminine to a lesser role; notwithstanding, there is a certain sympathy and love for this lower level of expression, often described as zharGUHN—not quite a language.

"At first Blackstock (who spoke fluent Polish aside from his *mama-loshen* Yiddish) was rather distressed that the agency had sent him a young woman who was a *goy* [should be GOYe] and who only had a smattering of Yiddish learned in a prison camp" (Styron *SC*).

MAmenyu/TATenyu Exclamations equivalent to "O Mother," "O Father," but both are diminutives: "dear little Mother," "dear little Father."

"*Momenyu*, Gold cursed his fate, and would have flung something heavy at someone. . . . *Tatenyu*, thought Gold, and threw himself into a chair" (Heller *GG*).

mamiLIge *n.* A cornmeal mush, the peasant dish often associated with Romanian Jews. The epithet roMAYNishe mamiLIge is the equivalent of calling an Italian a spaghetti bender. My father was a great maker of mamiLIge. He cooked up the mush to just the right consistency and then cut the sections with a thread rather than a knife, before serving. You eat it with your fingers, dipping it in hot butter and then in feta or pot cheese.

MAMzer *n.* Illegitimate child, bastard. As in English, MAMzer can be a general term of derision, but also an expression of begrudging affection. In *The Chosen*, when the young hero is knocked down by an opposing baseball player, his teammate exclaims, "That momzer! . . . You weren't in his way!"

"Mothers' hearts are broken by *mamzerim* like you" (Bellow *H*). As usual Bellow gives the accurate plural. Anglish is often MAMzerz.

" 'You should be dead. You should be in the ground where he is. *Podler* [from the town of Podel]. *Mumser*,' he shouted" (Elkin *CKKC*).

MANdelbroyt *n.* A hard, dry cookie with almonds (MANdln) in it. An extra-dry, crumbly version is toasted in the oven after being baked.

"Besides cholesterol-free, low sodium cookies and muffins, the mother-daughter pair [Arminee Shishmanian and her daughter Cathie Crosby] also make and sell a heart-healthy museli (a trail mixlike cereal that must do wonders for your gums as well as your heart), Italian biscotti, and Jewish mandelbread (hard, flat cookies)" (*Fresno Bee*, 13 August 1989).

MAtse *n.* The unleavened bread used during the celebration of Passover, It emphasizes the exodus from Egypt, during which the Jews had no time to wait for the bread to rise. MAtse is described during the Passover narration as "the bread of affliction." During the period of cleansing that takes place in preparation for the Passover festival, all "unclean" items, including bread, are removed from the household. Comedian Henny Youngman's line is,

"You work hard all year, comes Passover there isn't a piece of bread in the house."

A popular dish prepared during this time to break the monotony of eating plain MAtse is called MAtsebrai, a kind of omelet made of eggs and crushed MAtse. (German Brei means porridge or pulp.) One of Alex Portnoy's high school cheers:

> Ikey, Mikey, Jake, and Sam,
> We're the boys who eat no ham.
> We play football, we play soccer—
> And we keep matzohs in our locker!
> Aye, aye, aye, Weequahic High!

Alex concludes at length that "his superior Jewish brain might as well be made of *matzoh brei*" (P. Roth *PC*).

On California cuisine: "People here are very health-conscious. I've never sold so many egg whites; matzobrei with egg whites really blew me away" (*Los Angeles Times*, 6 August 1989)

From a *New York Times Book Review* discussion of the French-Canadian (Québecois) anxiety about using English: "Then last March, in the weeks before Passover, came Matzoh-gate. An astute-tongued trooper espied boxes of imported matzohs, unilingually labeled, on the shelves of a kosher grocery and ordered them removed at once" (Mordecai Richler, 1 June 1997).

MAYdele *n.* Little girl. A physically big girl is a moyd. Both words are often used ironically.

"And you're not a Jew, *meydeleh?*" (Ozick *TPR*)

MAYvn *n.* Connoisseur, specialist.

A cosmetics ad in the *New York Times* announces: "Amy Greene—our celebrated makeover maven—presides over her own do-it-yourself salon."

"Instead the president and Meese reached once more into the nether regions of the conservative movement populated by de-regulation experts, gold standard mavens and White House aides who wear Adam Smith ties to endless memorial services for dead Austrian economists" (Kevin Phillips, *Los Angeles Times*, 15 November 1987).

A restaurant review: When Charles Perry brought his "deli mavens" to the opening of the L. A. Stage Deli,

The mavens were impressed by the menu. There were 60-some sand-wiches, half a dozen fish platters, a lot of Jewish-mamma dishes and a fairly broad fountain selection. . . . But there was a growing restlessness as the meal proceeded. "The chicken soup, it's OK, but the matzo ball and the kreplech, they're so . . . light." "The potato pancakes have the wrong texture, too smooth." "The chicken liver is bland." "What is this, a potato knish wrapped in strudel?" And finally, the most damning thing of all: the bagel. It looked like a bagel, but it didn't have the dense, chewy, soft-pretzel texture of a bagel. It was a bun baked in the shape of a bagel. A Californianized bagel! . . . This had all been pretty dis-turbing, but everybody calmed down a little at dessert. There was a genuine Brooklyn egg cream, that ultra-simple drink of milk, chocolate syrup and seltzer water that is regularly ruined in California by being made with soda water. . . . But then a maven who had been strangely quiet over her plate of salmon, sturgeon, and whitefish bit into the rugelach, a sort of rolled butter cookie with cinnamon, nuts and raisins, and her eyes widened in horror. "Chocolate bits! There are chocolate bits in the rugelach!" "It's simple," I said, raising my hands in a characteristic helpless gesture. "Welcome to Hollywood. This is . . . the Soundstage Deli" (*Los Angeles Times*, 8 January 1988).

MAzl tuhv Exclamation meaning "good luck, congratulations." MAzl is a reference to a constellation, a good astrological sign.

A joke describes the father of a successful businessman who has changed his obviously Jewish surname. On the occasion when the son is honored as the young executive of the year, the father sneaks into a back row to observe the presentation of the award. But when the moment arrives, he blurts out, "MAzl tuhv—whatever that means."

meKHAIye *adj.* Pleasant, a pleasurable feeling. I learned the mean-ing of the word first from watching old ladies at the beach in Brooklyn. As they shipped water into the tops of their bathing suits, they murmured, "A meKHAIye!"

"A *farzayenisht* [not a Yiddish word] to his detractors, he was a ceaseless *mechaieh* to a biographer like Gold" (Heller *GG*).

meer far deer (or meer zuhl zain far deer) Literally, me for you. It means "let your misfortune be on me instead." It's what a mother says when she hears that something unfortunate has befallen her child. It reminds me of the folk motif, throughout the world, in which a lover is asked to prove his devotion by bringing his mother's heart to his beloved. As he is delivering it, he stumbles and falls—and the mother's heart cries out, "Did you hurt yourself, my child?"

MEESkait *adj.* Ugliness. It can be used to refer to someone who is physically or temperamentally very ugly: a real MEESkait. Someone who is exceptionally good-natured is a ZEESkait.

meGIle *n.* Hebrew for scroll, but usually it refers to the Book of Esther, which recounts the POOrim story. Even better known is the Anglish, meaning "too long a story." We say, "Don't make such a meGIle out of it."

"That letter—a strange *megillah* of which I was the Haman" (Bellow *HFM*).

Perhaps from the analogy to Magilla Gorilla of cartoon fame (it means big, but more for the rhyme than anything else), meGIle is sometimes used incorrectly for the equivalent of big shot: "She played the Big Megilla's stewardess sidekick in the action blowout, a part originally slated for a blue-eyed blond" (*Washington Post*, 4 January 1986).

In the following passage meGIle simply means story: "You recall that the first wind we got of this *megillah* was that the President's former national-security adviser had gone to Iran, looking to make friends, and had taken along some gifts—a Bible and a cake" (Molly Ivins, *Progressive*, January 1987).

"He tried to brief me about politics in this town. The main part of what he said was a regular megillah" (Bellow *MDH*).

A Wheaties commercial proclaims: "It's the whole megillah!"

melAmid *n.* A teacher, often of a KHAYder, with little training and almost no status. MelAmid is a term used to criticize someone's capabilities or competence. A melAmid was often the best that could be had for small towns that couldn't afford a rabbi or a teacher with advanced credentials. The writer Bernard Malamud probably had at least one in his family.

"At the usual early age, Levinsky was sent to *cheder*, where he was made to feel very keenly the disadvantages of poverty, as his teachers risked nothing in punishing a poor boy. His mother would intervene for him (this impulse was to prove fatal) and fought with many a *melamed* for laying hands on her David" (Rosenfeld *AE*).

"My father, a *melamed*, was a pauper. We occupied two rooms—one used for the cheder; the other for the kitchen, the bedroom, and everything else" (Singer *S*).

meNOra *n.* A candelabrum; generally refering to the one used during the celebration of KHANike. Ordinarily the temple candelabra have room for seven candles; the meNOra needs nine, to accommodate the eight candles lit during the festival and one for the "helper," or SHAmis, used to light the other eight. Many different designs for organizing the candles exist, and new patterns are constantly created.

mentsh *n.* Literally, person, or human being. But it also means to be a good person, to behave like a human being rather than an animal.

"You're not like those other university phonies. You're a *mensch*" (Bellow *H*).

" 'He's a very nice man . . .' she began. 'He's what you call'—resorting to Yiddish—'a *mensh*' " (Styron *SC*).

"Maybe the supreme gift of Yiddish to the English language is the word '*mensch*.' Its literal meaning, as in German, from which it came, is 'person,' but in Yiddish it reaches for an essence—character. A *mensch* is someone to emulate, a person of consequence whose character is both rare and undisputed. The question before the U.S. Senate can best be stated in Yiddish: Is William Rehnquist a '*mensch*'?" (Richard Cohen, *Washington Post*, 14 September 1986).

Performer Vincent Gardenia was awarded a Biffy from the Baltimore International Film Festival for achievement by a character actor. The trophy is inscribed, "Vincent Gardenia: Actor, Virtuoso, Mensch" (*New York Times*, 5 April 1991).

"As Billy Wilder recently implied, the all-woman Marlene [Dietrich] was a *mensch*" (Review by Walter Redefern, *TLS*, 14 February 1992).

An Ellen Goodman article discusses a heroic employer: "But in this celebration of Aaron, son of Samuel, grandson of Henry, there is a moral message for the competitive world. This is all it takes to be a hero. Be a *mensch"* (*Fresno Bee*, 22 December 1995).

From a review of Stephen Jay Gould's *Dinosaur in a Haystack:* "Mr. Gould's 'I,' as he chooses to represent himself, is first of all a *mensch:* the public school Jewish kid from Queens, a 'dinosaur nut' (ridiculed as 'Fossil Face' by his schoolmates); who became a lover of tolerance and reason, a 'humanist at heart,' a 'meat and potatoes man'" (*New York Times Book Review*, 21 January 1966).

A childhood friend of Louis Farrakhan: "I wish I could say otherwise, but Gene [Farrakhan] was a *mensch*. . . . I liked him tremendously" (*NYRB*, 19 September 1996).

A letter to the *Fresno Bee:* "It's over. Perhaps Rush Limbaugh, Ray Appleton [a local talk show host], George Will, William Safire and Mona Charen, just to mention a few, can now set aside their vitriol for one day and wish the first family congratulations and best wishes. We'll just call it 'Mensch for a day'" (Robert Levenson, 14 November 1996).

From a review of Arthur Miller's *Death of a Salesman:* "Charley is a man who manages quietly to make of his life everything Willy can't, raising a successful son while still being enough of a *mensch* to give Willy money for his insurance payments" (Sylvia Brownrigg, *TLS*, 15 November 1996).

In a column remembering San Francisco columnist Herb Caen: "Some of his best items never made the paper. 'Better said than read, mensch,' he'd say" (Eli Setencich, *Fresno Bee*, 3 February 1997).

Kate Jennings in a review: "Diane Ackerman comes across in her books, including *A Natural History of the Senses*, as a thoroughly nice person—a mensch with a large, ranging intellect" (*New York Times Book Review*, 2 March 1997).

MENTSHkeit (more likely, MENTSHlikhkeit) *n*. The essence of living a humane life, being a mentsh.

From a review of the film *City Hall:* "One of the film's running jokes is that Kevin [Calhoun] has a hard time with the Yiddishisms he hears around him, particularly menschkeit, literally 'a man's code of behavior,' used to refer to the unspoken rules by which politicians conduct their bargaining" (*New York Times*, 11 February 1996).

meTSIye *n.* A bargain. A GROYse meTSIye is a big deal.

"Ai-yi-yi—another *metzieh,* that General Alexander Haig, with his brain of a *golem's* a *gantsa k'nocker* [GANtser KNAKer—a big shot] under Nixon and Kissinger whose *goyisha kup* [GOYisher kuhp] divined some 'sinister force' behind the erasure of that eighteen and a half minutes from the incriminating Watergate tapes" (Heller *GG*).

meZOOze *n.* A small rectangular box placed on the right-hand side side of the door frame of a house; one kisses a finger and touches it on entering and leaving. Inside the box are paragraphs from the sheMA ("Hear O Israel, the Lord our God is one Lord"), and Deuteronomy 6:4–9, which includes the commandment "And you shall write them on the doorposts of your house and on your gates." The tradition is a strong remembrance of the Jews marking their homes so the Angel of Death will pass over.

"A mezuzah. Safe passage through a bad night" (Pynchon *GR*).

"I put on my short coat, a pair of boots, took the bag that held my prayer shawl in one hand, my stock in the other, and kissed the *mezzuzah*" (I. B. Singer, "Gimpel the Fool," in Bellow *GJSS*).

From a *Fresno Bee* item headlined "Noshing is always kosher at Noah's Bagels": "A *mezuza,* if you don't know, is a small piece of parchment, inscribed with a passage from Deuteronomy, that is rolled up and put in a case. It's attached to the doorpost to protect the home" (Vivian Taylor, 14 May 1997).

MIDrish *n.* From the Hebrew miDRASH, a parable that helps in the exposition and interpretation of biblical passages. MidRASHim are often quoted in attempts to comprehend the ultimate meanings of the Holy Scriptures.

"'Golde,' I say. 'You're sinning. We have a *midrash*—' 'What do I care about a *midrash?*' she says. 'We have a daughter to marry off. And after her two more are almost ready. And after these two, three more—may the evil eye spare them!'" (Sholom Aleichem, "Hodel," in Bellow *GJSS*).

"A professor at the Jewish Theological Seminary, [Burton] Visotzky teaches midrash, one of two intertwining streams of Torah interpretation that arose 2,000 years ago. (The other, Halakha, is the main source of Jewish law." From an article on the TV series

"Genesis," by Rodger Kamenetz (*New York Times Magazine*, 20 October 1996).

MIKve *n.* The ritual bath prescribed for Jewish women after menstruating. Pious men also use such a bath to greet the Sabbath. A convert is immersed in order to become officially Jewish. When Ethiopian Jews were airlifted to Israel in 1985, the Orthodox rabbinate demanded they be subjected to a MIKve. The women were incensed, since they adhere strictly to the laws concerning MIKve after menstruation. The men were equally insulted. An editorial cartoon showed the Ethiopians debarking from an El Al plane with a slide that went directly into a bathtub.

MILkhig *n.* Milk or other dairy products. The opposite of FLAYSHig (meat or meat products) in the Jewish dietary laws. The prohibition against mixing milk and meat derives from an obscure reference that warns against boiling a kid in its mother's milk. It's not clear why anyone should want to do this, but perhaps the point is that here, as elsewhere, Jews pointedly didn't do what some of their neighbors did, in order to establish their unique identity. Orthodox Jews also segregate the utensils, dishes, and pots used for milk and for meat dishes. My own family was not strict in this respect, but my mother never served milk with meat. The first time I thought about the prohibition was when I observed my family doctor eating a hot dog and washing it down with a glass of milk at a local luncheonette. It turned my stomach—but then I realized it couldn't be all bad if the doctor was doing it.

According to Rosenfeld,

The complex centering on *kashruth* [dietary laws] is not the only one that works on sex. There is also *milchigs* and *fleishigs;* and this, I think, is the arch taboo. My own Orthodox grandparents would tremble, as though some catastrophe had occurred, if *milchigs* and *fleishigs* ever came into contact with each other; and with good reason. This is the sexual taboo not only of exogamy, but of the sexuality of the tribe itself. It is the taboo of sex as such. *Milchigs,* having to do with milk, is feminine; *fleishigs,* meat, is masculine. Their junction in one meal, or within one vessel, is forbidden, for their union is the sexual act. (The Jewish joke about the man with cancer of the penis bears this out. He is advised by the doctor to soak his penis in hot water. His wife, finding him so engaged, cries out, "Cancer, shmancer. *Dos is a milchig teppel!*" (Who cares about cancer? You're using a *milchig* pot.) (Rosenfeld *AE*).

MINyen *n.* The quorum of ten male Jews necessary for most rituals and ceremonies. Perhaps best known through Paddy Chayefsky's play *Tenth Man.*

In an East Side school a MINyen was lacking and, as often was the case, the rabbi sent his wife to find a man to fill the vacancy. She leaned out the window and hailed the first passerby. "Listen, mister," she said, "would you like to be the tenth?" "To tell you the truth," he said after getting a good look at her, "I wouldn't even like to be the first."

"In the Winter Palace you had to walk up and down all day to find a *minyan*" (Bellow *H*).

"He had to be in *shul* before sundown. He had to get to the *minion*" (Elkin *CKKC*).

Joseph Heller's shaky Yiddish is redundant: ". . . furnishing the male adults needed to comprise the minyan of ten for the prayers at morning and sundown" (*GG*).

MISH-mash *n.* A mixture, a hodgepodge. Mish is Yiddish for mix, so perhaps it's a reduplication.

In Isabel Allende's novel *Eva Luna,* her boss comments: "'Keep writing, Eva. I'm curious about how you're going to end such a mishmash.'" Since this is a translation from the Spanish, MISH-mash has evidently become an international term.

"My files are full of folders with titles like 'Right-Wing Nincompoops' and 'This Is a Great Nation.' I'm strong on organizational principle. Among my favorites is 'Interesting Mishmash,' and from it comes the fodder for today's column" (Molly Ivins, *Fresno Bee,* 21 February 1966). Ivins follows with a collection of strange stories.

From a description of psychological diseases: "CFS [chronic fatigue syndrome], dubbed 'the yuppie flu' during the 1980s, is a mishmas of symptoms, including a mysterious and debilitating *malaise,* that affects primarily white middle-class men and women, and that many sufferers believe is caused by an unidentified environmental pathogen" (Mark S. Micale, *TLS,* 16 May 1997).

From a review of the 1997 film version of *Anna Karenina:* "Worse than the mishmash of accents is a Babel of language; for some reason, the servants usually speak Russian, their masters English (of a sort), interspersed by Tourette's syndrome outbursts of well-coached Russian" (Donald Rayfield, *TLS,* 6 June 1997).

From a review dealing with Casanova: "She has a gift for mathematics that shows up his vaunted capacity in that field as a cabalistic mishmas" (Clive James, *New Yorker,* 25 August and 1 September 1997).

miSHOOgener *n.* A madman. The feminine is miSHOOgene but American English usage fails to make the distinction. MiSHOOge is to be mad, mishiGAS is a madness, and the plural is mishiGOYim.

Portnoy's father on Christianity: "I assure you Alex, you are never going to hear such a *mishegoss* of mixed-up crap and disgusting nonsense as the Christian religion in your entire life" (P. Roth *PC*).

At the local ballgame: "And invariably Dr. Wolfenberg, who takes himself a little more seriously than your ordinary non-professional person (and is a German to boot), holds up his palm, halting an already Sokolow-stopped game, and says to Biderman, 'Will you please get that *meshuggener* back in the outfield?'" (P. Roth *PC*).

From an unsigned review of *Eve's Apple,* by Jonathan Rosen: "The novel includes several hilarious scenes, not least a luncheon at the Harvard Club during which a wise therapist with a keen appetite suddenly leads our hero to recognize his own ruling meshugas" (*New Yorker,* 9 June 1997).

Commenting on a Jewish gun fan who claims that gun control legislation creates anti-Semitism, David Corn notes: "As my grandmother might have said, that's one *meshuggeneh* Jew" (*Nation,* 4 June 1990).

A feature story about actress-writer Carrie Fisher: "Because these days, Fisher's own *mishegoss,* her extreme need for control that once prompted her to reach for drugs, is now making her reach for pens and yellow legal pads" (Irene Lacher, *Los Angeles Times,* 7 September 1990).

A company in San Rafael, California, sells what it calls "Mashuga Nuts," cinnamon-sugar spiced pecans. ("You were expecting maybe Brooklyn?")

From an article on Woody Allen's movie at the film festival in Venice: "although for the overwhelmingly Italian audience phrases such as 'world-class meshuggana cunt' probably lost something in translation" (Kurt Andersen, *New Yorker*, 15 September 1997).

mishPUHkhe *n.* Family, relatives.

Father: TAte	Mother: MAme
Son: zoon	Daughter: TUKHter
Brother: BROOder	Sister: SHVESter
Uncle: FEter	Aunt: TANte or MEEme
Nephew: pleMENik	Niece: pleMENitze
Cousin: KUZin, fem. kuZEEne	
Grandchild: AYNikl, pl. AYNiklekh	
Grandfather: ZAYde	Grandmother: BOObe or BUHbe
Father-in-law: shver	Mother-in-law: SHVIger
Son-in-law: AYDim	Daughter-in-law: SHNEEr
Husband: man	Wife: froy or vibe

misNAgid *n.* The Hebrew word for opponent. It refers specifically to the opponents of the khSEEdim, especially in the eighteenth century.

"On this withdrawn side she [Mother Herzog] often had a dreaming look, melancholy, and seemed to be seeing the Old World—her father the famous *misnagid*" (Bellow *H*).

mitn GRUHBn FINger With the thumb (the fat finger). The expression refers to the Talmudic gesture that places the thumb on a passage and lifts out the message in explication. (It's sticking in your thumb and pulling out a plum of exegesis.) My Brooklyn College English professor, Frederic Ewen, used to recall studying with the great philosopher Morris Raphael Cohen, "who taught mitn GRUHBn FINger."

MITSvuh *n.* Literally, a commandment, but it takes on the meaning of a good deed. Bar MITSvuh is literally "a son of the commandment," a boy of the age when he begins to be required to perform the commandments. Six hundred thirteen commandments are required of a pious Jew. Carrying out a MITSvuh can also be seen as performing a charitable or commendable act; we can say, "I know this is unpleasant, but do it anyway—it's a MITSvuh."

Former Massachusetts governor Michael Dukakis, speaking at a press conference reported by the *Washington Post:* "'I'm here for several reasons. First, George [Dukmejian] and I are the only two "dukes" who are governors. Second, Kitty [Dukakis's wife] is deeply involved in the Holocaust Council. Third, I'm of Greek descent—my dad came from Asia Minor, where there are a lot of Armenians. And fourth, the speaker of the Massachusetts House is Armenian. And a Greek as governor and an Armenian as speaker—as they say in Brookline, that's a "mitsvah". . . a good deed.' 'No, it's a double mitsvah,' piped in a friend. 'And don't forget you've got a Jewish first lady,' added Kitty Dukakis."

"It's a state of affairs, the journalist Gabrielle Glaser implies in 'Stranger to the Tribe,' that could be taken as further proof of the seeming Jewish affinity for having one's back forever aginst the wall, or as evidence of a more optimistic interpretation of history, one that casts intermarriage itself as an unexpected salvatory mitzvah" (Martha Fay, *New York Times Book Review,* 2 November 1997).

money-shmoney *n.* Example of a characteristic Yiddish locution (based on reduplication in its Yinglish form). In this approach the first word is repeated, but *sh* or *shm* is substituted for the initial consonantal sound of the second element (sick-shmick), or is added before it if the word begins with a vowel (old-shmold). This locution is primarily used to express lack of interest in a subject that another person has raised or to deflate a pompous statement. The *Dictionary of American Slang* calls it "a vocal way of shrugging one's shoulders" to undercut a statement that anticipates a respectful answer. A well-known expression is "money-shmoney—aBEE geZOONT," which means that health is more important than money. (There's also the whimsical "cancer-shmancer, as long as you're healthy.")

An old joke: Two women argue about the chastity of their daughters. "Virgin-shmirgin," one declares, "as long as she doesn't smoke."

A full-page ad in the *Los Angeles Times* (25 November 1979)

carried the headline: "Windfall-Schmindfall," as it argued against
the windfall profits tax.

Robert Mezey's widely reprinted poem "My Mother":

> My mother writes from Trenton,
> a comedian to the bone
> but underneath, serious
> and all heart. "Honey," she says,
> "be a mensch and Mary too,
> its no good to worry, you
> are doing the best you can
> your Dad and everyone
> thinks you turned out very well
> as long as you pay your bills
> nobody can say a word
> you can tell them to drop dead
> so save a dollar it can't
> hurt—remember Frank you went
> to highschool with? He still lives
> with his wife's mother. his wife
> works while he writes his books and
> did he ever sell a one
> the kids run around naked
> 36 and he's never had
> you'll forgive my expression
> even a pot to piss in
> or a window to throw it,
> such a smart boy he couldnt
> read the footprints on the wall
> honey you think you know all
> the answers you dont, please try
> to put some money away
> believe me it wouldnt hurt
> artist shmartist, life's too short
> for that kind of, forgive me,
> horseshit, I know what you want
> better than you, all that counts
> is to make a good living
> and the best of everything,

as Sholem Aleichem said,
he was a great writer did
you ever read his books dear,
you should make what he makes a year
anyway he says some place
Poverty is no disgrace
but its no honor either
that's why I say,
　　love,
　　　　Mother

A letter to the *New York Times* concerning Julia Roberts and Michelle Pfeiffer concludes: "Roberts, shmoberts. Anyone who has seen 'Into the Night,' 'Married to the Mob,' and 'The Fabulous Baker Boys' knows that the only actress to whom Michelle Pfeiffer might be compared is Carole Lombard" (22 October 1995).

Featured in a children's TV show: "two comic jugglers billed as 'Circus Shmirkus'" (*Los Angeles Times*, 4 September 1989).

The following locution leaves out a term but is still clear: "The Accord is a car of great styling because it is simplicity born of the gentle nondescript of previous generations. Nothing schmancy" (Paul Dean, *Los Angeles Times*, 22 December 1989).

In Margaret Atwood's novel *The Handmaid's Tale* there is the following conversation: "Cooking's my hobby, Luke would say. Hobby, schmobby, my mother would say. You don't have to make excuses to me."

From a review of the movie *The Secret Garden*: "Norman's book is effective when it sticks close to Burnett. But there's that big budget, 6.2 million demons shrieking for gewgaws to encumber a translucent tale that doesn't need Freud-Schmeud, Jung-Schmung symbolism grafted onto it" (*Newsweek*, 6 May 1991).

"Budget deal, shmudget deal, the media are missing the story again" (Molly Ivins, *Fresno Bee*, 10 January 1996).

moyl *n*. The person who performs circumcision.

From an article in the *New York Times Magazine*: "He is Dr. Fred Kogen (pictured above), and he is the most popular nonrabbinic mohel (pronounced moyle) in Los Angeles—meaning, for the untutored, that he is an M.D. who performs the bris, the ritual circumcision of 8-day-old Jewish boys" (15 December 1996). (Not every moyl is an M.D. See "bris.")

From a review in the *Fresno Bee:* "The mohel is no goil. . . . The second act appearance of Dr. Rosen, the mohel (pronounced *moyl*), becomes the catalyst that brings the plot to a boil" (23 May 1997).

MOYshe kaPOYer An expression that means doing things backward. MOYshe is the Yiddish for Moses (moSHE in Hebrew); kaPOYer means the wrong way, topsy turvy. The sense is "wrongway Moe."

"So, *Moishe Kapoyer,* the North was bombed to placate the South and salve the hurt feelings of the *mieskeit* [ugliness] and his *umgliks* [bad luck], not, as Kissinger falsely indicated, to force new concessions" (Heller *GG*).

MOYshe POOpik A put-down, a way of ridiculing someone. MOYshe (Yiddish for Hebrew moSHE) plus POOpik (belly button) means "Moe about-as-smart-as his navel."

A reference to Henry Kissinger: "*Moishe Pupik* was as good as gold when it came to finance and economics" (Heller *GG*).

MUHNtik oon DUHNershtik Monday and Thursday. Part of an expression that means regularly, on a continuing basis. In Yiddish we say, "YEder MUHNtik oon DUHNershtik" (every Monday and Thursday). Portions of the Talmud are read in the synagogue on Mondays and Thursdays.

"Every *Montik* and *donnershtik* the scampering lummox was in the papers again with some new *mishegoss* like a *shmegegge* from Chelm [a village in Poland famous for its folk tales about its pixilated population]" (Heller *GG*).

NAFke *n.* From the Aramaic word for whore. The other standard term for prostitute is KOORve.

". . . never so high never so high and gotta big itch for you-u-u-u, you little goy Fascist *nafka,* hey feel this" (Styron *SC*). Since Stingo is addressing a woman, the correct term is GOYe or SHIKse.

"'Shiksa! Hussy! *Nafka!*' Rashkes both scolded her and showered her with kisses. 'What's a *nafka*? Is that Hebrew?' 'Aramaic'" (Singer *CF*). Singer is ever a student of Jewish history and its linguistic sources.

In *RFJG*, Albert Fried quotes an early report on prostitution in

New York: "Almost any child on the East Side in New York will tell you what a 'nafke bias' [whorehouse] is."

NAkhis *n.* Joy or pleasure, especially the joy in some accomplishment of your children. The Yiddish expression is "shep NAkhis" (savor the the special pleasure). Anglish is "SHEPing NAkhis."

nar *n.* A fool. "A *naar* like him they make a Judge, while I don't even have one book in the Bible named after me" (Heller *GK*).

The adjective is NARish, plural NaRUHnim. There is a folk expression: "chasZUHnim ZEnen naRUHnim" (cantors are fools). It probably reflects the ongoing competition and antagonism in the United States between cantors and rabbis. A character in Pynchon's *Gravity's Rainbow* is called Klaus Narrisch.

NARishkait means foolishness. "First—O curséd spite—our disjointed times, and our burgeoning press, provide greatly enhanced opportunity for rehearsal of such narrishkeit ad nauseum; do we not feast upon trivialities to divert attention from the truly portentous issues that engulf us?" (Stephen Jay Gould *QTM*).

nash *v.* To snack between meals. The German *naschen* means to eat sweets on the sly, but nash refers to any appetizer or dessert that provides a bite rather than a full meal. NASHer and NASHing have become standard Anglish.

A New York billboard advertising frozen dinners reads, "A NASH IT'S NOT."

"'We'll eat at Morty's,' he replied cheerfully, 'don't worry. There'll be plenty for *noshing*—let's go'" (Styron *SC*).

"Oh, also they know how to go out in the fields with a gun, these geniuses, and kill innocent wild deer, deer who themselves *nosh* quietly on berries and grasses and then go on their way, bothering no one" (P. Roth *PC*).

"Her eyes were even different. They had become dark gray, not blue, as I remembered. Her hair was brown, and streaked with gray. She was plump and motherly, offering me tea or 'something to knosh on' every few minutes" (Alice Walker *TF*).

An article on diner chains is headlined, "Noshing on Nostalgia Is Big with Consumers and Developers" (*Los Angeles Times*, 4 February 1996).

From an article on automated highway systems: "Drivers will

be able to nosh, snooze, read or do work while cars cruise down the AHS" (*Fresno Bee*, 10 May 1997).

A headline in the *Fresno Bee:* "Noshing is always kosher at Noah's Bagels."

A *New Yorker* cartoon shows a restaurant window advertising: "NET 'n' NOSH (formerly BOOKS 'n' JAVA)" (Mike Twoby, 23 and 30 June 1997).

NEbish *n.* A nothing, a loser. Probably an Anglish version of NEbech; the suffix sounds more like German and may be easier for Americans to pronounce.

"And me a hungry Jewish youth, a poor *nebbish* with five dollars landing on Ellis Island not knowing a single individual" (Styron *SC*).

"In an early nightclub skit, Woody Allen told of an elevator that took umbrage at him, carried him to the basement, and tossed him out, saying in a hollow voice, 'You passed a remark.' Allen's nebbishy tale reflected my own paranoia and intimidation when confronted with complicated devices, these days meaning primarily the computer" (Charles Champlin, *Los Angeles Times*, 22 February 1990).

-nik The suffix that is equivalent to *-ist,* as in NOODnik, an annoying person. The Russian form is familiar in Sputnik (pronounced -nyik).

Hendrik Hertzberg, describing Bob Dole: "The country's leading aboutnik, of course, is Bob ('That's what Bob Dole's all about') Dole" (*New Yorker*, 9 September 1996).

William Safire: "At the annual conclave of executive heavies, political powers, scientific Nobelniks and media biggies . . . words have historic resonance and metaphors fly" (*New York Times Magazine*, 23 February 1997).

"'George Young,'" a Jet draftnik said, referring to the Giants general manager, "'has lost his mind'" (Dave Anderson, *New York Times*, 20 April 1997).

nisht aHEEN nisht aHEAR An expression that means "neither here nor there"; not definitive.

"Twisting and turning like a worm or a snake, the *vonz* [bedbug] was *nisht a heyn, nisht aher* on issues igniting the fiercest controversy" (Heller *GG*).

nooj *n.* Anglish for a pest. Nooj is really the verbal form. It comes from the Yiddish NOODni, which means the boring or tedious condition that the NOODnik, a person, causes. The Anglish has lost most of the Yiddish meaning and refers basically to one who pesters beyond endurance.

Of his father, Portnoy says, "Shout he could shout, squabble he could squabble, and oh *nudjh,* could he *nudjh*" (P. Roth *PC*).

It's hard to tell from this sentence by Texas satirist Molly Ivins that she means nooj: "Progressives are such worriers and nudges" (*Progressive,* December 1987).

nuhkh *adv.* Even more (than one can believe).

"And a professor at Princeton *noch*" (P. Roth *PC*).

nuhkh a muhl Once more, once again. Heller uses the phrase, as well as variants like "nukh mear" [in addition] and "vuhs nuhkh" [what else] in *Good as Gold.*

NUHKHshleppers *n.* Hangers-on, sycophants.

"Kissinger already had such *saychel* [good sense], as did according to this paragraph in *Newsweek,* several of his confederates and *nuchshleppers*" (Heller *GG*).

Alex Shoumatoff's study of kinship, *The Mountain of Names,* quotes a source that describes young men "shlepping for the in-laws. Sons-in-law the world over bend over with false courtesy and contorted deference, and parents-in-law think the bums aren't good enough." He confuses SHLEPpers with NUHKHshleppers.

oyf tseLOOKHis For spite; done purposely to annoy.

"For years I sniffed after an opportunity to think in print about the sacral Updike, and now that the chance is palpably here, it turns out to be not . . . those fictions of salvationism and eucharistic radiance. Instead, *oif tsulokhes* (the phrase of regret Bech's Williamsburg uncles would use and toward which Bech is amnesiac), here is Henry Bech, Jew. Rising, like Shylock and Bloom, out of a Christian brain" (Ozick *AA*).

oysgeMOOtshet *adj.* Worn down. MOOtshe means torture. Oysge-MOOtshet means exhausted, perhaps by a torturing experience.

"Look at him sitting there, so *oysgemitchet.* How he labored for the downtrodden—as will I" (P. Roth *PC*).

OYSvorf *n.* Outcast, bum, scoundrel.

"Thirty years I run this place without evicting nobody. Pride I've got in never kicking anyone out except for some weird *oysvorf* in 1938 I caught dressed up in girls' panties" (Styron *SC*).

oy vay O pain (or woe); "oy vay iz mir" is "O woe is to me." The American expression "O pain" is probably a direct translation.

"*Oy vey*, I groan silently, and fortify myself with a deep breath" (Heller *GK*).

Portnoy quips, "The perfect couple: she puts the id back in Yid, I put the *oy* back in *goy*" (P. Roth *PC*).

"George Will remarked: 'If everyone quit smoking today, it would be a calamity for Social Security.' Oy vey, and the program is already a wreck!" (Susan Douglas, *Progressive*, May 1997).

"Aside from its wide range of applications, another great thing about the word 'Oy' is that you can express degrees of dismay by how many times you say it—once or three times. 'Oy' means things are not great. 'Oy, oy, oy,' means things are really pretty terrible. Strangely, one rarely hears people say, 'Oy, oy'" (Mark Sherman, *Network*, Summer 1997).

parNUHse *n.* Livelihood, subsistence.

"And Gold was prepared to develop the thesis that Kissinger was not a Jew in a book of Kissinger 'memoirs' he was positive would excite attention and hoped it would earn him at least a discernible fraction of the *parnussheh* Kissinger was raking in from his own memoirs" (Heller *GG*).

pastrami *n.* A favorite item on the Jewish delicatessen menu, often served hot.

In an interview, Al Langer (of Langer's Delicatessen in Los Angeles): "Do you know the difference between pastrami and corned beef? . . . I mean besides the fact that pastrami's smoked and corned beef gets boiled? . . . Put your hand in the middle of your chest and you'll feel your breastbone. Underneath, where the breastbone starts to curve towards your side, that's called the plate, if you're a cow. And off each of the two plates you get one corned beef or brisket. But the pastrami comes from the belly button. That means you get two corned beefs off a steer but only one pastrami" (*Los Angeles Times*, 6 August 1989).

According to the *American Heritage Dictionary*, "A highly seasoned smoked cut of beef, usually taken from the shoulder." The derivation is Yiddish from Romanian, *pastrama*.

patsh *v.* To slap. Frequently, patsh in TOOKHis (to slap on the ass). Folksinger Sam Hinton (HINtn is another word in Yiddish for the behind) used to pun, "Pacem in TOOkhis."

"And why my mother weeps so is because my father refuses to potch my behind, which she promised would be *potched*, 'and good,' when he found out the terrible thing I had done" (P. Roth *PC*).

PISHerke *n.* The diminutive of PISHer, a little pisser or bed-wetter.

"Thirteen, his father was thinking, a *pisherke*, and you waved good-bye to the family? What was the matter? Was something the matter with them? What the hell were you waving good-bye to your family for at thirteen? No wonder you're *shicker* now" (P. Roth *AP*).

PISHke (or POOSHke) *n.* A small container (often with a coin slot) used to solicit donations. It is used for collecting money for various religious causes; but I can remember carrying one around when I was about nine for the Republican cause in Spain.

"Gold was astonished that a person of Kissinger's low stature and despicable achievements would be allowed into a respectable house, even the White House, but into a *house of finance*? Such a *geshrei* [outcry] should go up if he ever went near the *pishke*" (Heller *GG*).

pisk *n.* Snout, mouth of an animal. Pisk is a deep insult when applied to a human.

"The *pisk* he opens on him! (As my mother would put it)" (P. Roth *PC*).

"'Is it me or is it Sylvia Sidney?' asked Mrs. Plaut. 'I *used* to like her, I *used* to have with Teitelbaum the biggest arguments because he would say she has a certain little habit he couldn't stand, a little something she does with her *pisk*'" (Markfield *TW*).

"Such a *pisk* on the *pisher* to speak with such *chutzpah*" (Heller *GG*).

Two talkative sisters in Thomas Pynchon's *VI* are named Ditzah and Zipi Pisk.

plats *v.* To burst. It can be used two ways: as an insult—"PLATSn zuhl er" (may he burst); or as an exclamation—"ickh huhb sheer ge PLATST!" (I almost burst from surprise or pleasure).

Henry Roth often translates directly as Aunt Bertha curses, "Oh, may they burst" (*CIS*).

"From the geisha girl, Milty, she'll *plotz*" (P. Roth *PC*).

From a photo feature, "Women We Love": "When they speak we listen (except when they speak on, and on, and on, on *thirtysomething*, and we could *plotz* from the endless prattle)" (*Esquire*, August 1989).

POOpik *n.* Belly button. I once worked at a summer camp where the male counselors painted all the women's belly buttons with gentian violet. The next morning everyone showed up for breakfast with a purple POOpik. What accumulates in your POOpik is sometimes called FOONf.

"The fat guys pay out. They shiver in their pupick" (Bellow *H*).

POOrim (Purim) *n.* The festival that celebrates the victory of the Jews over evil Haman (HUHmn), the adviser of King Ahasuerus (akhashVERish) according to the Book of Esther. In an earlier Europe it was a lively and happy celebration marked by music and improvised plays based on the traditional story (with the current enemy of the Jews in the place of Haman) and performed by amateur POOrim SHPEELer (actors).

Prufrock The critical approach to T. S. Eliot's influential poems of the early decades of our century, "The Love Song of J. Alfred Prufrock" and *The Waste Land*, has changed considerably in recent years. Critics used to take at face value Eliot's insistence upon what he called his "impersonal theory" of poetry. To explain it, Eliot gave the analogy of a catalyst in a chemical reaction. The poet's mind is like the catalytic agent that is crucial to the result but shows no trace of itself. The mind of the poet "may partly or exclusively operate upon the experience of the man himself; but the more perfect the artist, the more completely separate in him will be the man who suffers and the mind which creates; the more perfectly will the mind digest and transmute the passions which are its material." In the famous essay in which Eliot tried to explain his position ("Tradition and the Individual Talent," published in 1917, the same year when "Prufrock" appeared), he argued that it is not the poet's "personality" but his poetry that should be the center of attention: "Impressions and experiences which are important for the man may take no place in the poetry, and those which become important in the poetry may play quite a negligible part in the man, the personality."

As the editors of an important literary anthology note, Eliot's position is that the poem should be "treated as a verbal object, with its own structure and meaning and emotional value, and not simply or even primarily as an outpouring of the poet's own personal anguish or ecstasy."

There is more than a little irony in the fact that Eliot wrote his poetry during this period partly as a desperate attempt to prevent a complete mental breakdown. As the editors of the same anthology note, "In 1921 Eliot had suffered a breakdown that forced him to take leave from his work at Lloyd's Bank in London and to enter a sanatorium in Lausanne, Switzerland. There much of *The Waste Land* was written." (It was published the next year; so was James Joyce's *Ulysses,* making 1922 the most important year of our century for the publication of modern masterpieces.)

Despite this obvious contradiction, well documented in a number of recent biographies of Eliot, "Tradition and the Individual Talent" makes a number of other interesting comments that have held up over time. Among them is Eliot's argument that "the historical sense compels a man to write not merely with his own generation in his bones, but with a feeling that the whole of the literature of Europe from Homer and within it the whole of the literature of his own country has a simultaneous existence and composes a simultaneous order." At the same time, he argues, when a really new work of art is created, what happens affects all the great works that preceded it as well. Anyone who thinks about this, he says, "will not find it preposterous that the past should be altered by the present as much as the present is directed by the past."

Eliot's comments came to mind when, several years ago, the *Bulletin of the American Association of Professors of Yiddish* published the following transliteration, asking for any clues to its authorship:

> Nu-zhe, kum-zhe, ich un du
> Ven der ovnt shteyt unter dem himmel
> Vi a leymener goylem af tishebov.
> Lomir geyn gikh, durch geselech vos dreyen zich
> Vi di bord bay dem rov.
> Oyf der vant

Fun dem kosheren restoran
Hengt a shmutsiker betgevant
Un vantsn tantsn karahod. Es geyt a geroykh
fun gefilte fish un nase zokn.
Oy, Bashe, freg nit keyn kashe, a dayge dir!
Lomir oyfefenen di tir.
In tsimer vu di vayber zenen
Redt men fun Karl Marx un Lenin.

. . . .

Ikh ver alt, ikh ver alt
Un der pupik vert mir kalt.
Zol ikh oyskemen di hor,
Meg ikh oyfesn a flom?
Ikh vel onton vayse hoyzn
Un shpatsirn bay dem yom.
Ikh vel hern di yam-meydn zingen Khad Gadyo.
Ikh vel zey entfern, Borech-abo.

I recognized it at once as a parody of the opening and closing sections of "Prufrock" by Isaac Rosenfeld, a hilariously funny writer whose death at the age of thirty-eight in 1956 cut short a brilliant career. Rosenfeld and Saul Bellow used to collaborate in translating Eliot into Yiddish, both well aware of Eliot's anti-Semitism. In the foreword to a collection of Rosenfeld's work, Bellow noted: "He was a marvelous clown. He imitated steam irons, clocks, airplanes, tugboats, big game hunters, Russian commissars, village poets and their girl friends. He tried on the faces of people in restaurants. He was great as Harry Baur in *Crime et Châtiment*, the inspector Porfiry Petrovitch, smoking cigarettes with an underhand Russian grip. He invented Yiddish proletarian poems, he did a translation of Eliot's *Prufrock,* a startling X-ray of those hallowed bones which brings Anglo-Saxons and Jews together in a surrealistic Yiddish unity, a masterpiece of irreverence."

"Prufrock" in Yiddish was especially funny in light of Eliot's persistent anti-Semitism. He liked to use Jewish images as a way of underscoring the commercialism and sensuality of modern culture—as if the Jews were uniquely responsible for the sordidness of modern life. Rosenfeld reacted with the time-hallowed device of undermining a vicious affront with laughter rather than anger. It was his standard technique. I met him when he taught humanities at the University of Minnesota in the early fifties. When he found out I knew Yiddish, he always had a good joke or a good line. And not only in Yiddish. "*C'est la vie*," he would say, "and you call this a *vie?*"

It's hard to reproduce the skill of his parody because, despite some inconsistencies, Rosenfeld has transmuted Eliot's poem into his own creation; it does, as Eliot predicted, alter our sense of the past as well as the present. But with a nod to Mark Twain, who once retranslated from French his "Jumping Frog" story, here is an English version of Rosenfeld's Yiddish version of "The Love Song of J. Alfred Prufrock":

Well then, come, you and I
When the evening stands under the sky
Like a clay golem on Tishebov [the date that commemorates
    the fall of both Temples].
Let us go quickly, through streets that curve
Like the rabbi's beard.
On the wall
Of the kosher restaurant
A filthy bedspread hangs
And bedbugs are folk dancing. There is the odor
Of gefilte fish and wet socks.
Oh, Bashe, don't ask, what do you care!
Let us open the door.
In the room where the women are
They are talking of Karl Marx and Lenin.
. . . .
I grow old, I grow old
And my belly-button is getting cold.
Shall I comb my hair?
May I eat a plum?
I will put on my white pants
And promenade near the sea.
I will hear the mermaids singing "An Only Kid" [the traditional
    Passover song].
And I will answer them, "Welcome."

puhGRUHM (pogrom) *n.* A massacre of Jews. But now it could be used of any attempt to massacre or destroy a group. The perpetrators are puhGRUHMtshiks.

"Gevalt, a pogrom!" (Malamud *IF*).

PUHnim *n.* A face.

"Let me get through this weekend without having to see his pathetic *punim*" (P. Roth *PC*).

puhts *n.* Obscene term for penis, the equivalent of prick. The diminutive, PETSl, shows up also in Anglish expressions like PETSLhead and PETSLbrain, the equivalents of "lamebrain." The expression putzing around, meaning playing around, not doing anything important, may be a combination of puttering and puhts, with no awareness of the obscene implications.

"But who wins an argument with a hard-on? *Ven der putz shteht, ligt der sechel in drerd.* You know that famous proverb? When the prick stands up, the brains get buried in the ground! When the prick stands up, the brains are as good as dead" (P. Roth *PC*). Roth gives a good gloss of the Yiddish. Drerd (a contraction of *der erd*) means earth or ground; in drerd means, literally, in the ground and also to be buried. SEKHl means sense or judgment. So the message is that when you are led by your sexual drives, your good sense is dead.

"I've heard Nathan call it his dork. Also his *putz*" (Styron *SC*).

razBOYnik *n.* Highwayman, thief. It's Russian and I have never heard it in Yiddish, but Bellow gives it as if it were. The Russian suffix is pronounced "nyik," the Yiddish "nik."

"I know these hooligans and *razboiniks*. They don't have skins, teeth, fingers like you" (Bellow *H*).

REbe *n.* The term used for the leader or teacher in Chasidic tradition. The more formal term for a traditional rabbi is ruhv. So when the khSEEDim use REbe, they mean it to be distinguished from the conventional position. The traditional Jewish communities make a similarly disdainful distinction.

RUGelach *n.* A dessert cookie.

From the article "Opening a Window on Hasidism": "Mr. Daum continued recently over coffee and rugelach in Mr. Rudavsky's office on Upper Broadway" (David Margolick, *New York Times*, 20 July 1997).

ruhshiSHUHne (Hebrew rosh hashaNA) and yuhm KIPer (Hebrew yom kiPUR) *n.* The High Holidays. RuhshiSHUHne means literally "the head of the year." Yuhm KIPer is the Day of Atonement, the most holy time in the Jewish calendar (other than the Sabbath). On that day pious Jews fast and ask forgiveness for their sins. High Holiday services in the United States are special events, and attendance usually requires buying a ticket. The last yuhm KIPer service I attended was marked by the rabbi's pitch for a new air-conditioning unit for the synagogue. It's the one time of the year that congregants will surely attend services.

A southern golf pro in a commercial seemed to be saying, "Ah never eat on the day of atonement [a tournament]."

A stranger in town tried to get into the services during the High Holidays without a ticket. "All right," said the SHAmis, "I'll let you in. But if I catch you praying—out you go." Such gags are obviously a critique of American vulgarizations of what should be the most spiritual occasion of the year. Usually a top-notch cantor is hired for the occasion, which often takes place in a Borsht Belt hotel.

sefIRos *n.* (*sing.* sefIRuh) From the Hebrew word for numbers, it refers to the kaBAle's notion of the ten emanations of the Divine presence. The sefIRos are "the ten names most common to God, and in their entirety they also form his one great Name. They are 'the King's faces,' in other words, his varying aspects, and they are also called the inner, intrinsic or mystical Face of God. They are the ten stages of the inner world, through which God descends from the inmost recesses down to his revelation in the Shekhina. They are the garments of the Divinity, but also the beams of light which it sends out" (Scholem *JM*). The very complicated idea is basically a way of dealing with the modes within which God operates in the physical world; since this is essentially a symbolic process, sefIRos has had a strong influence on literature and literary criticism. See, in particular, Thomas Pynchon, *Gravity's Rainbow,* and Harold Bloom, *Kabbalah and Criticism.*

"On the Kabbalist Tree of Life, the path of The Tower connects the sephira Netzach, victory, with Hod, glory or splendor. Hence the Golden Dawn interpretation. Netzach is fiery and emotional, Hod is watery and logical. On the body of God, these two Sephiroth are the thighs, the pillars of the Temple, resolving together in Yesod, the sex and excretory organs" (Pynchon *GR*).

"'At the creation,' explains [Pynchon's] Kabbalist spokesman Steve Edelman, 'God sent out a pulse of energy into the void. It presently branched and sorted into ten distinct spheres or aspects, corresponding to the numbers 1–10. These are known as Sephiroth. To return to God, the soul must negotiate each of the sephiroth, from ten back to one. Armed with magic and faith, Kabbalists have set out to conquer the Sephiroth. Many Kabbalist secrets here have to do with making the trip successfully'" (*GR*). Here, as elsewhere, Pynchon uses the name of a friend, Steve Edelman, in place of an established source.

sh/sch In transliterating from Yiddish one should not write *sch* (as in schmo, schtik) because it represents a basically German approach. (At least, staunch Yiddishists have always argued this point strongly.) In Yiddish the sound "sh" is made by one letter (sheen) so the spelling *sh* is closer and distinctive. I follow that practice here, but it can be seen that many writers vary and are inconsistent in their usage.

sha *v.* An exclamation equivalent to "shush," meaning "be quiet."

A famous Yiddish song goes, "Sha, quiet, don't make a stir—the REbe is about to dance again."

"'Sha,' says his son" (Malamud *TT*).

"And then this amazing creature—to whom no one has ever said 'Shah,' or 'I only hope your children will do the same to you someday!'—this perfect stranger . . . will kiss me" (P. Roth *PC*).

SHAbis *n.* The Sabbath, the seventh day, a day of rest. From just before sundown on Friday until slightly after sunset on Saturday, Jewish law prescribes a period of rest and meditation. SHAbis commemorates the covenant between the Jews and their God. "It is a sign between me and the children of Israel forever: for in six days the Lord made heaven and earth, and on the seventh day he rested, and was refreshed" (Exodus 31:17). Exodus also prescribes death for those who defile the Sabbath or perform any work on that day. If we could afford it, a Gentile (called a Shabis goy) was hired to light fires in the stove, turn on lights, and perform other tasks forbidden to Jews. My wife's grandmother used to turn lights on and off using a grandchild's little finger, on the grounds that a child would not be punished. Rabbinical commentaries have expanded on precisely what acts may or may not be engaged in on the Sabbath. (They have declared it a major MITSvuh for a married couple to have intercourse on Friday evening.) The Church Council of Nicaea in the year 325 officially changed the Christian Sabbath to Sunday in order to distinguish it from Jewish custom. Jewish religious schools may meet on SHAbis, but because of the proscription against writing, they usually meet on Sunday. (The children need to be trained to say "religious school" rather than "Sunday School," since the latter has obvious Christian connotations.) When the film *Never on Sunday* played in Israel, it created serious semantic problems. Some genius came up with a solution, retitling the film *Only on Weekdays*.

An AP story describes a young Japanese man who, while studying Hebrew in Israel, also becomes proficient in Yiddish: "He shares a dormitory apartment with an Orthodox Jew through whom he is discovering the intricacies of Jewish law, such as not mixing milk and meat dishes—a violation of kosher rules—and not switching lights on or off on the Sabbath. 'I've told him I'm willing to be a shabbes goy,'" says the young Japanese.

SHAmis *n.* A lay helper in the synagogue, having mainly janitorial duties (his wife is the SHAmeste); also the extra candle used to light the others on the meNOra during the celebration of KHANike. The SHAmis has charge of preparing the sanctuary for services and cleaning up afterward. Although his association with the religious institution gives him some small status, the term is often used derisively to emphasize the menial and custodial function.

In American tradition, SHAmis has spawned SHAYmis (usually spelled shamus), a private detective in underworld jargon. The implication is that the private eye is essentially a servant to the police, one who does their dirty work; or it may be that he is the servant of whoever hires him.

In the classic detective film *The Maltese Falcon*, Humphrey Bogart and other cast members say SHAmis rather than SHAYmis. The latter pronunciation suggests an Irish derivation.

"When the teacher had written all this down, Yisroel the *shammes* rolled up his sleeve, took the pen carefully with two fingers and prepared himself for the delicate operation. . . . And once more Simma the *shammeste* burst out crying" (Sholom Aleichem *SS*).

A review of *Kill Me Again:* "A conventional detective story, in which the filmmakers don't avoid clichés—the shabby shamus's office, the skeptical cops, the slick crooks" (Michael Wilmington, *Los Angeles Times*, 26 January 1990).

SHANde *n.* Scandal, shame. A common expression is "es iz a SHANde oon a CHARpe," CHARpe being a Hebrew word meaning the same thing. (So it's twice as shameful.)

"A bad boy! A *shande* to his family forever" (P. Roth *PC*).

A character in Heller's *Good as Gold* keeps saying to Gold, "You are a *shonda*." But that's not idiomatic. Shame on you is "shemt zikh!"

SHAYgits *n.* A male Gentile. It's always a derogatory term.

"Discovering the sinister Brock Vond on one of their films, Ditzah Pisk exclaims, 'Here's the little shaygetz again'" (Pynchon, *VI*).

sheMA *v.* To hear. It usually refers to the first word of the Jewish credo that in a shortened version states: "Hear, O Israel; the Lord our God is one Lord." The sheMA represents the central tenet of monotheism, the distinctive mark of Judaism. It was often the last words of Jewish martyrs. The entire statement is in Deuteronomy 6:4–9.

SHIdekh *n.* A marriage arranged by a matchmaker, known as a SHADkhn. Bernard Malamud's famous story involving a SHIdekh, "The Magic Barrel," characteristically never uses the Yiddish terms.

"There must be a few Yiddish words left in the old girl's memory—*shiddach, tachliss* [TAKHlis means purpose, the bottom line]" (Bellow *H*).

SHIKer *n.* A drunk.

"He drank his pay—a *shicker*" (Bellow *H*).

Joseph Heller quotes the old song: "'Shicka [SHIKer] is a goy,' was the tight-lipped snub of vindication she proposed" (*GK*).

"The guys stepped out in their fine duds on Saturday night and got shicker" (P. Roth, *ST*).

SHIKse *n.* A Gentile woman. It is a derogatory term comparable to GOYe, the feminine of goy.

A joke after Elizabeth Taylor and Debbie Reynolds had married Jewish men: Lounging by the pool in southern California, they spy Marilyn Monroe approaching (she had just married Arthur Miller). "Sha," Liz says. "The SHIKse koomt." (Shush. Here comes the SHIKse.)

"My beloved mama always said I was fatally attracted to blond *shiksas*" (Styron *SC*).

"This was a phenomenon I will call 'shiksa hunger': the longing for non-Jewish, crystalline Christian women on the part of Jewish men" (Daphne Merkin, *Esquire*, August 1989).

"Long before they ever laid eyes on each other, Josh had received the vaccine meant to inoculate him against all thought of running off with a shiksa" (from Martha Fay's review of *Strangers to the Tribe, New York Times Book Review*, 2 November 1997).

SHIme LEkhl Anyone who grew up in Brooklyn knows the term that describes the opening of a game of hide and seek. The one who is "it" turns her back to the group and covers her eyes. Then someone approaches and says, "You make a SHIme LEkhl and someone sticks it in." The person saying this traces a circle on the back of the one who is "it." At the end the circler sticks a finger in—and everyone runs while the one who is "it" begins to count to fifty or a hundred. LEkhl means hole, in this case, circle. SHIme may be nonsense, or it may refer to shimmy or some other term, but it is not Yiddish.

SHIve *n.* The seven-day period of mourning; the expression is "to sit SHIve." It's the custom to visit those in mourning (my mother used to bring oranges) and sit quietly with them in restrained conversation.

"When I got out of the hospital my mother was dead. She was a wonderful person. My father died when I was thirteen and all by herself she kept the family alive and together. I sat shive for a week and remembered how she sold paper bags on her pushcart" (Malamud *IF*).

"Worse yet, this last summer, instead of sitting *shiva* over a son running off to faraway Europe, you might have found yourself dining out on my 'deck' on Fire Island" (P. Roth *PC*).

Molly Ivins in the *Progressive:* "Progressives are expected to sit *shiva* over all this, mourning the corrupting influence of the tube and the debasing effect of advertising and public relations on our once-noble life" (November 1988).

shKHIne (Shekhina) *n.* The divine presence of God in the world. In the mystical framework of the kaBUHle, shKHIne represents a major sense of the feminine principle, an attribute of the Jewish God that is often lacking. As Gershom G. Scholem has pointed out, Kabbalism "is a masculine doctrine, made for men and by men. The long history of Jewish mysticism shows no trace of feminine influence. There have been no women Kabbalists; Rabia of early Islamic mysticism, Mechtchild of Magdeburg, Juliana of Norwich, Theresa de Jesus, and the many other feminine representatives of Christian mysticism have no counterparts in the history of Kabbalism." But the shKHIne is for the kaBUHle a feminine form of the immanence of God in the world. Scholem describes the shKHIne as "a sort of invisible Church, representing the mystical idea of Israel in its bond with God and its bliss, but also its suffering and its exile. She is not only Queen, daughter and bride of God, but also the mother of every individual in Israel. . . . In the symbolic world of the Zohar, this new conception of the Shekhina as the symbol of 'eternal womanhood' occupies a place of immense importance and appears under an endless variety of names and images" (*JM*).

shkooTS *n.* (*pl.* SHKUHTSim) Derogatory term for a male Gentile; SHAYgits is a synonym. The feminine, SHIKse, is much better known.

Portnoy's father reviling his Gentile colleagues: "Oh, the whole pack of them up there in Massachusetts, *shkotzim* fox hunting!" (P. Roth *PC*).

"*Treifes* is of the whole world of forbidden sexuality, the sexuality of the *goyim,* and there all the delights are imagined to lie, with the *shiksas* and the *shkotzim* who are unrestrained and not made kosher. . . . *Shaigetz* and *shiksa* are our yin and yang, the poles of sex" (Rosenfeld *AE*).

"With mother's milk they'd imbibed the good sense to think so realistically of such *momzehrem* [bastards] in government from Tsar Nikolai in St. Petersburg to the *chozzerem* [pigs] in City Hall and the *scutzem* in the social establishment in Washington, D.C." (Heller *GG*).

shlak *n.* Cheap stuff. Formerly used mainly for clothing: a shlak shop. But it works with almost anything and has general usage— shlak rock, a shlak movie. Shlak merchandise of any kind.

"I don't want the *schlak* stuff. Give me fresh or I'll take from somebody else" (Elkin *CKKC*).

"And there was Uncle in this fantasia of opulence, every morning wandering in the long room of Persian rugs and decorator drapes, lighted cabinets of Baccarat and Wedgewood, and schlock paintings from the eighteenth century of unidentified and (I'd say uncircumcised) personages from Austria or Italy" (Bellow *H*).

"By way of a Napoleonic self-coronation as the most cynical of all literary schlockmeisters, Gary had brought out the novel, *La Vie Devant Soi*, pseudonymously and revealed his authorship only after it had won a major literary award" (Thomas M. Disch, *Nation*, 24 October 1987).

"But in the current atmosphere of pop culture, it's hard not to root for Scott's old-fashioned hokum against, say, the vile cynical schlock of Adrian Lyne—another British director with a background in commercials, whose own New York City thriller, *Fatal Attraction*, is an enormous hit" (Terrence Rafferty, *Nation*, 24 October 1987).

"Both South and North Dakota, as well as Montana and Washington, are celebrating statehood centennials in this year with a smorgasbord of rodeos, parties, hoedowns and historical hoopla that combine the best of cowboy chic and the worst of American schlock" (Bob Sector, *Los Angeles Times*, 29 August 1989).

"'Donald, be kind,' said Sabbath. 'Don't disparage the Jews for wanting to be with it. Even the Jews are up against it in the Age of Total Schlock'" (P. Roth, *ST*).

From a *Newsweek* story about O. J. Simpson by Jonathan Alter: "The real legacy: après O. J., le déluge of schlock, destined to be auctioned at Sotheby's someday by his grandchildren" (17 February 1997).

Under the headline "Star Shtik," in *Newsweek:* "The inimitable 'Star Search' burned out two years ago, but the TV show's progeny have decamped to another semi-shlocky venue: Broadway" (28 April 1997).

From a review of *Barney's Version*, by Mordecai Richler: "When we meet him, he is sixty-seven, 'reeking of decay and dashed hopes,' though living high on Totally Unnecessary Productions, a company making television series 'sufficiently shlocky' to be syndicated all over" (D. J. Enright, *TLS*, 5 September 1997).

shlang *n.* Snake; also penis. The designation "snake" for the male sex organ is universal. In Yiddish we also refer to an evil, duplicitous person (usually a woman) as a shlang. After he came home from work, my father used to say, half-jokingly, "So what did the shlang do to you?" I used to say, "She hit me and KNIPt [pinched] me."

"And as for his *shlong* to me, with that fingertip of a prick that my mother likes to refer to in public (once, okay, but that once will last a lifetime) as my 'little thing,' his *shlong* brings to mind the fire hoses coiled along the corridors at school. *Shlong:* the word somehow catches exactly the brutishness, the *meatishness*, that I admire so, the sheer mindless, weighty, and unselfconscious dangle of that living piece of hose through which he passes streams of water as thick and strong as rope—while I deliver forth slender threads that my euphemistic mother calls a 'sis'" (P. Roth *PC*).

In *Gravity's Rainbow* Pynchon gives this engineer's limerick:

> There once was a fellow named Schroeder,
> Who buggered the vane servomotor.
> He soon grew a prong
> On the end of his shlong
> And hired himself a promoter.

shlep *v.* To drag or pull. The Anglish adaptations play variations on the idea of someone who barely manages to move along, hence the noun, shlep. For many years Jack Benny had a comic character on his programs named Mr. Shlepperman—a timid, weak-kneed character. He was clearly a drag.

"Some murderers, I thought. Shleppers is more like it" (Potok *TC*).

"Why should I *schlepp* out my guts" (Bellow *H*).

"Mistakenly, I had expected a stereotyped vulgarity. Anticipating in Lapidus *pere* someone like Schlepperman—the comic Jew of

Jack Benny's radio program, with his Seventh Avenue accent and hopeless solecisms" (Styron *SC*).

"'Quiet, schlep,' said the doctor, scrubbing" (Pynchon *V*).

A character in Pynchon's *Gravity's Rainbow* is called Max Schlepzig.

A *Los Angeles Times* story about delis: "His real love was New York's Carnegie [Deli], where he was known to spend a thousand dollars at one crack. Davis finally got tired of schlepping deli from New York and decided it was time for the deli to come to him" (Ruth Reichl, 6 August 1989).

"Prairie grabbed a kettle of institutional tomato soup, carried it on in, and for the next couple of hours she also schlepped racks of newly washed cups and dishes in and bussed dirty dishes out" (Pynchon, *VI*).

A news service report: "Have you noticed you don't hear much anymore about the yuppie? There's a good reason—he's dead . . . he's been replaced by the schleppy. That's a guy who has fallen by the fast track and is now 'living with less grandiose expectations'" (*Fresno Bee*, 26 February 1991).

"For eight months he has been maneuvering to get them . . . going so far as to find a screening room 100 miles away, and schlepping the widow there to see the film" (Diane K. Shah, *New York Times Magazine*, 22 October 1989).

From an opinion piece by Richard Reeves in the *Fresno Bee:* "He admitted he had been lying all along when he protested too much about honest schleppers who said they believed he was the one who wrote 'Primary Colors,' the campaign novel which revealed to non-readers of non-fiction that politicians lie and so do their wives" (29 July 1996).

From a *New York Times Magazine* article on weddings by Susan Shapiro: "Eric and Jill decided on a tiny French dinner, and my mother schlepped trays of 'Eric/Jill' candy to Ann Arbor" (29 July 1996).

"We're now in the era of databases, e-mail and the Internet, so people who call on customers can travel light. What do you call this trend? Ernst & Young [consulting firm] came up with "virtual schlepping" (*Fresno Bee*, 14 April 1997).

shliMEEL *n.* An incompetent, a loser. ShliMEEL is often confused with shliMAZL (literally, someone born under an unlucky star, a born loser.) The one is a hopeless dummy; the other is a cosmic victim. The classic definition: The shliMAZL is the guy the shliMEEL drops the bowl of hot soup on—every time.

Of Benny Profane: "Only something that, being a schlemihl, he'd known for years: inanimate objects and he could not live in peace" (Pynchon *V*).

"'Ah, schlemihl,' he whispered into the phosphorescence. Accident prone, schlimazzel" (Pynchon *V*).

On a work by Saul Bellow at the age of eighty-two (1997): "Entitled 'View from Intensive Care,' and casting the unlucky narrator in the role of the classic *schlimazel* (he calls himself 'a tabloid publisher') it describes Bellow's recovery from a near fatal illness" (*TLS*, 13 June 1997).

George Steiner describes Simone Weil as a "transcendent schlemiel" (*New Yorker*, 2 March 1992).

Molly Ivins on the flat tax: "You're makin' $10,000 a year, you pay your 10 percent, and you've got $9,000 left to raise your family on. Steve Forbes, he's makin' say $10 million. He pays his 10 percent, he's got $9 million left to raise his family on. What could be fairer than that? Except Forbes doesn't have $9 million left, he has $10 million left because his money is unearned income, you schlemiel. He's clipping coupons, he's earnin' interest, he's got capital gains from the stock market, so he didn't have to pay a nickel" (*Progressive*, March 1996).

In her critical review of a biography about Bruno Bettelheim, Sarah Boxer quotes Bettelheim's response to the parents of a former student: "Bettelheim called Mr. Pollak's father a simpleminded 'schlemiel' and his mother a false martyr" (*New York Times Book Review*, 26 January 1997).

From a review of Charley Rosen's *House of Moses All-Stars:* "As the Holocaust approaches, there are rumblings from Hitler's Germany which give Mitchel cause for argument with a Jew they meet who asks incredulously, 'The Austrian house painter? That little *shlemiel* with the Charlie Chaplin moustache?'" (*TLS*, 26 January 1997).

From an interview with Robert Brustein: "Among his recent projects is the klezmer musical 'Shlemiel the First,' which he conceived and adapted from a script by Isaac Bashevis Singer based

on the author's own stories" (Jan Breslauer, *Los Angeles Times,*
4 May 1997).

shloomp *n.* A sloppy incompetent.

"Don't be a *schlump.* It's not good for the organs" (Elkins
CKKC).

"To Dad, Benn was a schlump, an incompetent, his list of fail-
ings, his confused relations with women, made him on a charitable
view a fun figure" (Bellow *MDH*).

"In Gold's conservative opinion, Kissinger would not be recalled
in history as a Bismarck, Metternich, or Castlereagh but as an odi-
ous *shlump* who made war gladly and did not often exude much of
that legendary sympathy for weakness and suffering with which
Jews regularly were credited" (Heller *GG*).

From an article on portrait medals by Holland Cotter: "They
range in character from the regal beauty of Leoni's Andrea Doria
to the coarseness of Lorenzo de' Medici by Niccolo Fiorentino,
from the exoticism of the Turkish ruler Mehemed II, with his bull's
neck and watchful eyes, to the winsome Schlimpiness of the elderly Venetians" (*New York Times,* 1 July 1994).

shloonk *n.* A hapless person, probably an Anglish combination of
shloomp and shtoonk.

Roger Angell in the *New Yorker:* "De Niro doesn't throw or hit or
run very convincingly, but his awkwardness fits into his restrained
depiction of a poor schlunk; he never goes for the heartache in the
role" (31 July 1989).

shmalts *n.* Chicken or goose fat. The German *schmaltz* means lard.

Shmalts is used in cooking and as a spread on bread or MAtse. It
is the crucial ingredient in chopped liver. As a critical term it means
"dripping with sentimental gush," "melodramatic," "corny." A not-
too-bright young man I grew up with was known as SHMALTS-
head; a corpulent young woman was nicknamed SHMALTSee. In
Yiddish we describe a monetary coup (especially a rich marriage)
as falling into a "shmalts greeb [a pit full of shmalts]."

"They drugged you with schmaltz" (Bellow *H*).

"Sophie scarcely ever heard the music, indeed blanked most
of it out, for it was never anything but noisy German backyard
schmaltz" (Styron *SC*).

"The most inept of them, the two Momos—Max Loving and

Alex Paez—ages 13 and 17, crooned into their concealed mike with precisely the same degree of mechanical schmaltz" (Thomas M. Disch, *Nation*, 24 October 1987).

From a review of rock performer Elvis Costello: "The song has the gauzy, half-remembered shimmer of some lost pieces of early-sixties schmalz, which only compounds its essential perversity" (Mark Moses, *New Yorker*, 24 August 1989).

Singer Al Jarreau, talking about his repertoire: "Those songs are all the areas that are biologically, genetically Al Jarreau. From a sappy, syrupy, schmaltzy love ballad like 'Moonlighting' to the work I'm doing on the Hendricks album . . . that's me" (*Los Angeles Times*, 31 August 1989).

James Wolcott, reviewing *Mr. Holland's Opus:* "This schmalz fest is topped by a climactic tribute to Mr. Holland on the occasion of his retirement: an orchestra consisting of his former students plays the première of the symphony he's been scratching away at forever" (*New Yorker*, 29 January 1996).

SHMAte *n.* Literally, rag. But in Anglish SHMAte has the same meaning as "glad rags." People now say, "It's just a SHMAte I picked up at Saks Fifth Avenue."

A colleague who spotted me wearing a new linen sports coat commented, "I like your SHMAte." The Yiddish sense is still old clothes.

"And didn't I tell you that if you were ever with this guy Katz— ever again outside of work—that if you ever so much as walked ten feet with this cheap *shmatte*, I'd break your ass?" (Styron *SC*). This usage of SHMAte in reference to a person is not idiomatic.

Portnoy on his father's philandering: "For weeks he had been jabbering about the new *goyische* cashier ('a very plain drab person,' he said, 'who dresses in *shmattas*')" (P. Roth *PC*).

"She'll take off the business wardrobe and put on the dine-at-home *schmatte*, perfume herself" (Bellow *MDH*).

Shmate: A Journal of Progressive Jewish Thought was a quarterly published until recently in Berkeley, California.

"Mom, an old lefty dressed up like a gypsy in schmattes from the non-aligned nations, greets Henry at the door with a blast of Langston Hughes's poetry and protestations of horror at her own whiteness, and thereupon tells Daisy to go fix dinner while she gets down to some serious cocktail juju with the grandson of the great Harvey Burton" (Review of the novel *Primary Colors*, by Anonymous [Joe Klein], *New Yorker*, 29 January 1996).

On buying Princess Diana's castoffs: "An array of D.C. social presences were asked to speculate on just who would buy the royal shmattes . . . when they come up for auction June 25" (*Fresno Bee*, 19 May 1997).

SHMAYkhele *n*. A little smile.

"There passed over Beulah Lilt's eyes and cheeks a tentative, almost fearful, glimmer, what Brill's oldest sister Claire would have called a *shmeykhele*, the wraith of an amusement toyed with inside a desolation of solitude" (Ozick *TCG*).

shmeer *v*. To spread or smear; more widely used as a noun, meaning bribe in Anglish: "He'll arrange it if you give him a shmeer." The bribe is a kind of cover-up.

"For Jesus and Mary and Joseph and all the gang there in the manger, for the donkeys and the cows there in the manger, for the wise men and the myrrh and the frankincense, for the whole fucking Catholic shmeer that we need like a fucking hole in the head" (P. Roth, *ST*). Here the word means the whole shebang.

Molly Ivins writing about corporate welfare: "This would be good news, except that the whole schmear has been written by lobbyists practically killing one another for financial advantage, instead of by legislators representing the public interest" (*Fresno Bee*, 10 January 1996).

From an AP story: "Take the UnHoley Bagel—a hole-less bagel stuffed with cream cheese. No need to slice and *schmeer* this one" (Robin Estrin, *Fresno Bee*, 29 April 1997).

"A Russian cargo ship crashed into the Mir space station. . . . 'Fortunately no one was hurt, but now the station is known as Schmir,' Russ Myers says" (*Los Angeles Times*, "Laugh Lines," 28 June 1997).

SHMENdrik *n*. A callow youth, not to be trusted; the title of an opera by the Romanian Jewish composer, Abraham Goldfaden (1840–1908). It was a term applied to me often when I was a kid growing up in Brooklyn. Usually it was someone I didn't know who would beckon to me and call out, "Hey SHMENdrik, come over here." In current usage it connotes someone of no importance.

"Well, the poor *shmendrick* turned all different colors when the boss weighed me on the scales" (Perelman *TMP*).

"But at the time I believe it has largely to do with the fact that the elderly man who owns the place, and whom amongst ourselves we call 'Shmendrick,' isn't somebody whose opinion of us we have cause to worry about" (P. Roth *PC*).

"Where have you gone, Woody Allen? He was an American classic, the shmendrick who gets the girl by being sweet, funny, and true blue" (Maureen Dowd, op ed, *New York Times*, 1 October 1995).

SHMOOes *v.* To engage in light, casual conversation. It appears in Anglish almost always as shmoos, shmooze, and SHMOOZing.

A *Los Angeles Times* caption under a photo: "George Burns, Lee Strasberg, Art Carney schmooze with young director Marty Brest for 'Going in Style'" (12 August 1979).

"Once one morning during our coffee *shmooz* he asked if he might see some of the first pages I had written" (Styron *SC*).

"The original comic book, which lately reached its twelfth issue, was illustrated by a variety of underground artists. . . . And so Pekar's many-timbred voice—whining, schmoozy, tickled, resigned, wistful, self-accusing—was filtered through as diverse a range of graphic masks" (Thomas M. Disch, *Nation*, 12 December 1987).

An AP story datelined San Jose, California: "So-called 'live' telephone messages with 976 prefixes—ranging from sexually explicit discussions to dating services to teen-age schmoozing—will be shut down by Pacific Bell, officials said" (*Fresno Bee*, 21 December 1987).

Lanny Larsen, TV columnist for the *Fresno Bee*: "When I came down here [to Los Angeles], I remember how all of you seemed to think I was getting a three-week vacation, working on my tan, eating rich food, drinking good libations, schmoozing with the stars and watching the best that TV has to offer for the new season" (23 July 1989).

L. N. Haliburton in a food column: "You're welcome to taste before you buy—and affable owner Deely likes to schmooze about food." The headline for the story is "Schmoozing over Cheese and Pasta's Bounty" (*Los Angeles Times*, 18 August 1989).

"They will even share schmoozing anecdotes about corporate or religiously inversive occasions of rap usage to which they have been party" (Baker, *BSRA*).

From the Entertainment section of the *Fresno Bee:* "If your closest contact with downtown Fresno is from your car, here's your chance to see the place from a different perspective. Sort of schmooze with Fresno on foot" (22 September 1989).

"Izzy, who was eighty, had a sense of humor but not much of a following. His show was called the *Israel Rosenblatt Hour,* but he liked to call it "Shmooze for Jews"—and he kept it light, gossipy; no serious policy stuff for Izzy, mostly nostalagia and spritz" (Anonymous [Joe Klein], *PC*). The author of this work shows some knowledge of Yiddish in spelling the word *sh* rather than *sch*, and in interpreting it accurately.

A Boston College English professor, Paul Lewis, coins the term "schmoosoisie," meaning "the expanding class of people in the United States who make a living by talk, as on radio and television" (William Safire, *New York Times Magazine,* 3 December 1995).

From a story headlined "Power-schmoozing": "A power-schmoozer, according to Mandell, can work a room blindfolded, hop from table to table as if he were incited, schmooze even in an elevator and—a true art—escape from unwanted conversations. (Schmoozing, in case you have been living under a rock for some time, translates more or less as 'friendly, gossipy conversation.')" (Diana E. Lundin, *Los Angeles Daily News,* 26 May 1990).

More recently, SHMOOZing has taken on the meaning of powerfully persuasive talk. For example, a report on how to get a good room in a hotel: "Ms. De Geus's version of this catechism was: 'Schmooze [talk aggressively to] the reservationist. Get yourself a personal contact in the hotel, someone who will learn your likes and dislikes'" (Betsy Wade, *New York Times,* 10 December 1995).

Similarly, Michael Isikoff and Mark Hosenball, in an article about soft-money politicking, describe Clinton having "devoted an extraordinary amount of time to raising money, spending hours on the campaign trail schmoozing donors in private homes and hotel ballrooms" (*Newsweek,* 21 October 1996).

A satirical "Non Sequitur" cartoon shows Santa Claus besieged by advertisers: "Helpless against the riptide of schmooze, Santa watches himself sign a contract." Shmooze here means an aggressive argument rather than idle chit-chat.

An article on Bill Richardson's appointment as U.N. ambassador: "Richardson, who loves schmoozing journalists almost as much as he loves schmoozing dictators, could also prove tough competition for [Madeleine] Albright as a media darling" (*Newsweek*, 10 February 1997).

From a *Newsweek* story on one of Clinton's money-raising events: "Schmoozers included White House chief of staff Leon Panetta and Commerce Secretary Mickey Kantor" (24 March 1997).

A front-page story in the *Fresno Bee* on some alleged money laundering in local politics: "For three years, a young developer shmoozed his way around Fresno politics, not only contributing liberally under his own name, but feeding more than $24,000 into campaigns through friends, family and business associates" (Anne Dudley Ellis and Pamela J. Podger, 29 March 1997).

A *New Yorker* profile reports: "In contrast with Microsoft's reliance on E-mail, he described Katzenberg's love affair with the telephone, which he had come to see as a form of virtual schmoozing" (Ken Auletta, 12 May 1997).

From a *New Yorker* profile of Donald Trump: "An efficient schmoozer, Trump worked the room quickly—a backslap and a wink, a finger on the lapels, no more than a minute with anyone who wasn't a police commissioner, a district attorney, or a mayoral candidate—and then he was ready to go" (19 May 1997).

From a book review of Don J. Snyder's *Cliff Walk:* "He's embarrassed that sports scholarships and power schmoozing helped propel him into the professional ranks" (David Beers, *Los Angeles Times Book Review*, 1 June 1997).

A satirical poem about a statue in Central Park of an awful nineteenth-century poet, Fitz-Greene Halleck, who is sculpted holding a tablet but no pen:

> But never mind the mean gibes.
> Your grandeur won't be mocked.
> Your throne is hope to all scribes—
> The dull, the trite, the blocked.

For it was you, with keen ear,
Who first heard Gotham's muse:
Relax, you need no pen here
As long as you can schmooze.
(John Tierney, *New York Times*, 22 June 1997)

From a profile of Robert Morgenthau: "One reason Morgenthau can spend so many hours schmoozing is that he has built a vigorous and effective prosecutorial machine" (James Traub, *New Yorker*, 28 July 1997).

shmoots, SHMOOTSig *n., adj.* Dirt, dirty. Both words can have the connotation of moral filth.

"'You need to approach this place with more imagination,' she said. 'It looks grandiose and schmutsig. But I have memories of its better days'" (Bellow *MDH*).

A description of a Smithsonian Institution experiment in scrubbing shmoots: "Algae, which include your various scums, slimes, and seaweeds, are terrific at digesting schmutz, processing carbon dioxide and producing oxygen through photosynthesis" (Curt Suplee, "Brave Small World," *Washington Post Magazine*, 21 January 1990).

"One *schmutzig* mouth after another. *Schmutz* is her métier. . . . Seeing Michelle so enthrallingly kimono'd, his *schmutzig* clothes balled up under her arm—and with her geisha boy haircut lending just the right touch of transsexual tawdriness to the whole slatternly picture—he knew he could kill for her" (P. Roth *ST*).

shmuhGEgee *n.* A dope or incompetent. Probably another Anglish term from shmuhk.

"Who? That schmuck? I'm waiting for that affidavit. Tell him plaintiff will kick his ass if he can't produce it. He better get it this afternoon, that ludicrous shmegeggy!" (Bellow *H*).

"Why, you soapy schmegeggie" (Perelman *RG*).

"We've got a lawyer for you. Not a little shmegeggy just out of law school, but some guy who's been around for a while" (P. Roth *ST*).

shmuhk *n.* Obscene term for penis, equivalent to "prick." The diminutive is SHMEKl. It seems unrelated to the German *Schmuck* (ornament or jewel), unless it means "the family jewels," a well-

known euphemism for the male genitals. According to a folk etymology, shmuhk is an acronym from the Hebrew shma koLAYnu
(hear our voices). Shmuhk has also entered into American speech
through euphemisms often used by people who have no idea of
the original meaning or connotations. The best known are shmo,
SHMOho, and SHMOhawk, all of which mean stupid; the last is
also a derisive reference to a nonexistent tribe of Jewish Indians
(who are not too bright). Al Capp's shmoos probably take their
name from the same source, and this may help to explain their
blissful ignorance. Only a shmoo (shmo?) would dissolve with joy
while fulfilling the desires of human beings.

Many people who use shmuhk indicate they have no idea of its
obscene connotations. Charles Schulz had a "Peanuts" sequence
in which Lucy invented a new pitch called a "schmuckleball."
The sequence only lasted a few days before, I suspect, someone
explained to Schulz what he'd blundered into. "Doonesbury" featured a character named Albert Schmeckel. During televised football games you can often hear hundreds of fans chanting to millions of TV watchers: "The referee is a shmuhk!"

"Thrown out unopened—I thought in my arrogance and heartbreak—discarded unread, considered *junk*-mail by this schmuck,
this moron, this Philistine father of mine" (P. Roth *PC*).

Note the innocent use of shmuhk in this quote from a critic of
William Faulkner: "Appealed to by someone he thought of as a
business man rather than a schmuck, Warner agreed: Warner
Brothers would grant Faulkner an indefinite leave and renounce
claim to his novel" (David Minter, *Faulkner: His Life and Work* [Bal-
timore: Johns Hopkins University Press, 1980]).

A *San Francisco Chronicle* story quotes Lieutenant Colonel Robert Earl giving testimony to the Iran-contra committee about a
"General Buck Schmuck" being the originator of the plan to support the contras. "'That's a real name?' asked Chief Counsel
Arthur Liman, who obviously knows some Yiddish. When assured it was real, Liman commented: 'The only guy who should
have used a code name in this case didn't?' The Pentagon stated
there was no General Schmuck on active duty" (28 August 1987).

Actor Dustin Hoffman, talking about the prospect of working
again with director Sydney Pollack: "'I'm very excited about work-

ing with him again,' said the actor about the director. 'I spent a week waiting on pins and needles while he made up his mind. When he said yes, I called him up. "Is it true?" I asked him. He said yes. I said, "Ya schmuck, you'll never learn"'" (Deborah Caulfield, *Los Angeles Times*, 20 November 1987).

"His life has the pattern for Preston Sturges slapstick—Sturges might see him as a peppy fellow always fighting the storms and getting knocked into the water, the Emperor of China as a poor, sad, schmuck" (Pauline Kael, *New Yorker*, 30 November 1987).

"'Schmucks with Underwoods,' Jack Warner, the most pernicious of the brothers Warner, called screenwriters, and the impression persists, especially among the freeloading hacks on the show business beat, except that today writers are seen as schmucks with laptops" (John Gregory Dunne on *Hollywood: Opening Moves*, *NYRB*, 17 October 1996).

Larry Gelbart, in a review of a book about Hollywood in the *New York Times Book Review*, comments: "It is the rewrite of the rewrite of the play that is the thing. Which would, no doubt, have been news to Shakespeare. (You remember Shakespeare. He was that schmuck with a quill.)" (2 March 1997).

From a *New Yorker* profile of Donald Trump: "'If you have me saying these things, even though they're true, I sound like a schmuck,' he explained" (19 May 1997).

shnaz *n.* Nose. Jimmy Durante was known as shnaZOla. The *American Heritage Dictionary* gives the derivation from Yiddish SHNOItsl (snout), probably influenced by nozzle.

"Including—or should I say, especially—the fine, elongated, slightly uptilted Polish *schnoz*, as Nathan lovingly called it" (Styron *SC*).

shnook *n.* A stupid or incompetent person. Probably another Anglish euphemism from shmuhk.

Himmelstein says, "What do you mean—she's less of a whore than most. We're all whores in this world, and don't you forget it. I know damn well *I'm* a whore. And you're an outstanding shnook" (Bellow *H*).

"And when he started to talk about Matilda he was not the fellow who could claim a decent place in the hierarchy for himself; he was simply a schnook" (Bellow *MDH*).

SHNORer *n.* Beggar. But the Anglish usage connotes a sly chiseler who will manage to get money out of you no matter what you do. We would often say, "Watch out for Irv; he's on the shnor."

"To a malign imagination like Gold's, the specter of oil conjured up a miasma of Rockefeller influence and money that clung to Kissinger like a cloud of corruption and gave to his eyes, cheeks, and lips the glistening look of a *shnorrer* who has been very well lubricated" (Heller *GG*).

In *Animal Crackers* Groucho Marx sings, "Here comes Captain Spaulding, the African explorer—did someone call me, SHNORer?"

Shoah *n.* The Hebrew word for Holocaust. Also the title of a film on the same subject by Claude Lanzmann.

shool *n.* Synagogue, house of worship. German *Schule* means school or schoolhouse, but never a house of worship. The Yiddish reference is to the place where the texts and commentaries that expound and explain Jewish beliefs are studied and the rituals observed. SHOOLe in America means a school, especially a Jewish secular school.

"We'll live it up. We'll find an orthodox shul—enough of this Temple [Reform sect] junk" (Bellow *H*).

SHOYfer *n.* Ram's horn. Now it is usually blown only on ruhshi-SHUHne. Formerly it heralded special occasions and, it is said, it will be blown to announce the coming of the Messiah. The ram's horn is associated with the ram that was ultimately substituted for Isaac in the sacrifice by Abraham.

"If we blow into the narrow end of the *shofar,* we will be heard far. But if we choose to be Mankind rather than Jewish and blow into the wider part, we will not be heard at all; for us America will have been in vain" (Ozick *AA*).

Dirty joke: It pays to drive a car for a Jewish family because on the High Holidays they always blow the shofar.

shoyn farGESN I just forgot. It's the punch line in a widespread joke about changing names in America. An obviously Jewish man announces that his name is Sean Ferguson. "How could that be?" someone asks. "Well," he explains, "I was so frightened I might be sent back that when the immigration guy asked me my name, I

said, 'Shoyn farGESN.' So he wrote down Sean Ferguson." An obviously Asian guy says, "My name is Sean Ferguson, too." "How
come?" "Well, I was next in line and when they asked for my name
I said, 'Sam Ting.'"

"'That's his name,' Geronimo said, 'is all. And I am Peter
O'Leary and this here is Chain Ferguson'" (Pynchon *V*).

SHPILkes *n*. Pins. Sitting on SHPILkes—sitting on pins and needles.
An interesting connection is with Russian, as this comment in a
New York Times Magazine article about Moscow shows: "There is a
short lottery program, '*Spilke*,' on the state television network.
Spilke means either a woman's stiletto heel or a sarcastic, needling
comment" (1 June 1997).

shpits *n*. Tip or end.

"If you'll open for me the jar I'll eat marinated. Do you have also,
if you don't mind, a piece of rye bread—the shpitz?" (Malamud *IF*).

shprits *v., n*. To spray; a carbonated drink.

From a syndicated column, reprinted in the *Fresno Bee*, "Recently while schlepping past the counter at Dillard's, I stopped to
shpritz on some new fragrance and overheard the following"
(Myrne Roe, 7 October 1996).

SHRAIing *v*. Anglish, from SHRAIen, to scream.

"Jesus Christ, is that what this screaming and *shrying* is all about,
that I ate that sad sack's chocolate pudding?" (P. Roth *PC*).

SHREKlech *adj*. Terrible.

Talking of an old hospital: "That old Moses Maimonides. When
I was a kid that was a *schrecklich* name" (Bellow *MDH*).

shtark *adj*. Strong. The Anglish SHTARKe or SHTARKer means
tough, psychologically strong.

Portnoy imagines the devil greeting him in Hell: "'*Shtarkes*,' the
Devil will say" (P. Roth *PC*). The meaning here is ironic—"So you
think you're tough guys," the Devil says.

SHTEtl *n*. (*pl*. SHTETlech) The typical small Jewish town of Eastern
Europe. The values and attitudes of that experience (as shown in
the works of classic Yiddish writers like Sholom Aleichem) carried over to an extent in America, but the nature of life here has
been fundamentally different. Among many distinctions, in the
SHTEtl the Jews lived basically separate lives from their Gentile

neighbors. Here there has been an increasing tendency for the Jews to become integrated into American life even while maintaining strong elements of their own identity. The elements of YIDishkait are often nostalgically drawn from the values exhibited in SHTEtl life.

"Gold fiendishly planned using both [jokes] in a morbid and depressing chapter on Kissinger's humor. Neither reflected the ironic, fatalistic mockery of either the Talmud or the *shtetl*, and Gold greatly preferred as humor a joke *about* Kissinger circulated by the Danish news agency" (Heller *GG*).

shtik *n.* Piece or chunk; actions or behavior. We say in Yiddish, "a shtik ferd" (literally, a chunk of horse, meaning fat or big as a horse). NArishe shtik means silly behavior. American show business jargon uses shtik to mean bit or act; hence "That's not my shtik," meaning "It's not my style."

A *Los Angeles Times* review refers to "comedy club shtickla," which is Anglish for SHTIKlech (meaning small bits). The diminutive has a sexual connotation: a nice SHTIKl, meaning "a good piece [of ass]."

"'Let's cut out all the *shtick*,' said Gersbach. 'Let's say you're a crumb'" (Bellow *H*).

"The [CIA] manual is designed to set up a Machiavellian campaign of propaganda, indoctrination, and infiltration in Nicaragua, underwritten by the visible display and selective use of weapons. Shoot softly, it implies, and carry a big schtick" (Barbara Johnson, *A World of Difference* [Baltimore: Johns Hopkins University Press, 1987]).

A review of a Shakespeare in the Park production: "Where most Central Park productions offer one or two creditable performances and a not very well-unified vision of a play, which is further marred by incidents of shtick acting, this *Twelfth Night* consists entirely of shtick" (Mimi Kramer, *New Yorker*, 24 July 1989).

The term is coming to mean superficial acting techniques rather than deep characterizations, as in a review of the film *When Harry Met Sally:* "It's a Rohmer movie played as a sitcom. To keep us busy while we wait for Harry and Sally to figure out that they're in love, [director] Reiner and [writer] Ephron simply string together bits of shtick" (Terrence Rafferty, *New Yorker*, 7 August 1989).

A film review by Michael Wilmington: "*The Package* . . . looks like a bad dream culled out of newscasts and gussied up with *film noir* plot shtick" (*Los Angeles Times*, 25 August 1989).

A book review by John Updike: "[Thomas] Bernhard's curmudgeonliness here comes close to being as droll a shtick as W. C. Fields'" (*New Yorker*, 9 October 1989).

A photo caption: "Yes, it 's the most famous mugger of all, Jerry Lewis, shticking it up in Detroit Sunday to benefit cancer research" (*Fresno Bee*, 21 May 1990).

A review by Thomas A. Disch: "The production at Playwrights Horizons is directed and choreographed by Gaciela, who earlier this season, in *Dangerous Games*, did for the dance traditions of Argentina what she now does for those of the Caribbean—turns them into shtiks" (*Nation*, 11 June 1990). Disch consistently uses shtik in the plural: "Do cornball jokes and comic shticks suddenly become racist because a person of color delivers them?" (*Nation*, 17 December 1990).

A review of TV chef Martin Yan: "Those who have seen the Chinese chef on his popular PBS show or in any of his appearances on 'Live with Regis and Kathie Lee' or 'The Tonight Show with Jay Leno' might be familiar with the shtick. He is an energetic package who's been quipping and wokking on public television for 16 years" (Elizabeth Evans, *Fresno Bee*, 1 November 1995).

Evaluating Vice President Al Gore, John Jacobs writes, "In the meantime, Gore has time to work on a persona that is often so wooden that he has made it part of his schtick" (*Fresno Bee*, 28 January 1997).

"No schticking, no nudging knowingly, no winking or pandering to the grown-ups at the expense of the kids" (Maurice Sendak, *New York Times Book Review*, 16 November 1997).

shtoonk *n.* A stinker, a nasty person who is also an incompetent.

"Don't think their lawyers are like my shtunk who couldn't get you thrown out for what you did to me" (Malamud *TT*).

shtoop *v.* To push or shove. The Anglish SHTOOPing means fucking.

"Doctor, could he have been slipping it to her? . . . With those legs—why, *of course*, he was *shtupping* her" (P. Roth *PC*).

Pynchon mentions "Mme. Sztup" in *Gravity's Rainbow*.

Heller uses the term to mean "bribe," though shmeer is the more likely Yiddishism: "He was probably making more in undisclosed compensations than Gold earned in salary, even without any under-the-counter *shtupping* he might still be getting from the Rockefellers" (*GG*).

SHTRAYml *n.* The broad-brimmed black hat trimmed with fur that is worn by khSEEdim. Jews were often commanded by repressive regimes to wear certain kinds of clothing. The SHTRAYml, like other articles of clothing, is an instance of turning the restriction into an ornament.

SHUHlim aLAYkhim (Sholom Aleichem) *n.* The pen name of Sholom Rabinowitz (1859–1916), one of the classic Yiddish writers; best known as the author of the text from which the musical *Fiddler on the Roof* was taken. His name is the same as the traditional Hebrew greeting, which means "peace unto you." The response is aLAYkhim SHUHlim—"and to you peace." It is still the standard greeting in Yiddish.

SHVARtser *n.* A black person. Often abbreviated to shvar in Anglish. The gender distinctions in Yiddish (*m.* SHVARtser; *f.* SHVARtse) are usually ignored in Anglish. SHVARtser is a derogatory term (roughly equivalent to "colored"). NEger is the acceptable term.

Portnoy notes the hypocrisy in his mother's attitudes toward Dorothy, the black cleaning lady: "Once Dorothy chanced to come back into the kitchen while my mother was still standing over the faucet marked H, sending torrents down upon the knife and fork that had passed between the *schvartze*'s thick pink lips" (P. Roth *PC*).

"You should be ashamed to dance like a shvartzer, without any clothes on" (Malamud *TT*).

Newsweek magazine created a great flap when it quoted comedian Jackie Mason's description of mayoral candidate David N. Dinkins as a "fancy shvartzer with a mustache." The *New York Times* correctly defined the word as "a derisive Yiddish term for a black."

"'How long have you been here?' Sabbath asked, though he knew the answer already: long enough to learn to say 'schvartze'" (P. Roth, *ST*).

From a review of *Barney's Version*, by Mordecai Richler: "we gather that, despite Barney's unkind jokes about *schvartzers*, in his will he is leaving a tidy sum to set up a scholarship at McGill University for a black student gifted in the arts" (D. J. Enright, *TLS*, 5 September 1997).

From a *New Yorker* piece by Joe Klein on elections: "They go to places like the Brighton Beach Baths, in Brooklyn, where Mario Cuomo once tried to sell his opposition to capital punishment by saying 'They don't have the death penalty in Israel.' 'They don't have *schvartzes* in Israel,' a woman replied" (3 November 1997).

shvarts yuhr Literally, a black year. But when directed toward a person it means "may the devil take you," "may you fall on evil times."

shvits *n.* Steam bath. The word means sweat, but usually the reference is to the place where you go to sweat—the steam bath. It used to be a popular activity for Jewish men, perhaps acting as a reminder of the MIKve. When I was a young man in New York, it was a ritual for the gang to spend the night before the wedding with the groom in a shvits.

"Once a month my father took me with him down to the *shvitz* bath, there to endeavor to demolish with steam and a rubdown, and a long deep sleep—the pyramid of aggravation he has built himself into" (P. Roth *PC*).

A critique of Gloria Allred, Friar's Club gate crasher: "Anyone who wants to take a shvitz with Uncle Miltie that bad should have a prune danish stuffed in her Jockeys" (*Esquire*, August 1989).

David Remnick on the 1996 Olympics: "Rising above us—the lowly and various beasts, *shvitzing* in our 'authorized' Olympic shorts and 'fully licensed' Olympic T-shirts—are the looming trees of a new age: thirty-foot-high inflatable beer cans and Atlanta's true Olympic symbol, a sixty-five-foot Coke bottle" (*New Yorker*, 5 August 1996).

TALmid (Talmud) *n.* The collection of commentaries on Jewish law and tradition (from the Hebrew word for instruction). One section, MISHne, represents originally oral tradition; another geMORe, contains commentaries on the MISHne. The TALmid includes two separate compilations: the more influential is the Babylonian TALmid; the other is known as the Palestinian (not

Jerusalem) TALmid and is about one-fourth the size of the Babylonian TALmid.

What is the Talmud? The bulk of it is taken up with debates of ancient
rabbis. It is primarily concerned with questions of conscience, religious duty, and human sympathy—in short, with the relations "between man and God" and those "between man and man." But it practically contains a consideration of almost every topic under the sun,
mostly with some verse of the Pentateuch for a pretext. All of which is
analyzed and explained in the minutest and keenest fashion, discussions on abstruse issues being sometimes relieved by an anecdote or
two, a bit of folklore, worldly wisdom, or small talk. Scattered through
its numerous volumes are priceless gems of poetry, epigram, and
story-telling. It is at once a fountain of religious inspiration and a
"brain sharpener." We were sure that the highest mathematics taught
in the Gentile universities were child's play as compared with the Talmud (Cahan *RDL*).

TANte *n.* Aunt (also MEEme or Mume). Uncle is FEter.
"Come here, little Moses, and sit on your old *tante*'s knee. What
a dear little *yingele* [little boy]" (Bellow *H*).
TAtele *n.* A term of endearment toward a child. TAte is father; TAtele
is the diminutive. When a parent uses the term in reference to a
child, it's like invoking the memory of one's father. One of the main
characters in E. L. Doctorow's *Ragtime* is referred to only as Tateh
(father).
"Sweet, passive Milton, you wouldn't hurt a fly, would you,
tateleh?" (P. Roth *PC*).
TCHOTCHke—see TSAtskele
TFIln *n.* The paraphernalia of the phylacteries, consisting of two
small leather boxes attached to straps, one placed on the left arm
and the other on the forehead every morning except on the Sabbath and holidays, Passages from the Scriptures are contained in
the boxes, and the ritual is according to Exodus 13:9: "And it
shall be to you as a sign on your hand and as a memorial between
your eyes, that the law of the Lord may be in your mouth; for with
a strong hand the Lord has brought you out of Egypt." The connection with the exodus from Egypt suggests that TFIln are a sym-

bol (like the mark on the door of Jewish homes) that God protects the Jews. The ritual begins after bar MITSvuh. Several years ago, when I was a visiting professor at Brooklyn College, Chabad khSEEDim associated with the MITSvuh-mobile (a traveling van run by Orthodox groups) used to accost me in the morning on my way to school and yell in Yiddish, "Huhst geLAYgt TFIln haint?" ("Did you lay TFIln today?") I used to reply, "I haven't laid anyone today." On a recent visit to the Wailing Wall in Jerusalem, one of my sons was shown on the spot how to put on TFIln and what brief prayer to say. He went along with the operation, which obviously was a MITSvuh for the khSEEDim who talked him into it.

Thomashevsky, Boris (1868–1939). An active figure in the New York Yiddish theater as both actor and director. He was associated with a heavy, melodramatic, and often sentimental style of acting. His grandson is the well-known conductor Michael Tilson Thomas.

"Even as an actor I wasn't one of the best. Thomashevsky, Jacob Adler [1855–1926], [Maurice] Schwartz [1890–1960]—all were better than me" (Malamud *IF*).

TISHebuhv (Tish'a b'Av) *n.* The ninth day of the Hebrew month Av (July–August). The date commemorates the fall of both Temples. It is a fast day and an occasion of double mourning. Whenever my father wanted to say something was far off, he'd say, "Next TISHebuhv."

"The day that Zelig and Bahele moved from No. 7 Krochmalna street was like Tisha Bov for me" (Singer *S*).

"'Why would Picker do it?' Adler said. 'He could only lose. He's smart, he'll say Yeah sure I want a "conversation" and then work us on the details until Tishah-b'Ab [a long way off]'" (Anonymous [Joe Klein], *PC*).

T.L. (TOOKHis LEKer) *n.* The Yiddish expression for ass licker. Anyone who ever cooperated with a teacher, policeman, or any other adult was a T.L. in my Brooklyn neighborhood.

TOOKHis *n.* Ass, buttocks. English diminutive is TOOSHee or toosh. "Kish meer in TOOKHis" means "kiss my ass." Roth gives Alex Portnoy's high school cheer:

> Aye-aye ki-ike-us
> Nobody likes us,

> We are the boys of Weequahic High—
> Aye-aye ki-uchis
> *Kish mir in tuchis*
> We are the boys of Weequahic High!

In *A Prophetic Minority* Jack Newfield describes meeting civil rights activist Stokely Carmichael in Mississippi at a time when local whites were terrorizing the black community: "Stokely broke that fear by taunting the sheriff, walking behind him in broad daylight, mocking his stride, mimicking his dress, and cursing him in Yiddish: 'Kish mir tuchas, baby' he said." (It's hard to tell whether it's Newfield or Carmichael who didn't get the idiom right.)

My high school girl-watching buddies in Brooklyn used to be on the lookout for what they called "a MOOSHee TOOSHee."

In a joke a notorious bigot maintains, "Some of my best friends are Jews. In fact, my friend Goldberg always says how much he admires my ability to use my TOOKHis [pointing to his head]."

Zydeco (black Creole tradition) musician Rockin' Sydney does a version of the song "Toot, Toot" that includes the lines:

> Don't you mess with my toosh.
> Find yourself another bush.
> If you want to keep your nose,
> Keep your hands off my rose.

In a review of the largely gay Wagnerian spoof *Der Ring Gott Farblonjet,* by Charles Ludlam, Thomas A. Disch quotes a Rhinemaiden's observation about the Dwarf Alverrück: "Er kommt nicht der wasser zu trinken," to which the Dwarf replies, "I came some tuschies zu pinchen" (*Nation,* 21 May 1990).

From a review of Dennis Rodman's autobiography: "Rodman is a certifiable star in a mainstream sport, and yet one is curious about how, as a matter of literary history, we got from the herculean tales of Mantle and Mays to the confessional style of an athlete who poses on the book jacket with his bare *tuchis* flush to the camera and who writes that to 'put on a sequined halter top makes me feel like a total person and not just a one-dimensional man'" (David Remnick, *New Yorker,* 10 June 1996).

TOOKHis licker—see T.L.

TOOKHis OIFn tish Literally, "ass on the table"; it means "put your money where your mouth is."

TOOMling *v.* Anglish for making a stir; in show business, it means acting with energy. Yiddish TOOMl (din or noise) can have the same meaning.

In a Los Angeles *Times* interview headlined "Henny Is Tummling through Town Again," comic Henny Youngman is described as engaging "in what he calls *tummling*, Yiddish for being 'on.' He picked it up as a teen-age Borsht Belt comic required to keep summer-camp guests amused night and day" (1 February 1981).

TOYre (Torah) *n.* The first five books of Moses, that is, the first five books of the Hebrew Bible, known also as the Pentateuch: Genesis, Exodus, Leviticus, Numbers, and Deuteronomy. In a general sense TOYre refers to the philosophy of Judaism in all its aspects. The TOYre is read in the synagogue throughout the year, section by section. When the end is reached and a new cycle begun, there is a joyous celebration, SIMkhis TOYre (joy in the TOYre) in which the scroll is carried around the synagogue and those present are even encouraged to be a little tipsy. (A cantor I worked with used to call me back to his little office for a quick shot of whiskey. He felt it gave you a head start in the celebration.)

Trayf *n.* Absolutely unkosher. But ordinarily used in American literature outside the context of dietary restrictions.

"To me he's as *trayf* as pork" (Singer *S*).

The conclusion of John Updike's sequel to *Bech*, entitled *Bech Is Back*, concludes with the profoundly pessimistic notion that America is somehow spoiled beyond redemption, "*Treyf*, he thought. Unclean."

"But in Madamaska Falls Sabbath kept his retort to himself. He had got into difficulty enough explaining to one of Roseanna's fellow teachers that he could take no interest in her specialty, Native American literature, because Native Americans are *treyf*" (P. Roth, *ST*).

From a profile of playwright Wendy Wasserstein: "With a characteristic mixture of amusement, detachment, and enthusiasm, she said, 'What am I doing here, eating *treyf* at two o'clock in the morning?'" (Nancy Franklin, *New Yorker*, 14 April 1997).

From the article "Opening a Window on Hasidism": "America was a trefina medina, an impure and unholy place where even rabbis shaved their beards" (David Margolick, *New York Times*, 20 July 1997).

TREPverter *n.* Words heard on the stairs. Bellow's Herzog explains the meaning: "At first there was no pattern to the notes he made. They were fragments—nonsense syllables, exclamations, twisted proverbs and quotations or in the Yiddish of his long-dead mother, *Trepverter*—retorts that come too late, when you were already on your way down the stairs."

truhg es geZOONter hayt "Wear it in the best of health." The traditional formula when someone tries on a garment for the first time. (Or as we sometimes say, "Tear it in the best of health.") I turned it into a song for children on the Folkways album *Songs of the Holidays*. It's also on *Good Morning Blues* (see Discography).

TRUHMbenik *n.* A shiftless no-goodnik. There are strong intimations that the TRUHMbenik is unreliable with money and potentially dishonest. But the main connotation is an irresponsible youth. English includes TRUHMbeniking around.

"The gaudy militarism of the portly *trombenik* was more Germanic than Jewish, and at least one newsman had fortuitously spied in Kissinger a puerile compulsion for 'Teuton his own horn'" (Heller *GG*).

TSAdik *n.* (*pl.* tsaDIKim) Saint. The term was often applied to the Chasidic teachers, whose holiness extended beyond ordinary human capabilities—at least in the eyes of their followers.

TSAtskele (TCHOTCHke) *n.* Literally, a doll or children's plaything; now used often to describe someone (usually a young woman) who is pretty but spoiled rotten. The implication is that she needs to be treated like a precious doll. TCHOTCHke usually refers to a knickknack or other cute but insignificant object.

"O you virtuous Jewess, the tables are turned, *tsatskeleh*" (P. Roth *PC*).

An entry in *Metropolitan Home* under the title "Chotchke Cuisine": "'Chotchke,' as the more erudite among you will realize, is a Yiddish word (more correctly spelled 'tchochke,' I am told) . . . meaning a trifle, a gimcrack, a piece of fluff—something pretty but ultimately useless. Chotchke Cuisine isn't trifling food, exactly, but rather food served in a trifling manner—food accompanied by lots of 'extras,' free stuff, empty gestures. . . . It is cuisine with bells on, and the bells aren't just announcing dinner; they're ringing false" (September 1989).

An article by Paul Goldberger in the *New York Times*, dealing with trinkets sold at Monticello, is headlined "Thomas Jefferson, From Statesman to Tchotchke." Goldberger notes that much of "Monticello's inventory consists of what most people would call high-quality tchotchkes."

"With the money he'd had to pay Drenka that first time with Christa, she bought the power tools for Matthew; with the hundreds that Lewis, the credit-card magnate, slipped into her purse, she bought *tchotchkees* for the house—ornamental plates, carved napkin rings, antique silver candelabra" (P. Roth, *ST*).

"While a singer rasps 'Give Me the Simple Life,' a paean to Spartan family values, the camera pans a series of Tchotchkes that the lyrics ('A cottage small is all I'm after') make an ironic counterpoint" (Ingrid Abramovitch, *New York Times*, 3 December 1995).

From an article on prenuptial arrangements: "It's like you're dividing up the tchotchkes you collect on vacation before you've even bought them" (Julie Salamon, *New Yorker*, 25 August and 1 September 1997).

Playwright David Mamet, quoted in a *New Yorker* profile: "'Being a writer is all so ethereal that I think most of us tend to surround ourselves with tchotchkes so we can actually be sure we have a past" (John Lahr, 17 November 1997).

TSHUHLnt *n.* A stew or baked fish put into the oven on Friday afternoon so that it can be served on Saturday without breaking the proscription against cooking on the Sabbath. The word is a good example of the influence of French on Yiddish, deriving from *chaud* and, beyond that, the Latin *calere*, of which the present participle is *calentum* (from Max Weinreich *HYL*). In the Old Country, people developed a special taste for TSHUHLnt, since it was SHMALtsy, different from ordinary cooked meals. The technique doesn't quite work in modern ovens, which don't retain heat the way the Old World ovens did.

I. B. Singer recalls: "One place or another, we always went as a three-some. On the Sabbath, after the *cholent,* he took Altcha to the Yiddish theatre" (*New Yorker,* 1 July 1985).

TSIbile PLETsl *n.* Onion roll. This is one of the many New York culinary delights that appear only in ersatz forms outside the city. It should not be confused with BYAlee, which has a different (harder) consistency.

TSImis *n.* A kind of vegetable stew with carrots and prunes. It is often part of the festive table prepared for Passover, a special and complicated concoction, and that is the essence of the Anglish "to make a TSImis," that is, to make a fuss about something, or expand it beyond its normal proportions.

Bellow recounts this joke: "A Jew enters a restaurant. Supposed to be good, but it's filthy. . . . And there isn't any menu. You order your meal from the tablecloth, which is stained. You point to a spot and say, 'What's this? *Tzimmes?* Bring me some.' . . . And the waiter writes no check. The customer goes straight to the cashier. She picks up his necktie and says, 'You ate *tzimmes.*' But then the customer belches and she says, 'Ah, you had radishes, too'" (*HFM*).

"Someone who laughs like this is ready for a feast—*flanken* [flank steak], *tsimmes, rosselfleysh* [pot roast]" (Ozick *TPR*).

TSITsis *n.* The fringes attached to the four corners of a garment that Orthodox Jews wear under their vests and jackets. (Similar fringes are on the prayer shawls worn in the synagogue.) In the Hebrew Bible Moses says, "Speak unto the children of Israel, and bid them that they make them fringes in the borders of their garments and throughout their generations, and that they put upon the fringe of the borders a ribband of blue; and it shall be unto you for a fringe, that you may look upon it, and remember all the commandments of the Lord, and do them; and that ye seek not after your own heart and your own eyes, after which ye used to go a whoring: That ye may remember, and all my commandments, and be holy unto your God" (Numbers 15:38–40). Like many ancient Jewish practices, one of its aims is to distinguish the Jewish people from other nations of the world. (TSITsis should not be confused with TSITSkis, women's breasts.)

TSOORe *n.* (*pl.* TSOORis) Trouble or calamity.

A *Los Angeles Times* headline: "For the Israelis, *Tsouris* Is Spelled

A-W-A-C-S." (AWACS is the acronym for the U.S. Airborne Warning and Control System.)

Portnoy's mother: "'*Hamburgers,*' she says bitterly, just as she might say *Hitler,* 'where they can put anything in the world in that they want—and *he* eats them, Jack, make him promise, before he gives himself a terrible *tsura,* and it's too late'" (P. Roth *PC*).

"Half consciously I heard myself imitating Nathan: 'Oy, have I got tsuris!'" (Styron *SC*).

"Zipi and Ditzah would fly into a rage at the impossibility of getting any of these hippie chicks to do anything on the beat. 'It's tzuris I don't need!'" (Pynchon *VI*).

uhlevaSHUHLem From the Hebrew aIAV hashaLOM, "may he rest in peace," "blessed be the memory." Said after the name of one departed.

"Kaplitzky—*alehasholem*—took care of everything" (Bellow *H*).

uhngePATSHket *adj.* Careless and disorganized, tastelessly overdone.

"That boyish matter-of-factness is what saves this passage and dozens like it from seeming *ongepotchket*" (Evan Eisenberg, *Nation,* 28 November 1987).

vants *n.* Bedbug. Often a term for a despicable person. But I had a summer camp friend knowns as Vants because he was diminutive and a little tricky.

A sequence of the TV series "M*A*S*H" hinged on discovering the crossword puzzle entry for a five-letter word that means a small bug.

On Kissinger praying with Nixon: "With his own people he don't go to Temple, but on his knees he goes down on a carpet to pray with that *vontz*" (Heller *GG*).

vear farBLUHNjet Literally, "get lost!" It is apparently the source of the English expression.

In a comment about President Clinton's alleged refusal to discuss the budget problems with him and other Republican leaders, Senator Dole remarked, "It's as if he just said, 'Get lost!'" (*Los Angeles Times,* 11 November 1995).

vear geHARgit Literally, get killed! The equivalent of "drop dead!"

"'*Vehr Gehargit!*' the old man roared in reply to the baleful Chinese manager when he at last found his voice" (Heller *GG*).

voo den What else (would you expect)?

"No, I'll rise from my seat—and (*vuh den?*) make a speech" (Roth *PC*).

vu shtayt es geSHRIBn? Where is it written? Where does it say? It's a standard phrase for quibbling about the meaning of a law or precept. Strictly, it refers to Scripture, but it can be used in any context.

"But where is it written that the cure is better than the disease?" (Singer *S*).

"Where does it say that I have to be good? Isn't it enough that I'm God?" (Heller *GK*).

An ad showing a taco quotes Jake "Jefe" Hefferman, strategic chef–Acapulco Restaurants: "Where is it written that this is the national dish of Mexico?"

Fresno County supervisor Doug Vadim, defending his vote: "As to the vote on the housekeeping contract, where is it written that a board member can't have a change of mind once the facts and merits of an issue have been viewed in the total budgetary magnifying glass?" (*Fresno Bee*, 16 August 1989).

who-er *n.* Not exactly Yiddish, rather the New Yorkish pronunciation of whore. It was many years before I realized that who-er and whore were the same word.

"Did I ever once say anything about how you used to sneak away to Mexico with those skinny dress models so often your smart wife here would know, or how my younger son here keeps downtown an apartment for his who-ers he calls a studio and never once invites me to sleep there but makes me ride all the way home at night to Brooklyn?" (Heller *GG*).

YARmoolke *n.* The skullcap worn at all times by Orthodox Jews. The source of this tradition is not clear, but it is obviously intended to be a sign of respect for the Deity. I once asked a religious-school teacher why Gentiles remove their hats while Jews keep the YARmoolke on. He said, "Because we do it one way, they do the opposite." This is partly true and occasionally vice versa. In recent times the wearing of the YARmoolke (in the armed forces, for example) has become a controversial issue. I'm especially intrigued by the modern tradition of keeping the YARmoolke in place with a bobby pin.

"He said Look what you did to it momzer murderer and Look at the mark you made on an all-silk yarmalka, even the stitching is silk" (Markfield *TW*).

In an article about Jews on TV: "[Professor] Turow says the hope is not that all Jews on prime-time series wear yarmulkes, but that they at least occasionally partake in traditional Jewish habits or are allowed to question how much assimilation is too much" (Michele Willens, *Los Angeles Times*, 6 September 1990).

An article reprinted in the *Fresno Bee* explains that "cartoons of Mickey Mouse, Donald Duck and Pluto as well as characters from Batman and Sesame Street have been turning up wearing skull-caps, known as yarmulkes, worn by young boys at Temple Beth Emet in Burbank, where the Disney Co. is based. 'If it brings people closer to God, I don't mind being known as a Mickey Mouse congregation,' said Rabbi William Kramer, who heads the temple. . . . But you won't find an official Mickey Mouse yarmulke, because Disney officials in Burbank said the product has not been sanctioned" (13 May 1990).

Joseph Epstein in a *TLS* review: "Two Jewish bees, in a less than riotous but sociologically interesting joke, are flying about, when one of them places upon his head a *yarmulka*. 'Why are you doing that?' asks the other. 'I'm doing it,' says the first bee, 'so I won't be taken for a WASP'" (31 May 1991).

On growing up Jewish: "Yaphet Kotto grew up fighting for his religion, wearing his yarmulke on the streets of the Bronx. . . . Kotto, who was raised a Jew, attended Roman Catholic schools, and is the son of a Cameroonian crown prince. . . . 'It was rough coming up,' he said. 'And then going to *shul*, putting a yarmulke on, having to face people who were primarily Baptists in the Bronx meant that on Fridays I was in some heavy fistfights'" (*Fresno Bee*, 2 February 1997).

YEke *n.* The title applied to Jews of German origin in Israel. It is an insulting term and refers mainly to the stereotype of compulsive, authoritarian, rigid German behavior. But it is obviously not a new term, as indicated by this reference from a Yiddish story by Joseph Opatashu published in 1928: "They envied 'Yeke Fool' (so they called the German) and his easy-going life" (Bellow *GJSS*).

YEnemz *p.* Masculine possessive form of the pronoun "that." It means in Yiddish "that one's" or "someone else's." And that is the connection for a well-known expression: In response to the question, "What brand of cigarettes do you smoke?" the answer is, "YEnemz."

YENte (YENtl) *n.* The generic term for a gossipy old woman. Max Weinreich argues that Yentl, which sounds like a diminutive, was the older form, derived from French *gentille* or *gentil*, and that the actual diminutive was YENtlin; later it was assumed that YENtl or YENtlin was the term of endearment for a child, and the adult form was thus inferred to be YENte. Weinreich notes that YENte has been in Ashkenazic tradition for nearly a thousand years. He points out that "the contemptuous attitude to it (through association with loquacity disorganization, gossip) is new; as late as the twentieth century the name Yentl was still given, mostly in small towns. But after it began passing out of style there came a time that only old women, and provincial ones at that, had the name Yente; the name (just like Yakhne and Vikhne) assumed the associate meaning that it has today." A nonsense reduplication was YENte tileBENte, another version of gossipy old woman. In recent American usage YENte is applied to anyone who talks too much or carries tales, including fussy old men.

A button reads: MARCEL PROUST IS A YENTE.

A reviewer in the *NYRB* referred to Anaïs Nin as "an ethereal *yente.*"

The chief program adviser for PBS commented in a *Los Angeles Times* interview: "To accomplish that, Weil believes her role as programming chief calls for her to be part yenta and part bargain hunter. The 'yenta factor,' as she calls it, brings together the ideas that come through her Washington office with the production teams at the various public television stations from which much of the PBS fare originates."

A business that will do onerous household and shopping tasks is called Renta Yenta.

"The night before, for example, out in the truck, Blood had been singing, 'End up eatin' some fast food I know / Will taste like shit—' referring to an argument that had been going on all week about where to take the third partner at V&B Tow, Thi Anh, to lunch on her birthday, whose date Blood, the company yenta, had in her folder" (Thomas Pynchon *VI*).

"If Merry had been *her* daughter, things would make sense. If only Merry had fought a war of words, fought the world with words alone, like this strident yenta" (P. Roth *AP*).

yents *v.* To fuck. In Anglish the verb more likely means to screw someone in the sense of cheating, but YENtser and YENtsing are Anglish in the first sense of the word.

yeSHEEve (Yeshiva) *n.* A school for advanced study of the Talmud; a Talmudic college.

In my neighborhood (and other sections of Brooklyn) it was a euphemism for the local poolroom, where in fact a good deal of higher education took place.

yeSHEEve BOOKHer *n.* (*pl.* yeSHEEve booKHIReem) A student in a Hebrew school that concentrates on religious study.

Describing his father's generation, Philip Roth notes, "Encouraging us to be such *yeshiva buchers,* they little knew how they were equipping us to leave them isolated and uncomprehending" (P. Roth *P*).

Writing about Jerusalem, Bernard Wasserstein says, "Yet [Meron] Benevisti knows his city more intimately . . . its beggars, prelates, mukhtars, street musicians, muleteers, *yeshiva bochers,* poets, painters" (*TLS* 7 March 1997).

YHVH *n.* The Tetragrammaton, representing the four Hebrew letters designating the name of God, usually translated as Lord. Since the vowels that would give the word its meaning are missing, we speculate that it was originally Yaweh or Yaveh. An arbitrary vocalization using the vowels of Adonai (*e, o, a*) resulted in the mistranslation "Jehovah." In any case, this is an example of the notion that the name or names of God must never be spoken or written. In ancient times the name was spoken only by the high priest in a state of ritual purity in the Holy of Holies.

"If Yahweh wanted me to be calm, he would have made me a goy" (P. Roth *ST*).

YIDish *n.* The fusion language that became an almost universal vernacular and literary language of European Jews during the tenth century. According to Max Weinreich, the term is much younger than the language itself, originating around the middle of the seventeenth century. Ordinarily known as MAme LUHshn (the mother tongue) and disrespectfully as zharGUHN (meaning something less than a language), YIDish has many qualities that endear it to modern Jews. Cynthia Ozick, for example, has proposed establishing what she calls a New Yiddish: "Like Old Yiddish before its massacre by Hitler, New Yiddish will be the language of multitudes of Jews: spoken to Jews by Jews, written by Jews for Jews. And, most necessary of all, New Yiddish, like Old Yiddish, will be in possession of a significant literature capable of every conceivable resonance. . . . The human reality will ring through its novels and poems, though for a long time it will not be ripe enough for poetry; its first achievement will be mainly novels" (*AA*).

Undercutting the standard notion that God speaks Hebrew, Heller arranges for a character to address the issue: "'In what language did God address you?' 'In Yiddish of course,' said Nathan" (*GK*).

"His Yiddish, however, fevered on itself, bloated, was still Yiddish, it was still *mamaloshen*, it still squeaked up to God with a littleness, a familiarity, an elbow poke, it was still pieced together out of *shtetl* rags, out of a baby *aleph*, a toddler *beys*—so why Ostrover?" (Ozick *TPR*).

"Her grandmother pretended she was German in just the same way that Faith pretends she is an American. Faith's mother flew in the fat face of all that and, once safely among her own kind in Coney Island, learned real Yiddish, helped Faith's father, who was not so good at foreign languages, and as soon as all the verbs and necessary nouns had been collected under the roof of her mouth, she took an oath to expostulate in Yiddish and grieve only in Yiddish, and she has kept that oath to this day" (Paley *EC*).

"Talk Yiddish? *How?* I've got twenty-five words to my name—half of them dirty, and the rest mispronounced!" (P. Roth *PC*).

"You may have heard charming, appealing, sentimental things about Yiddish, but Yiddish is a *hard* language, Miss Rose. Yiddish is severe and bears down without mercy. Yes, it is often delicate, lovely but it can be explosive as well. 'A face like a slop jar,' 'a face like a bucket of swill.' (Pig connotations give special force to Yiddish epithets.) If there is a demiurge who inspires me to speak wildly, he may have been attracted to me by this violent language" (Bellow *HFM*).

Yiddish names: The tradition is to name children after a deceased relative. Naming a child after someone still alive is seen as an invitation to the Angel of Death. My daughter is named after her late maternal grandmother; my first cousin, who has the same name, was furious and terrified when she found out what I had done. The relationship between Yiddish names and American names sometimes is simply a matter of using the same initial letter. If grandpa was Abraham, the descendant might be Arnold, Arthur, Aaron, or Albert. Traditionally a child gets a Yiddish as well as a Hebrew name, and the latter is used for ritual and formal occasions. These days Hebrew names are in vogue.

YIDishkait *n.* The collection of qualities that define the broad meanings of Jewishness; within the YIDish connection lies the epitome of Jewish culture, manners, and traditions. As I have suggested elsewhere, even the existence of the state of Israel has not made YIDishkait an obsolete term.

yids *n.* A derogatory Anglish term that means Jews. The proper Yiddish is yeed, plural YEEDn.

In a review of a book about Ezra Pound, William H. Gass notes that Pound said about his biblical name, "the yitts pinched it as they did everything else" (*TLS*, 20–26 January 1989).

In *Bonfire of the Vanities*, Tom Wolfe gives a redundant version with both a Hebrew plural suffix and the English plural form: "Yiddims."

Joseph Epstein in a review of Sander L. Gilman's *Smart Jews:* "'Every poet,' said Paul Celan, 'is a Yid'" (*TLS*, 7 March 1997).

"Or else, in the language of myth, 'heavy-money Yids,' representatives of the powers of darkness and the secret rulers of the world?" (P. Roth *AP*).

YIKHes *n.* Pedigree; ancestral background and pride. You can also gain YIKHes by marrying into a family with a distinguished background. The greatest YIKHes is derived from being a member of a family of scholars.

Himmelstein says: "And you—it's all too much for you. Who told you you were such a prince? Your mother did her own wash;

you took boarders; your old man was a two-bit moonshiner. I know you Herzogs and your *Yiches*" (Bellow *H*).

YITZkhak *n.* A Hebrew first name almost always spelled YITZhak in the United States and thus erroneously pronounced "YITZak." As with many other Hebrew words (Hanukah, for example) the *h* was at one time written with a dot under it, which gave it the guttural "kh" sound. But since the dot dropped out, most non-Hebrew-speakers mispronounce the name. A form of Isaac, it should be pronounced as written in Yiddish or Hebrew: YITZkhak. Similarly spelled is KHOOTSpe, to prevent pronouncing "ch" as in chicken.

YIZker *n.* The opening word of a prayer in memory of the dead, recited on three holidays and the Day of Atonement. It is often associated with special remembrances, of the victims of the Holocaust or those who died defending Israel. YIZker means "He [God] shall remember." It has been a recent tradition to compile a YIZKer book in memory of the dead, a custom redoubled as a consequence of the Holocaust. A YIZker book, for example, will be compiled to commemorate the slaughter during World War II of an entire town.

You should excuse the expression . . . Yinglish, from "ZUHLst mich anTSHOOLdikn" (you should pardon me). It's a clever way of enabling you to say something obscene or outrageous: "He is, you should excuse the expression, a first-class shmuhk."

you shouldn't know from it Yinglish, from "ZUHLST nit VISn foon aZA zakh" (you shouldn't know about such a thing). It means "you should be protected from such an experience."

YOYsher *n.* Justice. It's a Hebrew word but regularly used in Yiddish, especially as an exclamation, demanding that justice be done.

"You can't imagine what I endure with three sick women around my neck, you're a writer, Lesser. You can appreciate the nasty little tricks of life, so yoishe, anyway, for Christ's sake. I can't go on like this forever. I'm not such a bad person. I beg you, yoishe" (Malamud *TT*).

yuhm KIPer *n.* The Day of Atonement. Next to the Sabbath, it is the holiest day in the year, when one confesses all sins and asks God and man for forgiveness. It is a day when old antagonisms are often patched up. The term High Holidays refers to ruhshiSHUHne (New Year's) and yuhm KIPer.

YUHRtsait *n.* The annual commemoration of a death. It is marked by the lighting of a special YUHRtsait candle and the reciting of KAdish. The candles used to come in heavy glasses and burn overnight. Thereafter we used to see the glasses around the kitchen. Often written YAHRtsait, which suggests Austrian or German dialect or spelling.

From a *New York Times Magazine* article on weddings by Susan Shapiro: "The Scrabble board was set out, the yahrzeit candle flickering, as if she were playing with a ghost" (23 February 1997).

yuhts *n.* An Anglish combination of puhts and yuhld (fool).

"You can leave talking to Doctor, who can be funny when he goes after those *yutzes* in City Hall, gets those salamandrine streaks on his face and lifts his brows like a Shavian wit" (Bellow *MDH*).

ZAFTig *adj.* Juicy. Zaft literally is "juice." But the main connotation (especially in Anglish) is of a well-built, voluptuous woman.

A *Los Angeles Times* review of the classic Greek comedy *Lysistrata* notes: "Women's age-old weapon, the erotic principle, is heightened with zaftic verve, building, finally, to a burlesque of monstrous phalli and the ridicule of male pomposity" (10 November 1979).

"Slothrop settles back sighing, taking his helmet off and lets sweet saftig Trudi have her way with him" (Pynchon *GR*).

In a "B.C." cartoon series, drawn by Johnny Hart, Grog is seated on a hill, reading aloud from a book. He says, "Zignorf . . . zagerif . . . zee . . . zorr . . . zah," and just as a young cave woman goes by, "ZAFTIG!" She turns immediately and runs up the hill to give him a big kiss.

Some TV gossip from Gail Shister in a syndicated column: "Ricki Lake, the zaftig star of John Waters' big-screen hit 'Hairspray,' is joining the cast of ABC's 'China Beach'" (*Fresno Bee*, 1 August 1989).

From a review of *Waiting to Exhale*, a film about four middle-class black women: "And, at one screening, the audience chanted 'Go, Glo. Go, Glo. Go, Glo' when zaftig single mother Gloria (Loretta Devine) found Mr. Right right across the street" (Karen De Witt, *New York Times*, 31 December 1995).

From an article on Europe: "a leopard lolls about like the tamest tabby cat; and a zaftig Pax nurses a chubby Plutus, the baby god of riches" (Simon Schama, *New Yorker,* 28 April and 5 May 1997).

From a *New Yorker* profile of Frank Sinatra by John Lahr: His agent "also persuaded Sinatra to record 'Tennessee Newsboy,' with washboard accompaniment, and 'Mama Will Bark,' with the zaftig Dagmar, and Donald Bain barking like a dog" (3 November 1997).

zai nisht NARish Don't be a fool; idiomatically it's zai nisht kain nar.

"A voice inside cautioned, *Zei nisht naarish.* Where does someone like you come off being Secretary of State?" (Heller *GG*).

ZAYde *n.* Grandpa. But more likely to be used is the Anglish ZAYdee.

"We all do. We all get to screw the girl. Even my old *zaydeh* gets to screw her. My rabbi gets to screw her. Everybody gets to screw her except you, St. Johns. You get to go home and screw your wife" (P. Roth, *ST*).

From an AP article about Zayde's Bagel & Bake Shop: "Zayde—Grandpa in Yiddish—may be surprised by the bagel explosion" (Robin Estrin, *Fresno Bee*, 29 April 1997).

ZEESe niSHUHMele *n.* Sweet (or gentle) soul. It is one of Bellow's many epithets that define Herzog (whose name suggests "heart-felt") as a basically good and sensitive person.

"Very well Moshe Herzog—if you must be pitiable, sue for aid and succor, you will put yourself always, inevitably, in the hands of these angry spirits. Blasting you with their 'truth.' This is what your masochism means, *mein zisse n'shamele.*"

zharGUN *n.* The French term employed to describe Yiddish as a non-language. Max Weinreich quotes Moses Mendelssohn: "This Jargon contributed no little to the immorality of the common Jews." My parents' generation almost always used the term to represent Yiddish—an apology for its commonness.

zhluhb *n.* A dullard, an awkward blockhead. Zhluhb is effectively onomatopoeic.

In accord with Thomas Pynchon's affinity for Yiddish tag names, he mentions, in *Gravity's Rainbow*, "Richard M. Zhlubb, night manager of the Orpheus Theater on Melrose."

"You know why Ma? My personality is nice conner I take after you, you dumb old shlub" (Markfield *TW*).

"Lieberman was the worst. Lieberman was a real *zshlub*" (Heller *GG*).

Uncle Benn's father-in-law wonders, "'So why had Matilda picked this *zhlobb!* This was what doctor longed to know'" (Bellow *MDH*).

From a review by Stephen Holden of the revival of *The Graduate:* "As most of us remember, Mr. Hoffman plays Benjamin Braddock, a 20-year-old high-achieving schlub who upon graduation from a fancy East Coast college, flies home to Los Angeles to be greeted by his family like a returning war hero" (*New York Times*, 9 February 1997).

ZOhar *n.* The Book of Splendor, the central text in the tradition of Kabbalism, written in the thirteenth century by the Spanish Castilian Moses de Leon. The Zohar is written in artificial Aramaic in the form of a mystical novel.

"Its place in the history of Kabbalism can be gauged from the fact that alone among the whole of post-Talmudic rabbinical literature it became a canonical text, which for a period of several centuries actually ranked with the Bible and Talmud" (Scholem *JM*).

Appendix 1

Portnoy's Complaint: The Jew as American

Even taking into account his more recent work, Philip Roth's *Portnoy's Complaint* (1969) is likely to endure as his most important contribution to American literary tradition. Despite his disclaimers, one of the strengths of the book is his virtuoso use of Yiddish, Anglish, and Yinglish. He raises some themes that other Jewish-American writers have not been able to deal with candidly, and he explores them on a level of diction that has been equally taboo in the history of Jewish-American literature. Given the basically puritan cast of that tradition, it is not surprising that Roth's treatment of sex appeared so scandalous—almost as scandalous as his attitudes toward Jews. At this distance in time it is possible to see that in 1969 he was employing shock techniques that, especially in the sexual themes, recall Walt Whitman and Henry Miller. As happened with both Whitman and Miller, the first responses of critics invariably missed the serious thematic intentions of the author because they were so outraged at what seemed to be the immorality of the work. It is an old American custom, as the *Wall Street Journal* noted not long ago when it reprinted the comments of a nineteenth-century Boston critic who characterized the author of a book of poetry published in 1855 as "some escaped lunatic raving in pitiable delirium," suggesting finally that "he be kicked from all decent society as below the level of the brute." The author, of course, was the founder of modern American poetry, Walt Whitman. The accusation is not very far from those leveled at Roth.

As a matter of fact, few of our important authors have escaped such condemnation. The clue to Philip Roth's place in this history comes not only from his candid use of sexual materials: "Obscenity,"

Roth has noted, "as a usable and valuable vocabulary, and sexuality as a subject, have been available to us since Joyce, Henry Miller and Lawrence." The great shock comes from Roth joining the sexual themes to the Jewish issues that have always been one of his main literary concerns. Shock values aside, *Portnoy's Complaint* marked a major moment in the history of Jewish experience. But, just as Ralph Ellison's equally significant *Invisible Man* (1952) is not only an important black book but also a central insight into the nature of the American experience, so also Roth's Jewish book provides a major illumination of American values. For both authors, the American connection is logical and necessary.

Although his mode is comic, Roth deals seriously with most of the themes (especially sex and identity) that have preoccupied American writers, and does so in a way that is actually reminiscent of Whitman in "Song of Myself." When asked by an interviewer if he had been influenced by Lenny Bruce and other stand-up comics, Roth quipped that he was "more strongly influenced by a sit-down comic named Franz Kafka and a very funny bit he does called 'The Metamorphosis.'" What he likes about American comics, and especially groups like the Second City, Roth continued, is the "joining of precise social observation with extravagant and dreamlike fantasy."

But I think Roth's main thrust is to question the assumptions of Jewish *exceptionalism*, assumptions that have been implicit in the work of every Jewish-American writer up to the present time. *Portnoy's Complaint* attempts to document a new level of consciousness for American Jews. In the process it strips them of some illusions that they and many of their Gentile brethren in this country have accepted all too easily. I think that helps to explain why it is such an important book and also why it has been attacked so furiously from all sides.

Once the ad hominem arguments are disposed of, the main objection from Jewish quarters is that Roth has done a disservice to his people by portraying them in such negative terms while exposing his own "self-hatred." The underlying argument is that a writer owes a certain allegiance to his tribe (whether it be regional or national in designation), the same argument that some southerners used to attack Twain and Faulkner because their portrayal of the South was "negative." The first barrage of such criticism in Roth's case came after the publication of *Goodbye, Columbus* (1960). Perhaps the best answer to this criticism came from Saul Bellow, in the introduction to his collection *Great Jewish Short Stories* (1963). For the Jewish writer in the diaspora, he notes, "it seemed most important to present Jewish life as sympathetically as possible. Because the Jews were remorselessly oppressed, all the good qualities of Jewish life were heaped up in the foreground of their stories. Raw things—jealousies, ambitions, hatreds, deceptions—were frequently withheld."

Bellow recalls that the Jewish slums of Montreal where he grew up were not very far removed from the ghettoes of Poland or Russia, but that it was difficult to recognize the realities of life there in the work of modern Jewish writers. "These writers," he says, "generally tended to idealize it, to cover it up in prayer shawls and phylacteries and Sabbath sentiment, the Seder, the match-making, the marriage canopy; for sadness the Kaddish, for amusement the schnorrer, for admiration the bearded scholar. Jewish literature and art have sentimentalized and sweetened the ghetto; their 'pleasing' pictures are far less interesting of course than the real thing." With a considerable change of diction this could be Portnoy trying to explain to his father why "the saga of his people" or the Talmud has no meaning for him; the traditions have been vulgarized and sentimentalized, "fiddlerized on the roof."

But Bellow is speaking as a writer, and here the issue (as it almost always does) goes beyond the Jewish Question and becomes one of art versus propaganda. Bellow gives as an example the attitude of some propagandistic critics of Leon Uris's novel *Exodus*. Though patently not a very sophisticated or technically proficient book, it was praised by critics because it was "extraordinarily effective as a document and we need such documents now. We do not need stories like those of Philip Roth which expose unpleasant Jewish traits. The Jews are much slandered, much threatened, greatly sinned against— should they for these reasons be unfairly represented in literature, to their alleged advantage?" Such arguments for covering up the range of Jewish experience remind Bellow of Soviet attempts to purify writers so that they will not lend comfort to the enemy; for Bellow there are no acceptable political standards for writers, only literary ones.

But there is also a broader cultural framework for this question. We may recall the agony of James Joyce's Stephen Dedalus, who concludes that in order to become an artist it is necessary to over-come the restraints of nationality, language, and religion. Talking about his native Ireland, he says, "When the soul of a man is born in this country, there are nets flung at it to hold it back from flight. You talk to me of nationality, language, religion. I shall try to fly by those nets." In quoting Joyce, Bellow's point (and it is Roth's as well) is that the artist cannot bend his axis of vision to conform with the provincial needs of his tribe (however defined); in fact, it becomes the function of a writer to be most critical of his closest sources and values, and in that sense Joyce is most faithful to the Irish when he excoriates them to the fullest extent. (Similarly, when Naomi, the Sabra, accuses Portnoy of being a "self-hating Jew," he replies, "Ah, but Naomi, maybe that's the best kind.") Bellow and Roth would both agree with Joyce's final formulation: "I will not serve that in which I no longer believe, whether it call itself my home, my fatherland, or my church; and I will try to express myself in some mode of life or art as freely as I can, using for my defense the only arms I allow myself to use—silence, exile and cunning." The funny thing is that Joyce didn't even look Jewish, but it's no accident that the earliest draft of what finally became *Portnoy's Complaint* was entitled by Roth *Portrait of the Artist.*

If the battle for the right to artistic integrity has universal implications for the modern writer, it poses special problems for Americans. The nets of which Joyce speaks were woven over a long period of time and were solidly entwined in the psyche of the Irish writer. But he had a clear target for his complaints and, though the agony of a struggle for self-expression was no less, Joyce at least faced a more readily identifiable monolith. American writers are new men and women in a new land; they must first create their own tradition and then, almost in the same act, attack it in order to ensure their integrity and freedom; or as Hemingway puts it, avoid obstacles that prevent you "from knowing truly what you really felt, rather than what you were supposed to feel and had been taught to feel." Hemingway is talking about conventions (literary and social) that interpose themselves between the writer's perception and what is really out there. It is another version of the fear that one may become fettered by commitments that hinder the free flight Joyce talks about.

Yet despite these demands, there is at the same time a compulsion for writers to be rooted in a tradition that will provide a framework and a texture for their vision. This is a precarious balance, for on one hand writers demand freedom to pursue their art, while on the other they know that their most precious resource is language, which emanates from a clearly defined cultural matrix and is often regional in character. In an essay on American literature and language, T. S. Eliot identifies what he conceives to be "the two essential characteristics of a national literature—a strong local flavour combined with unconscious universality." Universality, he argues, "can never come except through writing about what one knows thoroughly . . . And though it is only too easy for a writer to be local without being universal, I doubt whether a poet or novelist can be universal without being local too. Who could be more Greek than Odysseus? Or more German than Faust? Or more Spanish than Don Quixote? Or more American than Huck Finn? Yet each one of them is a kind of archetype in the mythology of men everywhere."

Eliot is dealing here with the same balance between individual and national expression, and his solution is to recommend just the right combination of regional roots and unconscious universality. But that is precisely what American writers have found most difficult to accomplish, largely because they have not been sure what their national identity is. And that is why "identity" is such an obsession in American literature, where the issue is complicated by the double heritage of individuals who live in a country that defines itself (to use Whitman's phrase) as "a nation of nations." Eliot points out that "a national literature comes to consciousness at the stage at which any young writer must be aware of several generations of writers behind him, in his own country and language," emphasizing that "the importance of this background is incalculable." As we know from their own comments, our early writers complained that there was no such background, except for strong pressures (which they tried to resist) from British traditions.

For later writers a similar double consciousness comes from the identification as an African American, or a Jewish American, or even a Native American, and the consequent necessity for dealing with both halves of these terms. As Whitman put it (in a slightly different context), writers need to be both "in and out of the game"—to be independent but also to celebrate the connection with their cultural sources. Only in America do we encounter a strange phenomenon:

when asked their nationality, Americans habitually say where their parents or grandparents came from. We almost always say Italian-American, Polish-American, Irish-American—the more the merrier, unto the "57 varieties"—when in fact the accurate response is "American." Well, in fact, that, too, is inaccurate because we should say (in deference to Mexicans, Canadians, and Costa Ricans, all of whom are Americans), "United Statesians." But of course we have no such locution. I once went around the room in a class and got all the hyphenated responses, except from one person who said "French." I asked, "Franco-American?" "No," he said, "I was born in Paris." "And your grandfather?" "Born in Italy." The point is that he didn't say "Italo-French."

Every hyphenated American must face the implications of this complex fate (to use Henry James's term), for the simple solution of jettisoning the "second" consciousness seems sterile or, as in the case of African Americans, almost impossible. At this stage in our national development, when almost everyone is pursuing national or ethnic backgrounds in response to what we often call the *Roots* phenomenon (after the Alex Haley novel), there emerges a curious and comic inferiority complex on the part of those who have most fully assimilated; namely, the WASPs, who often envy the blacks, Jews, Italians, Irish, Indians, or Chicanos. (An early example is Norman Mailer's essay "The White Negro.") Each group has its unique problems but, as we have seen in the context of African-American literature (and are beginning to see in groups like American Indians and others), to raise the question is to provide an important framework for understanding what is meant by "American" in general. What I want to emphasize is that Jewish-American writing has had its own evolutionary process. The importance of *Portnoy's Complaint* is that Roth seems aware of just such issues and is pointing out some consequences that have not been dealt with before in Jewish life and literature.

In some ways the problem for Jewish Americans is just the opposite of what has faced black Americans. As Melville J. Herskovits pointed out in *The Myth of the Negro Past* (1941), it has been widely held that slavery wiped out entirely the African heritage of the slaves, leaving them literally without a past. Blacks have had to rediscover their African heritage and define it in American terms, hence the preference for "African American" as a designation. It is, as I have noted, a very American preoccupation. Jews, on the other hand, face the difficulty of dealing with an inheritance that is ancient and continuous and that, since the Diaspora, has had a built-in double consciousness. The inferences that have been drawn from Jewish history are manifold, but several bear directly on the American experience. The basic one Roth seems to be concerned with is what I referred to earlier as "exceptionalism." Stephen Spender notes, along these lines, that although other modern poets also find it difficult to deal with the anguish of contemporary existence (he is thinking of Ted Hughes's *Crow*) the struggle is different for Jews: "In the poetry of Nellie Sachs and Abba Kovuer, for example, the holocaust, while being the terrible center of their poetry, is also in some way redemptive, because it has restored to them, as Jews, the sense of belonging to a whole Jewish history, punctuated with exile and destruction, and given them a new awareness of the sacred consciousness of the Jewish people, beyond their own individuality."

The assumption is that the split consciousness of the modern world, which forces Gentile poets to what Spender calls "survival poetry," is an advantage for the Jews. It brings to mind the traditional image of the Wandering Jew, and though Spender implies nothing pejorative, the idea is difficult to separate from its demonic connotations (recall the Jew in Hawthorne's story "Ethan Brand"). Spender comes close to stating the view that Roth deals with, in which the force of Jewish history saves the Jew from the evils of the "host" country. This motif was notable in Jewish-American writing before *Portnoy's Complaint*. The Jew is intrinsically an outsider, kept pure by his association with the "saga of his people." Everything depends, however, on the interpretation of that history, which, contrary to popular belief, lacks a central and overriding unity.

A case in point is Bellow's treatment of Herzog, who is a good foil to Portnoy. Faced with the existential problems of his life in America, Herzog weaves a blend of his ancient heritage (the Hebrew Bible, the Talmud, Jewish folklore, and Spinoza, among others) with the traditions he comprehends as an American, including a number of ideas he associates with Emerson and Whitman. All these are functional in his consciousness; they substantiate the notion that the Jews, who can syncretize the ideas in both their past and their present, have a special ability to deal with the chaos of modern life. Bellow does not sentimentalize or oversimplify Herzog's predicament. *Herzog* well illustrates what Alfred Kazin insists is the real theme of Jewish-American literature: divorce. But it is also clear that the Jewish-American heritage as Bellow defines it provides an intellectual and philosophical framework for Herzog's struggles in life. The key word, perhaps, is functional, for Herzog is of a generation close enough to its European antecedents that the legacy of the Old World still works—and Herzog is after all a professor of humanities. To put it another way, Herzog is well equipped to function in the realm of cultural pluralism, which is what the term "nation of nations" implies; and he even controls both Hebrew and Yiddish, the two main languages of the Jews. Recall Herzog's disdain for his antagonist in the novel, who is always mispronouncing Yiddish words and expressions.

Portnoy's complaint about his approach to Yiddish is more complicated. "I've got twenty-five Yiddish words to my name," he cries, "—half of them dirty, and the rest mispronounced!" As a matter of fact he has closer to a hundred, and they reflect accurately the development of Anglish and Yinglish—precisely in line with the main point of this study. The fate of Yiddish is not unlike that of the Jew in America—for both, the generation gap (between Herzog and Portnoy and truly between Bellow and Roth) has exhibited some central changes in the relations between the Jews and their ancestral culture.

Before I examine these in detail, recall that it is Herzog's Jewishness that makes him the natural target for the anti-Semitism that is the other side of the equation propounded by Spender. A classic formulation appears in David Shetzline's novel *Heckletooth 3* (1969), in which one of the characters is Kendricks, a goy: "the Jew was the hope of America, if only because the Jew, as Kendricks cleaved to the promise, was a man so long and predictably fucked over, no matter how he insinuated himself into the paper credentials of any given society, he was always at call to be shat upon, defiled, purged, hauled forth and dispatched like a dwarfed calf." Kendricks notes of the Jews that no matter what their accomplishments in education, intelligence, or wealth, "they were always ripe for a slaughter, and what was truly something: they could be lynched by the local Minutemen Birchers and know, as the rope tightened, the fire burned, somehow, the something that was themselves, their Jewishness would survive. You could never kill a Jew." The most interesting aspect of Shetzline's rendering is Kendricks's envy of the Jews:

> Kendricks wished he were Jewish—not the ignorant sort who trusted in the abracadabral magic of bans, but a real American Jew who could never be liked nor killed; who was heir to so much racial battle fatigue, he possessed a fantastic dignity, a trust of time. The commitment to time, the inviolableness of a People haunted Kendricks. He possessed none of it. He had come to believe that living was so very much attitude, and his own was so bereft of even a death-bed optimism, he accepted himself as sterile. Not only atheist, but misogamist, misanthropist, a missed-by-his-own-doing of anything that might have made him different, Kendricks, in accepting his own limits, projected upon his understanding of the American Jew the only thing he could honorably salute and serve.

Shetzline has not only chronicled the demise of the WASPs, he has also caught something important in their attitude toward their Jewish compatriots. It is an ambivalence that matches the confusion of values in a character like Portnoy and his response to GOYim. For if, on the one hand, the Jew is a ready scapegoat, he is also envied for his ability to make it on his own despite all handicaps, while preserving the sense of his own identity as an American *and* as a Jew. This is another instance of the WASP's inferiority complex in the face of "ethnic" Americans. Kendricks feels sterile in comparison with the Jew's "different" identity, especially his commitment to time and the history of his people. But underlying Kendricks' statement is something more important: The Jew is not so much an alien as he is someone who has fulfilled the destiny of the true American.

Here is the source of a curious form of anti-Semitism, not based on the traditional charge of the Jew as Christ-killer or as the practitioner of arcane rituals. Rather it is that the Jew is too close for comfort when viewed by Gentiles in the framework of their own success formula. The earliest speculations about the national character of the American (in the guise of the Yankee) reproduce almost all the stereotypes associated with the Jew. Constance Rourke has caught this well in her classic *American Humor: A Study of the National Character* (1931).

The Yankee is seen as shrewd, conniving, penurious, almost demonically intelligent, and supremely on the make. Rourke points out that similar values survive in another typically American figure, the frontiersman, and we may recall the axiom of a famous frontier hustler, Simon Suggs—"It pays to be shifty in a new country."

But if all these attitudes and approaches recall Jewish outlines, the Jew has one quality that the inhabitants of the New World lack—a history that provides an indelible identity, despite the dispersion and wandering. Edmund Wilson has traced a variation of this American envy of the Jews by recounting the obsessive identification of James Russell Lowell with Jews, to the point that he wore a skull cap and liked to be called "Rab." Almost predictably, Wilson notes, Lowell in his later years became a fanatical anti-Semite. Wilson also reminds us that, from the beginning of our history, Americans have tended to see themselves as a chosen people in a new Jerusalem, bearing similar burdens and enjoying the same special relationship with the Creator as the ancient Hebrews. In an important sense, according to this approach, the Jew comes to be seen as the archetypal American who has realized the American dream—and more. The Jews accomplish all the positive goals of the Golden Country and suffer none of the shortcomings, including the lack of a historical base. The Jew has a usable past.

Roth's main point in *Portnoy's Complaint* is that the American Jew can no longer claim either the exceptionalism of an earlier generation or the nice balance of being both Jewish and American without enduring a good deal of anguish. Alex is afflicted by the generation gap, a disease that has been endemic since the second generation of Puritans settled in New England. The children's main charge against the parents is always the same—hypocrisy. Although the Portnoys regularly eat nonkosher food in a Chinese restaurant, Sophie tortures her son because she knows he eats KHAzerai (literally, piggish food) outside the house. The traditional lore of the Jews has become, as Alex states, "hysteria and superstition. . . . I was raised by Hottentots and Zulus! I couldn't even contemplate drinking a glass of milk with my salami sandwich without giving serious offense to God Almighty." Most of the conflicts between Alex and his parents stem from the son's recognition of the changes that have taken place in the attitudes of American Jews since the turn of the century, and most critics have missed the fact that Roth has taken great pains to set the novel at a particular time in American history. Portnoy is thirty-three and the action takes place in 1966. Alex is of a generation that had not been dealt with very much in American fiction—Jewish or otherwise. Born at the height of the Great Depression, Portnoy has no real sense of it nor of the other great cataclysm—World War II—that has figured so prominently in recent American fiction. (Alex was fourteen in 1947.)

Politically, Alex is "a child of the forties, of network radio and World War Two, of eight teams to a league and forty-eight states to a country." He knows all the patriotic songs of his time as well as the anthems of all the armed forces. Having lost the sense of Jewish exceptionalism, Alex naturally takes up the central theme of our literature—a quest to discover the relationships between his identity and the meaning of American life. The sexual theme is clearly associated with both aspects of the quest: "There's more than just adolescent resentment and Oedipal rage—there's my integrity!" As Alex explains to his psychiatrist, Doctor Spielvogel: "What I'm saying, Doctor, is that I don't seem to stick my dick up these girls, as much as I stick it up their backgrounds—as though through fucking I will discover America." The difference among the generations is clear. "Oh America! America!" Alex says, "it may have been gold in the streets to my grandparents, it may have been a chicken in every pot to my father and mother, but to me, a child whose earliest memories are of Ann Rutherford and Alice Faye, America is a *shikse* nestling under your arm whispering love love love love!"

The economic and political implications of the American experience have been superseded by starlets, movie queens, and, above all, the mass media. Roth provides a brilliant catalogue of the main currents in that high-water period of American liberalism, which has been recently derided and deflated. The period is depicted not only in terms of film, but also by references to radio programs like Jack Armstrong (he is to Portnoy "the All-American Goy"), Allen's Alley, Ralph Edwards, Fibber McGee and Molly; snatches from pop songs; and especially through memories of such icons of liberalism as the newspaper *P.M.*, Frank Kingdon, Marian Anderson, Howard Fast's novel *Citizen Tom Paine*, and the American Veterans' Committee, of which Alex's future brother-in-law, Morty, is the membership chairman. With Morty, Alex takes part in the Henry Wallace presidential campaign, "a crusade for the rights of the people." When Mr. Portnoy warns Morty, "You're going to turn that kid into a Communist," Alex notes that his father is one of those "who vote Democratic but think Neanderthal."

Alex is most completely under the control of his "master," Norman Corwin, whose celebration of v-e Day, *On a Note of Freedom*, has inspired Alex to write his own radio play, *Let Freedom Ring*. This is a foreshadowing of Portnoy's role as assistant commissioner of human opportunities—which also brings with it the Monkey's constant threat to expose him as a "hypocrite" himself. (The Monkey is Portnoy's girlfriend.) But at this same point in his life, Portnoy experiences the most significant movement toward his quest. "I am reborn," he says. "Free, I find, of shameful secrets! So clean-feeling, so strong and virtuous-feeling—so American!" There are several targets for Roth's satire here, not the least of which is the naïveté of Portnoy's sense of being reborn cleansed and virtuous. The Monkey's threat is not without foundation. Portnoy snobbishly decides to educate her about her origins, "origins, of course, holding far more fascination for the nice left-wing Jewish boy than for the proletarian girl herself." He dubs the course of study "Professor Portnoy's Humiliated Minorities, an Introduction," and the purpose is to "save the stupid *shikse*; to rid her of her race's ignorance; to make this daughter of the heartless oppressor a student of suffering and oppression; to teach her to be compassionate, to bleed a little for the world's sorrows. . . . The perfect couple: she puts the id back in Yid, I put the *oy* back in *goy*."

Portnoy's resurrection as an American is built on the traditional role of the Jew as outcast, which suggests a "natural alliance" with oppressed groups like the poor whites and blacks of the South. But in his parents Alex has already seen the inefficacy of that idea: His father tries to collect insurance payments from poor blacks, who take out their frustrations on him; Sophie crows about how good she is to the black domestic, "meanwhile running scalding water over the dish from which the cleaning lady has just eaten her lunch, alone like a leper." Roth saw the traditional political alliance between blacks and Jews crumbling, partly as a consequence of black power movements and to some extent because the Jewish position had shifted fully into the power structure.

Just as Americans have often seen themselves as missionaries to the world, so Alex attempts to fulfill the special function of the Jews: "If you loved Arthur Miller as saviour of *shikses* [the reference is to Miller's marriage to Marilyn Monroe], you'll just love Alex! . . . The Saintliest Commissioner of the City of New York . . . seen here with his pipe and his thinning kinky black Hebe hair, in all his Jewish messianic fervor and charm." But neither the Jewish nor the American values will support Alex's political or psychic needs. Sophie and Jack Portnoy are middle-class Americans for whom the humanistic (and often radical) ideology of Judaism has little meaning. Portnoy himself finds both Jews and Gentiles provincial: "The Jews I despise for their narrowmindedness, their self-righteousness, the incredibly bizarre sense that these cave men who are my parents and relatives have somehow gotten of their superiority—but when it comes to tawdriness and cheapness, to beliefs that would shame even a gorilla, you simply cannot top the *goyim*."

What has been taken for "self-hatred" in Roth is a critique of an American society that has abandoned its deepest commitments to political and economic equality, and the only really shocking element is that Roth will not find an excuse for exempting the Jews: "How can they possibly *believe* this shit? Not just children but grownups, too, stand around on the snowy lawns smiling down at pieces of wood six inches high that are called Mary and Joseph and little Jesus—and the little cut-out cows and horses are smiling too! God! The idiocy of the Jews all year long, and then the idiocy of the *goyim* on these holidays! What a country! Is it any wonder we're all of us half nuts?" And, of course, Reaganism, with its sectarian religious crusade and its demand that the reforms of the New Deal be abandoned, was just around the corner.

Roth defines this social dislocation most fully in psychological terms and, though many critics have refused to take his political analysis seriously, they have accepted the Freudian analysis at face value. It is worth taking a closer look at the diagnosis of "Portnoy's

Complaint," which Roth derives from Freud's paper "The Most Prevalent Form of Degradation in Erotic Life":

Portnoy's Complaint (pôrt'-noiz kəm-plānt') *n.* [after Alexander Portnoy (1933–)] A disorder in which strongly felt ethical and altruistic impulses are perpetually warring with extreme sexual longings, often of a perverse nature. Spielvogel says, "Acts of exhibitionism, voyeurism, fetishism, autoeroticism and oral coitus are plentiful; as a consequence of the patient's 'morality,' however, neither fantasy nor act issues in genuine sexual gratification, but rather in overriding feelings of shame and the dread of retribution, particularly in the form of castration." (Spielvogel, O. "The Puzzled Penis," *Internationale Zeitschrift für Psychoanalyse,* vol. XXIV, p. 909.) It is believed by Spielvogel that many of the symptoms can be traced to the bonds obtaining in the mother-child relationship.

Roth's attitude toward psychiatrists is very clear. The Monkey's therapist is called Harpo because he never says anything. Portnoy's is Spielvogel, which means the bird that talks (or spiels), that is, the parrot. And, indeed, Spielvogel simply parrots Freud's description of the difficulty that results in the puzzled penis. Portnoy paraphrases it himself: "In the 'Degradation' essay there is that phrase, 'currents of feeling.' For a 'fully normal attitude in love' (deserving of semantic scrutiny, that 'fully normal,' but to go on—) for a fully normal attitude in love, says he, it is necessary that two currents of feeling be united; the tender, affectionate feelings, and the sensuous feelings. And in many instances this just doesn't happen, sad to say, 'Where such men love they have no desire, and where they desire they cannot love.'" The ultimate source of this problem, Freud argues, is the unnatural relationship to the mother. Freud's analysis was meant to be universal. For Roth, of course, it is not just the mother, it is the Jewish Mother. And here again the Jewish and the sexual motifs are joined in what for many has been the most shocking theme of all.

The response of non-Jews to this theme, however, should have been the best clue to Roth's intentions. Hardly anyone who has reacted to the book fails to identify with Portnoy; in my own experience this has included the WASPiest of WASPs, blacks, Lutherans from the Midwest, and easterners regardless of ethnic background. There are several explanations. In part Roth is describing the immigrant mother (including those of Anglo-Saxon origins), who combines a provincial sense of the ancestral heritage with a killing pressure for success in the New World. It is a very American experience, one that obviously cuts across ethnic lines and has no special connections with Jewish women and the Freudian analysis I have been discussing. Roth dramatizes a Jewish version that is different from, say, the Irish-American attitude only in tone and nuance, and is quite similar to the circumstances of Italians, blacks, and others. It is therefore neither a specifically Jewish problem nor even basically a sexual one. Portnoy himself questions Freud's use of the term *normal*, and in the section immediately following the invocation of Freud's theory, Alex and the Monkey find a moment when "there was a sensual feeling mingling with the purest, deepest streams of tenderness I've ever known! I'm telling you, the confluence of the two currents was terrific! and in her as well. She even said as much!" So much for the Most Prevalent Form of Degradation.

On the other hand, it is possible to give a diagnosis of "Portnoy's Complaint" in strictly cultural terms. The war between ethical and deeply felt instinctual drives defines effectively the breakdown of liberal ideology and, at least since *Candide*, sex has been the most effective metaphor in the attempt to puncture rationalist predispositions. We have been all too conscious of this deflation of liberal values in our recent political life, and one of its main symptoms has been the estrangement between blacks and Jews. Roth provides a brilliant description of the predicament and its consequences. Alex is placed clearly in the generation that, still committed to a postwar euphoria, has the basis for its optimism pulled out from under it. Among the first signs are the breakdown of family life and estrangement of the generations. The next stages include black militancy, hippies, and the disillusionment of Watergate. Roth sees that the Jews experience the same dislocations as other middle-class Americans who perceive only dimly that many of their basic values are being called into question. None of these issues depends to any significant degree on the special role of the mother, sexual or otherwise.

Roth has insisted that he writes about Jews and their behavior because that is what he knows best. In the process he has uncovered some interesting circumstances in Jewish history. Why such emphasis on the Jewish *mother?* Psychiatrists are generally furious about Roth's treatment of their profession, but most agree that Roth is quite accurate in his description of the American immigrant family as matriarchal. (The same is true for blacks, perhaps for other reasons.) This is largely due to the pressure on the father to become successful in a new culture. In first-generation immigrant families the father is often defeated or fails to achieve gracefully the transition necessary to ensure his patriarchal position. The pressure is then on the second generation, especially the son, who also finds himself questioning the adequacy of the father. (There is some controversy about the way this develops among blacks, but there is nevertheless a strong Jewish-mother effect among black women.) In *Portnoy's Complaint* the motif is worked out in terms of baseball. Jack Portnoy (though apparently American-born, like Roth's parents) doesn't quite find the sport amenable to his skills. Alex, on the other hand, in a passage reminiscent of both Hemingway and Salinger, invokes the names of DiMaggio, Duke Snider, and Al Gionfriddo:

> Yes, every little detail so thoroughly studied and mastered, that it is simply beyond the realm of possibility for any situation to arise in which I do not know how to move, or where to move, or what to say or leave unsaid. . . . And it's true, is it not?—incredible, but apparently true—there are people who feel in life the ease, the self assurance, the simple and essential affiliation with what is going on, that I used to feel as the center fielder for the Seabees? Because it wasn't, you see, that one was the best center fielder imaginable, only that one knew exactly, and down to the smallest particular, how a center fielder should conduct himself. And there are people like that walking the streets of the U.S. of A.? I ask you, why can't I be one! Why can't I exist now as I existed for the Seabees out there in center field! Oh, to be a center fielder, a center fielder—and nothing more!

Center field is for Roth what the catcher is for Salinger—the core position—and the skills entailed unite physical and psychological strength; above all it implies confidence, maturity, and a sense of integrity. If Roth underscores the basic escapism of American athletic activity, he also seems to support Virginia Woolf's quip that baseball is what Americans have in place of society.

But from his family's point of view, Portnoy's interest in athletics is scandalous—a prospective surgeon cannot afford to endanger his hands in so physical an activity. Here, as elsewhere, Sophie's approach is based on a series of scare techniques practiced "solely for the sake of humbling and frightening me into being once again an obedient and helpless little boy." The special force, the almost demonic power of the Jewish Mother, seems peculiar in a Judaic tradition that is fiercely patriarchal. But as Raphael Patai has demonstrated in his study *The Hebrew Goddess* (1967), the symbol of the "divine woman" has persisted in Jewish folk culture despite her exclusion from official religious doctrine. The Jewish Mother, it seems to me, fulfills that need for the feminine principle; like her analogues, she encompasses both life and death, the overwhelming power of love as well as the threat of destruction. Roth has found her in New Jersey, just as Patai has unearthed evidence of her existence in both ancient and modern Jewish communities. Judging from the cries of outrage (especially from Jewish sources) about Roth's mistreatment of the Jewish Mother, one can argue that exceptionalism is at work again. The mother may be seen as pious and loving, but any attempt to extend her range of power, in accordance with the teachings of comparative religion, is viewed as an ungrateful affront. Roth has sinned again, if sin it is, by insisting that the history of the Jews is consonant with that of most other human cultures.

What does Roth really want for his hero? He emphasizes it often enough, and not surprisingly the plea turns out to be very much in the American grain. It is to be "oneself," a center fielder perhaps, a centered, autonomous individual who is free enough in spirit to acknowledge all aspects of his personality—including sexuality. Just before Portnoy has his final debacle in Israel (the last episode in rejecting the notion of Jewish exceptionalism, for he is impotent in Israel), he recalls what he might have been: "a robust Jewish man," heading home to wife and family from a gloriously exhausting softball game, or wedded to the Pumpkin, a "poetic American girl . . . someone who knew who she was! Psychologically so intact as not to be in need of salvation or redemption by me!" (Of course, he realizes, she would be rejected because "she wouldn't be Jewish.") Portnoy quests for the possibility of a new life in Israel. "How my life would change! A new man!—with this woman." But this is no more a possibility than his earlier essay. Roth provides no practical solutions to Alex's problems; he has no easy program for the survival of the Jews, or the rest of humanity for that matter. He has met Bellow's criterion, however, for an unsentimentalized view of Jewish life; and I think he has succeeded in creating a thoroughly local yet universal work of art along the lines that Eliot has proposed. If he has not put to rest the mystique of Jewish exceptionalism in American life, it is not for lack of effort. Yet the idea remains, in the work of Jewish and non-Jewish writers alike. A perfect example is seen in a passage from Mary McCarthy's *Birds of America* (1971). Her partly Jewish hero, Peter Levi, comments that being an American

> was like being Jewish, only worse: you recognized "your people" everywhere in their Great Diaspora and you were mortified by them and mortified by being mortified. . . . It was worse than being Jewish, Peter felt, in the sense that nobody was excluding you and you made your own ghettoes around Army bases and in "exclusive" hotels abroad, eating your own version of kosher like his tablemates on the boat, who were always clamoring for ketchup. . . . Being a Jew gave you a history of martyrdom that at least was old and dignified. If you were a Jew you were "one of the chosen," while an American was just a Philistine.

Short of becoming fanatically Orthodox, Roth is probably right in suggesting that American Jews can claim nothing special—perhaps only the exceptionalism of being Americans. But even Roth himself has tried to save something distinctive from his Jewish heritage, and it is significant that Yiddish has some part in it. Asked by a *Times (London) Literary Supplement* interviewer to assess the impact on him of Hebrew and Yiddish, Roth noted that the Hebrew and Yiddish languages in themselves had been of negligible influence. What reached down to him

> wasn't the Yiddish language but the values and the cultural style that had been associated with the Yiddish world of the Jewish immigrants who'd come to America around the turn of the century. Skillful and energetic as the Jewish adaptation to America was in the first and second generations, the impact of the lost Yiddish world upon American

Jewish sensibilities remained considerable right down to my own generation, so that even if one couldn't read, speak, or write Yiddish, what was said or written in English might well be affected by a feel, however attenuated, for Yiddish expressiveness and wit, and for a turn of mind previously unfamiliar to Protestant America. It isn't Yiddish that influenced the way I write, but rather this turn of mind that influenced how I came to see the Americans I eventually began to write *about*, both the Jews and the non-Jews.

Portnoy is right, and not for the first time; for as we have seen here, the impact on American life and literature now comes less from Yiddish than from Anglish and Yinglish. NEbech.

Appendix 2

The Revival of Klezmer Music

KLEZmer is the Yiddish version of the Hebrew klayZEmer, which means vessels or instruments of music; hence it came to mean also the SHTEtl musicians who provided music and entertainment for weddings and other festivities, especially in connection with the folk dramas associated with Purim. From the time of the Middle Ages, Jews were well known as musician specialists; they performed not only for Jews but often for Gentile groups as well. In *The Cherry Orchard* Chekhov refers to the family's Jewish orchestra, which was obviously a klezmer band. The stage directions for act 3 state: "Jewish orchestra is playing—the same one that was mentioned in Act II." There Gayeff explains, "It is our famous Jewish orchestra. You remember, four violins, flute and double bass."

Klezmer groups were in fact often string bands. In view of later developments in this country, it is worth noting that klezMOrim often had exactly the instrumentation of the early New Orleans jazz bands—clarinet, trumpet or cornet, trombone, and tuba. Sometimes these would be joined by violins or cellos. There are numerous references to hammered dulcimers from as early as the seventeenth century. Felix Mendelssohn heard a concert by a famous klezmer musician who had invented a version of the dulcimer that sounds like a xylophone (he placed blocks of wood on a bed of straw). In describing the musician, named Gusikow, Mendelssohn proclaimed, he "is quite a phenomenon, a famous fellow, inferior to no virtuoso in the world, both in execution and facility." The Yiddish term for hammered dulcimer is TSIMbal, as in Efrem Zimbalist (there were probably some klezmorim in that famous theater family). There have been a number of American hammered dulcimer performers, including Joseph Moskowitz, the famous New York musician and restaurateur, whose performance has been included in the reissue of klezmer music edited by Martin Schwartz (see Discography).

The repertoires of the klezmorim comprised both Jewish and non-Jewish sources, so that even today one hears "Jewish tunes" in the bands of Gypsy, Greek, Slavic, and Armenian musicians. One of the superb Armenian oudists in my hometown of Fresno, California, plays a tune that features in a middle section what we know as "HAva naGEEla." (The oud is a lutelike instrument featured prominently in Middle Eastern music.) A. Z. Idelsohn notes that "the *klezmorim* in Central and Eastern Europe were the forerunners of the host of musicians of Jewish extraction, both composers and performers, who, from the beginning of the nineteenth century on, contributed enormously toward the upbuilding of European art-music."

It is equally important to recall that the klezmorim borrowed much music from their neighbors as well as from traveling groups, especially Gypsies. Although we tend to emphasize the separation of Old Country Jews from their neighbors, the Soviet folklorist Moshe Beregovski notes that "Jewish musicians used to play frequently at non-Jewish weddings and festivities where they undoubtedly played Jewish tunes in addition to the Ukrainian dance-repertoire. In the same way they brought their Ukrainian repertoire to Jewish weddings (e.g., kazatskes, skotsnas)."

The fate of the klezmorim themselves was to be much more complicated. They persisted into the twentieth century as a crucial element in the transmission of folk materials into European popular culture. In that sense they are comparable to the string bands of the twenties in the United States, who performed the same function for country-and-western music. Klezmer musicians also emigrated to this country and, because of the outstanding records that were made here in the twenties and thirties, a significant body of their music is available. Actually, the earliest recordings of Jewish music were made in 1895. And as Henry Sapoznik has pointed out in the notes to his album of early klezmer music, commercial companies like Columbia and RCA Victor produced large numbers of ethnic recordings, including Jewish materials. The records were directed toward specific communities, such as urban blacks and rural whites, and a number of ethnic groups, including Jews. These companies did very well until the Great Depression either cut back their scope or brought their operations to a halt.

The existence of so many old recordings has been crucial to the revival of klezmer music in this country. For although the strains of klezmer music can be heard in various classical compositions (the first movement of Mahler's First Symphony is a good example), the tradition was almost totally destroyed in the Holocaust. What remains has been heard by most of us in wedding and bar MITSvuh music in any city where there has been a large Jewish population. Almost everyone, for example, has heard the klezmer tune for the favorite Jewish wedding dance, the shear (scissors), which is done by four couples, like an American square dance. (The name comes from one of the figures in which the dancers cross each other like the blades of a scissors.)

Klezmer musicians also were active in other musical areas in the United States, including some early recordings for cartoons ("Betty Boop" among them) and gigs with many jazz bands. One famous incursion is memorable because it took place in the Benny Goodman Band. One of his musicians, trumpeter Ziggy Elman, had recorded a klezmer tune on his own (a dance known as a FRAYlechs), and Goodman later said, "I knew it was a great piece of material for us as soon as I heard Ziggy's record of it on Bluebird. I'd known that melody for years. It was an old Hebrew song and it was a Greek song too. Seems to me I had an old record of it once—Jewish on one side and Greek on the other. It must be thousands of years old." (The tune was known as "SHTILer bulGAR" and might have been a hundred years old, at most.)

Elman (his real name was Harry Finkelman) may have heard the same old record, or perhaps he picked up the tune from his father, who was a cantor. Goodman continued, "Anyway, when I heard Ziggy's record [called "Fralich in Swing"] it had no vocal, and I thought it could be a big hit with lyrics. So I contacted Johnny Mercer and asked him to write some for us." The vocalist was "Liltin'" Martha Tilton. The record was cut by Goodman for Victor records on 1 February 1939 in New York City and issued under the title "And the Angels Sing."

In Goodman's version the band breaks into a traditional klezmer rendition in the middle of the piece and then segues back into the swing style that Goodman had popularized. That segue seemed to be the end of klezmer swing. But the story of the klezmer revival is typical of the development in this country of many forms of traditional music and their characteristic repertoires and instruments. Unlike most other industrial societies, the United States has witnessed a unique revival of many elements in its traditional culture, as well as folk materials brought from other countries. Very often the results appear in popular or FUHLKStimlech styles rather than in authentically folk modes. The revivals sometimes come about when young musicians discover (or rediscover) performers from an earlier time. This happened to me when I rediscovered the fabulous Kentucky banjo player Buell Kazee, who had recorded fifty-two sides for Brunswick in the twenties and then disappeared from sight. He was a preacher in Lexington, Kentucky, when I ran into him and made a documentary record of his life and art for Folkways Records (see Discography).

More often it is the fact that records of the music survive, and dedicated young musicians listen carefully and learn the styles, sometimes only through feats of inspired research. Like the early New Orleans jazz musicians, the klezmorim were often jealous of their skills and not always eager to share with others. Naftula Brandwein, one of the great klezmer clarinetists, was notorious for turning his back on the audience so that any visiting musicians would not be able to see the fingering for some of his sensational passages. (There are similar stories about early jazz musicians who did the same thing when white musicians or some of their jazz rivals were in the audience.) Surviving klezmer musicians too have sometimes been openly hostile to some of their youthful admirers, many of whom they feel are still wet behind the ears.

Most of the American klezmer revivalists are folk, bluegrass, or European folk music aficionados who became aware of the klezmer tradition and abandoned their former enthusiasms. Among the crucial influences in California, where some of the first groups developed, was the extensive collection of old 78s in the possession of Martin Schwartz, a linguist at the University of California at Berkeley. Professor Schwartz made his material and expertise available to many musicians and was especially close to such important bands as the Klezmorim and Kapelye.

Like the folkies of earlier times, the klezmer groups are very eclectic in responding to many levels and styles of musical activity. One of the most important and exciting developments is the revival of a rich repertoire of Yiddish songs that has been untouched for many years. They include the FUHLKStimlech compositions of poets like Mark Warshavsky and Morris Rosenfeld as well as the work of Jewish tunesmiths of Second Avenue and Tin Pan Alley like Sholem Secunda, whose "Bei Mir Bist Du Schoen" became a huge success for the Andrews Sisters in a bilingual recording.

Begun in the seventies, the klezmer revival was still going strong in the mid-nineties, and it is likely to hold its own as a special category of American pop music. The list of recordings keeps growing for the older as well as the newer music, and the repertoires of klezmer music have developed in contemporary terms. Much of the music is dance oriented, including the wedding dance (shear), FRAYlechs, bulGAR (done much like a HOra but more delicately), and the exotic-sounding Romanian DOYne. Other tunes are marches that show the military band connections of some of the early European groups.

Another significant area is traditional or popular Yiddish materials. The songs of Mark Warshavsky, composer of "OYfn PRIPitshik" ("On the Hearth") and "dem MILner's TREnm" ("The Miller's Tears"), are popular with the new groups, as are settings of the proletarian poems of Morris Rosenfeld, whose sweatshop songs "Mein Rooe Plats" ("My Resting Place") and "Mein Yingele" ("My Little Boy") have been done by several groups. The latter is a poignant ballad about an immigrant father whose work hours prevent him from seeing his little son while awake. (A bilingual version is part of the Bluestein Family album *Where Does Love Come From?*)

Among the most interesting of the revival materials is a pop tune that was widely known but condemned in highbrow Yiddishist circles because it was neither folk nor literary in its origins. The song, called "Dee GREEne kooZEEne" ("The Greenhorn Cousin"), documents the downfall of a beautiful and vital immigrant girl, who is destroyed by the sweatshop. Like many immigrant songs, it plays on the idea of the United States as a golden country—but more in theory than reality. The Greenhorn's last line is "BRENen zuhl Columbus' medEEne" (may the kingdom of Columbus burn in Hell). Because it is a jazzy tune that mixes Yiddish with American diction (including words like PAYdi, meaning paycheck), Yiddishist intellectuals steered clear of it, labeling it "vulgar Second Avenue shlock." But it is a very moving and effective song, and it reveals that Jewish Americans endured the same hardships as other immigrant groups. (The Yiddish song is also on the Bluestein Family album, along with a singable English translation.)

In addition to holiday and religious songs (especially those in Chasidic style), another important component of klezmer repertoires is music that has jazz sources. Most of the contemporary American klezmorim have grown up listening to jazz, but when they play traditional music (except for blues) they have little opportunity to tap such sources. But the klezmer musicians active in the thirties were very closely involved with jazz, and it is a logical and inevitable step for the current groups to use a good deal of jazz material. Dixieland is a natural because the instrumentation is similar, but one can also hear ragtime approaches as well as other jazz styles, including Yiddish-inspired or Yiddish-sounding pieces from the repertoires of the Duke Ellington and Cab Calloway big bands.

There is also an interest in the characteristic instrumental styles of the klezmorim. Several of the early musicians, like Brandwein and Dave Tarras, were virtuoso clarinetists, and the work of exceptional fiddlers, trumpeters, and hammered dulcimer players has also been preserved on records. Some of the surviving old-time klezmer musicians have been willing to share their instrumental skills with younger players, thus providing a direct continuity of the tradition.

A more difficult problem arises for the young singers who attempt the Yiddish song repertoire. Here they are often largely on their own, and few are as capable as Michael Alpert, the stunning interpreter of Yiddish materials along with the group Kapelye. But, as was the case for many revival musicians of the past, the young singers work hard to reproduce the styles that interest them, and many will be successful in the long run.

The revival of klezmer music has by no means run its course. Given the mishiGAS of American popular music, with its penchant for integrating folk styles into the most outrageous and far-fetched combinations, there is no way to predict what hybrid will crop up next. One of the klezmer groups is preparing a Broadway special based on the tradition. Recordings of new and old groups continue to appear. And it is worth emphasizing that one of the most important consequences of klezmer music is its re-presentation of a great many significant and entertaining Yiddish songs. For that reason alone the modern klezmorim have been receiving wide support both in Jewish communities and from the general public. It is neither the first nor the last revival movement of traditional music in the United States.

Klezmer music in this country was originally represented by several big bands that played traditional tunes, in recordings made during the twenties. There were also several virtuoso performers who occasionally passed on their skills to younger ones. Then during the 1970s there was a major explosion, and klezmer, as predicted by some, became its own genre, peopled by young, often traditional musicians who became obsessed with the music that existed once in the SHTETlech of the Old World.

As is the wont of musicians, these zealots soon began adding to and changing klezmer music, under the influence of folk, jazz, rock, and other ethnic sources. Such making of traditional music by recognized musicians (rather than by the anonymous authors of older times) is what I call poplore—old-time music that is influenced by commercial sources. (See my book *Poplore: Folk and Pop in American Culture*.)

So when we listen to contemporary klezmer bands, we can hear everything from the reworking of traditional tunes by such groups as the Klezmorim (still the best, though the personnel have changed) to the commercially inspired work of such groups as Kapelye and the Klezmer Conservatory Band. Even more poplorist is Brave Old World, which has specialized in creating its own tunes and songs. (This group has an immense European following, especially in Germany—an amazing circumstance in light of the Holocaust.)

Klezmer, in short, has developed into a worldwide phenomenon, performed by groups in almost every American city, which has long since left the traditional sounds of Eastern European SHTETl musicians far behind. Not only that, but the genre is still developing, so no one can predict its ultimate future. Such is the destiny of all American music that has been influenced by folk styles.

We can get a good idea of the state of klezmer music today by listening to the album *In the Fiddler's House,* an Angel recording of violinist Itzhak Perlman together with Brave Old World, the Klezmatics, the Andy Statman Klezmer Orchestra, and the Klezmer Conservatory Band. Perlman says in the introduction, "As a boy, growing up in Israel, I heard the sounds of klezmer music on the radio. . . . When I was approached to do this recording, my first thought was 'Great! Let's do it!' But then I paused. I wondered what business I, a classically trained musician, had playing this soulful, passionate music." Perlman is a superb musician, but his great skills have little in common with traditional klezmer music. On the other hand, almost every tune by each of the various groups on the album is their own concoction, though based on klezmer originals. And that precisely is what has happened to klezmer music—it has gone from anonymous folk style to the composed and organized approach that defines it today. Where klezmer music will go tomorrow is anyone's guess.

Appendix 3

A Note on Leo Rosten

Leo Rosten, who died in 1997, was the most important figure in the story of Yiddish as represented in print. At the ripe old age of eighty-eight, he seemed capable of attaining the life span described by the traditional Yiddish toast: "Biz HUNdert and TSVANtzig" (May you live to be one hundred twenty). According to the Hebrew Bible, that was the age of Moses when he died. Once when there were "giants in the earth," who mated with the daughters of men, God interceded and reminded them that as a consequence they would have not immortality but a life span of only one hundred twenty years. (I recall seeing a TV evangelist hushing a disciple who had suggested that, according to that story, there must be a race of angels on earth somewhere.)

Rosten will be sorely missed. For many years, almost single-handedly, he argued for the legitimacy of Yiddish even when many Jews still considered it a zharGUN, not quite a language, especially when compared with Hebrew. This despite the solid accomplishments of Yiddishists like Yitzkhak Layb Peretz, Sholom Aleichem, Sholem Asch, and Nobel Prize winner Isaac Bashevis Singer.

In Rosten's works—like *The Joys of Yiddish*, and *Hooray for Yiddish*, and, as far back as 1937, *The Education of H*Y*M*A*N K*A*P*L*A*N* (which he wrote under the pseudonym Leonard Q. Ross)—he succeeded in disseminating Yiddish to millions of readers around the world.

It was difficult for a man of his generation to deal with the realities of certain taboo words. Like William Safire, the self-styled "literary maven," Rosten bowdlerized Anglish words such as shmuhk. Both shmuhk and other euphemisms like shmo mean penis. There is another Yiddish expression for penis that translates as something innocuous, like "the male member," but the closest translation of shmuhk in English is "prick," a vulgar term. There's no way it can be used in polite company.

The same is true for the scatological word drek, usually defined as dirt. It means shit, as in the witty phrase "drek from Broadway," slang for shlocky materials from the Great White Way. (I was once asked by the California Department of Motor Vehicles to rule on the definition of a vanity license plate that read DREK. The owner insisted it meant dirt, which is true, but any Yiddish-speaking person knows the literal meaning. The driver got to keep his plates anyway.)

Rosten often argued that Yiddish was unique in its expressibility, but that quality is shared by any language that's close to its folk roots, like Irish or the American English of Mark Twain in *Adventures of Huckleberry Finn*. (Not *The Adventures*, as it is often misprinted.)

Rosten was on firm footing, however, in giving his definitions through jokes. Take KHOOTSpe (chutzpah), probably the most often used Yiddish word in the American lexicon, best defined by the story of the guy who murdered his parents and then threw himself on the mercy of the court because he was an orphan. That's chutzpah— arrogance. Or take the distinction between a shlemiel and a shlimazel: The first is the clumsy oaf who spills hot soup on the latter— the natural-born loser.

Many words have shifted in meaning since Rosten began his work. Shmooze is one such. The Anglish verb SHMOOes means to engage in small talk, idle chatter. But lately shmoozing means attempting to influence strongly, as in the expression "power-shmoozing" so as to get a good room in a crowded hotel. A similar case is TCHOTCHke, from the Yiddish TSAtskele, meaning doll. Tchotchke, sometimes spelled chotchke, means cheap gewgaws, insignificant trinkets.

Recently we've seen the expression "glatt kosher" on many a Chinese restaurant's sign. Glatt means flat or smooth, hence rigorously KUHsher. Kosher is widely used to mean acceptable or O.K. Its original meaning is "passed" under the supervision of a rabbi or an authorized butcher.

Rosten will be remembered for his wit as well as his erudition. I can imagine him thinking of the many who attempt to succeed him, rehearsing in his mind the joke about the rabbi and the cantor, always fierce competitors. The two prostrate themselves, proclaiming loudly, "O Lord, I am nothing." Observing them, the SHAmis (Yiddish for deacon) likewise throws himself down, saying, "O Lord, I am nothing." Whereupon the cantor and the rabbi say in unison, "Zay nor ver vil zayn a goornisht!" (Look who wants to be a nothing!).

Bibliography and Discography

SS Aleichem, Sholom. *Selected Short Stories of Sholom Aleichem.* Ed. Alfred Kazin. New York: Modern Library, 1956.

EL Allende, Isabel. *Eva Luna.* New York: Knopf, 1988.

AHD American Heritage Dictionary. Ed. William Morris. Boston: Houghton, 1969.

PC Anonymous [Joe Klein]. *Primary Colors.* New York: Random, 1996.

TD Ansky, S. *The Dybbuk.* Trans. Henry G. Alsberg and Winifred Katzin. 1926. New York: Liveright, 1971.

THT Atwood, Margaret. *The Handmaid's Tale.* Boston: Houghton, 1986.

BSRA Baker, Houston A., Jr. *Black Studies, Rap, and the Academy.* Chicago: U of Chicago P, 1993.

SHJ Baron, Salo Wittmayer. *A Social and Religious History of the Jews.* 2d ed. 17 vols. New York: Columbia U P, 1952.

TV Bellow, Saul. *The Victim.* New York: Vanguard, 1947.

AAM ———. *The Adventures of Augie March.* New York: Viking, 1953.

H ———. *Herzog.* New York: Viking, 1964.

HFM ———. *Him with His Foot in His Mouth and Other Stories.* New York: Harper, 1984.

MDH ———. *More Die of Heartbreak.* New York: Morrow, 1987.

A ———. *The Actual: A Novella.* New York: Viking, 1997.

GJSS ———, ed. *Great Jewish Short Stories.* New York: Dell, 1963.

PR Bernays, Anne. *Professor Romeo.* New York: Weidenfeld, 1989.

KC Bloom, Harold. *Kabbalah and Criticism.* New York: Seabury, 1975.

HTD Bruce, Lenny. *How to Talk Dirty and Influence People: An Autobiography.* Chicago: Playboy Press, 1965.

RDL Cahan, Abraham. *The Rise of David Levinsky.* New York: Harper, 1917.

FG Chametzky, Jules. *From the Ghetto: The Fiction of Abraham Cahan.* Amherst: U of Massachusetts P, 1977.

DAS *Dictionary of American Slang.* Ed. Harold Wentworth and Stuart Berg Flexner. New York: Crowell, 1960.

CKKC Elkin, Stanley. *Criers and Kibitzers/Kibitzers and Criers.* New York: Random, 1965.

AMT Feldman, Susan, ed. *African Myths and Tales.* New York: Dell, 1963.

LJA Fiedler, Leslie. *The Last Jew in America.* New York: Stein, 1965.

FR ———. *A Fiedler Reader.* New York: Stein, 1977.

MM Freud, Sigmund. *Moses and Monotheism.* Ed. and trans. James Strachey. London: Hogarth, 1974.

RFJG Fried, Albert. *The Rise and Fall of the Jewish Gangster in America.* New York: Holt, 1980.

K Ginsberg, Allen. *Kaddish and Other Poems: 1958–1960.* San Francisco: City Lights, 1961.

JWM Gold, Michael. *Jews without Money.* 1930. New York: Carrol and Graf, 1984.

QTM Gould, Stephen Jay. *Questioning the Millennium: A Rationalist's Guide to a Precisely Arbitrary Countdown.* New York: Harmony, 1997.

SIA Hamill, Pete. *Snow in August.* Boston: Little, Brown, 1997.

GG Heller, Joseph. *Good as Gold.* New York: Simon, 1976.

GK ———. *God Knows.* New York: Knopf, 1984.

JMH Idelsohn, A. Z. *Jewish Music in Its Historical Development.* New York: Schocken, 1975.

DA Levine, Philip. *Don't Ask.* Ann Arbor: U of Michigan P, 1981.

MB Malamud, Bernard. *The Magic Barrel.* New York: Farrar, 1958.

IF ———. *Idiots First.* New York: Farrar, 1963.

TT ———. *The Tenants.* New York: Farrar, 1971.

TW Markfield, Wallace. *Teitlebaum's Window.* New York: Knopf, 1976.

APM Newfield, Jack. *A Prophetic Minority.* New York: Signet, 1967.

NYRB *New York Review of Books.*

TPR Ozick, Cynthia. *The Pagan Rabbi and Other Stories.* New York: Knopf, 1971.

BTN ———. *Bloodshed and Three Novellas.* New York: Knopf, 1976.

L ———. *Levitation.* New York: Knopf, 1982.

TCG ———. *The Cannibal Galaxy.* New York: Knopf, 1983.

AA ———. *Art and Ardor.* New York: Knopf, 1983.

EC Paley, Grace. *Enormous Changes at the Last Minute.* New York: Farrar, 1973.

HG Patai, Raphael, *The Hebrew Goddess.* New York: KTAV, 1968.

TMP Perelman, S. J. *The Most of S. J. Perelman.* New York: Simon, 1957.

RG ———. *The Rising Gorge.* New York: Simon, 1961.

TC Potok, Chaim. *The Chosen.* New York: Simon, 1967.

V Pynchon, Thomas. *V.* 1963. New York: Bantam, 1979.

CL ———. *The Crying of Lot 49.* 1966. New York: Perennial Fiction Library, Harper, 1986.

GR ———. *Gravity's Rainbow.* New York: Viking, 1973.

VI ———. *Vineland.* Boston: Little, Brown, 1990.

MD ———. *Mason & Dixon.* New York: Holt, 1997.

AE Rosenfeld, Isaac. *An Age of Enormity: Life and Writing in the Forties and Fifties.* Cleveland: World, 1962.

JY Rosten, Leo. *The Joys of Yiddish.* New York: McGraw, 1968.

CIS Roth, Henry. *Call It Sleep.* 1934. New York: Avon, 1964.

GC Roth, Philip. *Goodbye, Columbus.* New York: Houghton, 1959.

PC ———. *Portnoy's Complaint.* New York: Random, 1969.

RM ———. *Reading Myself and Others.* New York: Farrar, 1975.

P ———. *Patrimony.* New York: Simon, 1991.

ST ———. *Sabbath's Theater.* Boston: Houghton, 1995.

AP ———. *American Pastoral.* Boston: Houghton, 1997.

VOP Rubin, Ruth. *Voices of a People.* 2d ed. New York: McGraw, 1973.

JM Scholem, Gershom. *Major Trends in Jewish Mysticism.* New York: Schocken, 1961.

H3 Shetzline, David. *Heckletooth 3.* New York: Random, 1969.

CF Singer, Isaac Bashevis. *A Crown of Feathers.* New York: Farrar, 1973.

NL ———. *Nobel Lecture.* New York: Farrar, 1978.

S ———. *Shosha.* New York: Farrar, 1978.

TP ———. *The Penitent.* New York: Farrar, 1983.

OJFM Slobin, Mark, ed. and trans. *Old Jewish Folk Music: The Collections and Writings of Moshe Beregovski.* Philadelphia: U of Pennsylvania P, 1982.

TS ———. *Tenement Songs: The Popular Music of the Jewish Immigrants.* Urbana: U of Illinois P, 1982.

SC Styron, William. *Sophie's Choice.* New York: Random, 1979.

TLS *Times (London) Literary Supplement.*

B Updike, John. *Bech: A Book.* New York: Knopf, 1970.

BB ———. *Bech Is Back.* New York: Knopf, 1982.

RP Van Gennep, Arnold. *The Rites of Passage.* 1908. Chicago: U of Chicago P, 1960.

TF Walker, Alice. *The Temple of My Familiar.* San Diego: Harcourt, 1989.
HYL Weinreich, Max. *History of the Yiddish Language.* Trans. Shlomo Noble and Joshua Fishman. Chicago: U of Chicago P, 1980.
MYD Weinreich, Uriel. *Modern English-Yiddish, Yiddish-English Dictionary.* New York: McGraw, 1968.
RBBO Wilson, Edmund. *Red, Black, Blond and Olive.* New York: Oxford, 1956.

Discography

SH Bluestein, Gene. *Songs of the Holidays.* Folkways FC7554, 1958.
BK ——, ed. *Buell Kazee Sings and Plays.* Folkways FS3810, 1958.
WLCM Bluestein Family. *Where Does Love Come From?* Greenhays/Flying Fish, 1986.
GMB ——. *Good Morning Blues.* EVTA, 1987.

Klezmer Recordings

Kapelye. *Future and Past.* Flying Fish FF249. 1981.
——. *Levine and His Flying Machine.* Shanachie 21006. 1985.
Klezmer Conservatory Band. *Klez.* Vanguard VSD 79449. 1981.
Klezmorim. *East Side Wedding.* Arhoolie 3006. 1977.
——. *Streets of Gold.* Arhoolie 3011. 1978.
——. *Metropolis.* Flying Fish 258. 1981.
——. *Notes from the Underground.* Flying Fish 322. 1984.
Perlman, Itzhak. *In the Fiddler's House.* (With Brave Old World, The Klezmatics, The Andy Statman Orchestra, and The Klezmer Conservatory Band.) Angel 7243 5 55555 2 6. 1995.
Sapoznik, Henry, ed. *Klezmer Music, 1910–1942: Recordings from the YIVO Archives.* Folkways FSS 34021. 1981.
Schwartz, Martin, ed. *Klezmer Music: Early Yiddish Instrumental Music— The First Recordings, 1910–1927.* From the collection of Martin Schwartz. Folklyric 9034. 1982.
Statman, Andy, and Zev Feldman. *Jewish Klezmer Music.* Shanachie 21002. 1979.
——. *Klezmer Orchestra.* Shanachie 21004. 1983.